HELL
— HATH NO FURY —
LIKE HER
THE MAKING OF CHRISTINE

By LEE GAMBIN

Hell Hath No Fury Like Her: The Making of *Christine*
Lee Gambin

Published in the USA by:
BearManor Media
P O Box 71426
Albany, Georgia 31708
www.bearmanormedia.com

ISBN: 978-1-62933-392-2
BearManor Media, Albany, Georgia
Printed in the United States of America
Text design by Robbie Adkins, www.adkinsconsult.com
Cover design by Darren Cotzabuyucas, DC DESIGN

To my beloved pooch Buddy and to my human friends
who care (you know who you are)...

The following people have been interviewed for this book, and I would like to thank each and every one of them for their wonderful contributions:

Cast:
Keith Gordon – "Arnie Cunningham"
Alexandra Paul – "Leigh Cabot"
William Ostrander – "Buddy Repperton"
Malcolm Danare – "Moochie"
Steven Tash – "Rich Cholony"
Doug Warhit – "Bemis"
John Richard Petersen – high school student (uncredited)

Crew:
John Carpenter – director / co-composer
Richard Kobritz – producer
Bill Phillips – screenwriter
Donald M. Morgan – cinematographer
Marion Rothman – editor
Virginia Katz – assistant editor
Alan Howarth – co-composer
William C. Carruth – music editor
Roy Arbogast – SFX supervisor
Kim Gottlieb-Walker – on set photographer
Caroline Paul – Alexandra Paul's sister/prank on John Carpenter

And the following people have contributed some critical insight, and I would like to thank them also:

Lisa Rae Bartolomei – critic on sound design
Clementine Bastow – critic on themes regarding gender
Adam Devlin – critic on songs used throughout the film
Bill Gibson – president of the Christine Car Club / collector
Elissa Rose – critic on costuming

A massive thanks to the following people who provided photos for the book:

Kim Gottlieb-Walker, Richard Kobritz, Steven Tash, John Richard Petersen and Bill Gibson.

Additional thanks go out to:

Adam Dallas, Justine Ryan, Sean Sobczak, Chris Schwab, Cinemaniacs, Antony Botheras, Kelly Preston, Ben Ohmart, Alan Duffin, Sandy Grabman, Marsha DeFilippo, Robbie Adkins, Stephen King and christinemoviecar.com

The human stars of the film, Keith Gordon as Arnie Cunningham, Alexandra Paul as Leigh Cabot and John Stockwell as Dennis Guilder pose with the titular star, the Plymouth Fury herself, Christine.

CONTENTS

"BAD TO THE BONE": The birth of Christine, Detroit, 1957

During the late seventies and early eighties, Columbia Pictures would only produce a handful of horror films, which would be a strange decision made by the studio when the genre was turning in healthy profits for fellow companies at the time. Clearly, the most bankable of horror subgenres during this period was the much written about and discussed slasher boom that dominated the scene with writer/director John Carpenter's *Halloween* (1978) being a massively influential force jettisoning a slew of stalk and slash "knife pictures" for years to come. As well as being the most successful independent feature film at the time, *Halloween* also launched Carpenter's career (albeit he had made a number of films prior) and branded this talented maestro of the moving camera, king of frame composition and dedicated craftsman of mood, as a new master of horror. Clearly Columbia Pictures was on board when they were approached by producer Richard Kobritz to take on Carpenter to adapt popular horror novelist Stephen King's latest book about a supernatural car named Christine that takes out the bullies that persecute "her" owner – the put upon nerd Arnie Cunningham.

A haunted car movie could be considered a risky venture for the studio, however, Columbia's horror choices varied in content, theme and style in the late seventies and early eighties. The studio most certainly followed trends and took on slasher films including the sports-themed riff on the "Ten Little Indians" motif *Graduation Day* (1981) starring genre regular Christopher George and the complex and beautifully crafted J. Lee Thompson Canadian venture *Happy Birthday To Me* (1981) which featured Melissa Sue Anderson of *Little House on the Prairie* (1974-1983) fame as well as Hollywood veteran Glenn Ford. But Columbia also tapped into the eco-horror fad that hit its peak in the seventies with the serious in tone *Nightwing* (1979) which featured bubonic plague carrying bats as its featured threat and the directorial debut of James Cameron who delivered a Euro-sleaze style "follow up" to Joe Dante's excellent socially aware Roger Corman produced film *Piranha* (1978) with *Piranha II: The Spawning* (1981). Adding to the mixed bag of varied horror films was *When a Stranger Calls* (1979) which would feature one of the most terrifying opening sequences ever put to film, where a wide-eyed Carol Kane answered a constantly ringing telephone asking if she has "checked the children", *Night of the Juggler* (1980) starring James Brolin as a man chasing down a psychotic played by the googly eyed Cliff Gorman who has his kidnapped young daughter, and *Eyes of Laura Mars* (1978) – which incidentally would have a screenplay written by *Christine* director John Carpenter – which was a stylish American Giallo starring Faye Dunaway, Tommy Lee Jones, Brad Dourif and featuring a theme song by superstar Barbra Streisand. *Christine*, from 1983, would be yet another offering of the horror genre for Columbia and here, this brilliantly conceived and constructed character study and acute commentary on the role of "possession" would become a cult classic, a critical triumph and a perfectly realised adaptation of Stephen King's rich and provocative novel.

With the Columbia Pictures logo making way for the credits (white over black), John Carpenter's *Christine* opens much like many films of the late seventies and early eighties – simple, ambiguous and evoking a sense of ominous foreboding. When you look at this trend, it seems to surface in varied films that have directors at the helm wanting to keep the sense of drama at bay because the audience will be punched in the face with it as the film moves forward. Michael Anderson's *Orca* (1977) does this – it features the credits rolling over a black screen with the haunting sound of whale cries simmering in the audio-distance, while Alan Parker's *Fame* (1980) features an even more foreboding soundscape where the High School of Performing Arts is just waking up and coming to life, before we are faced with the onslaught of the gruelling audition sequence that sets off the film. Here in *Christine*, John Carpenter has his credits sequence accompanied by the roar of the Plymouth Fury's mighty engine – she is birthing, she is breathing, she is fuming. In a film, much like the aforementioned *Fame*, that is so musically driven, it is a clever choice from Carpenter to have the title sequence music-free and completely devoted to the sound of a revving machine; in this regard, it makes the music (the first number being "Bad to the Bone" by George Thorogood and The Destroyers) even more dynamic and forceful – just like Alan Parker's use of a quiet opening, followed by a monologue from the play "The Dark at the Top of the Stairs" is all the more disconcerting when he then hits his audience with the loud energetic frenzy of a young boy playing rock 'n' roll drums. Ultimately Carpenter, much like Parker and Anderson, understand sound as a dramatic tool, and *Christine* is a perfect testament to this.

The title card for *Christine* is also an inspired invention of design combining classic American muscle car imagery while evoking an image of female genitalia (something that the film will be thoroughly invested in). The shiny golden V-shaped chrome would replace the Plymouth Fury's cursive "Fury" emblem, and the slick CHRISTINE lettering would be sprawled across it like a flag celebrating both the world of automobiles and the strength and beauty (and danger) of women.

The opening scene of the film would also be the first day of filming and John Carpenter would later share the story of being late to the shoot having been stopped midway to have a breathalyser test by local police. Shot in the Californian Valley in an abandoned factory, the sequence is what would be the "birth of Christine", as she would come together in an assembly line. Opening on a large metallic fan that helps keep the building air-conditioned at best it can, this image pushes the energy of movement and progress whilst commenting on the world of machines and industry – the story of *Christine* will open in 1957 and during this year a number of events would spark the concept of change and endeavour. For instance, the teen-centric rock 'n' roll TV show *American Bandstand* (1952-1989) would premiere on ABC while Elvis Presley would purchase Graceland. In regards to *Christine*, a film that plays with the notion of the "dangers of rock 'n' roll", these two major pop-cultural events would leave an impression on the film's subtext: young people are slaves to their subculture, heroic icons like Presley become an institution represented by a Memphis mansion and so forth.

The thunderous sound of "Bad to the Bone" spews out and welcomes us into this secret world of cars and auto-industry. The song was released in 1982 and was a mainstay for the newly invented MTV, which would ultimately be the eighties equivalent of *American Bandstand*. "Bad to the Bone" would not compliment the title card of "Detroit, 1957" but it would also completely summarise Christine herself as an entity that is born a bad seed – she is evil incarnate, and nothing demonic or human has influenced her in any way. Christine's birthplace is Detroit – America's motor city and a city of industry – and she is tended to men working in trenches, lifting their tools up towards her, fine tuning her rivets, codeplane and debouncifiers. Christine is a stunning piece of machinery, a blood red Plymouth Fury with a brilliant sheen and vibrant energy. Even in her placid state, of being pulled across the production line, she commands attention and is viewed by John Carpenter's camera like a gorgeous woman walking the streets in a tight fitted skirt, exposed legs, breasts heaved up and sporting high heels. Christine is the only painted up Plymouth on the factory line and she is presented as the star of the film in an instant – a glamorous diva who is in charge, self-possessed and ready for action. Her fins, her hood, her lines and the way she cruises down the bearing pull is completely fetishized and made to look sleek and sexy; the garage attendants are working class Joes completely dwarfed by her supernatural magic that Carpenter successfully manages to get across. Outside of the image of Christine herself, the entirety of this sequence is shot in a bronze sheen, which is a masterful turn from Carpenter and his director of photography Donald M. Morgan who sets the illusion of yesteryear in this curtain raiser. The look of the orange hue comes up in previous Carpenter works such as his TV miniseries musical biopic *Elvis* (1979) where early years are given the golden touch, setting the tone of an older period of time as the child Presley experiences growing up in the impoverished south. In *Halloween*, this glorious use of color and light gives the film an unworldly sensibility, and leaves the impression that not all is right in the safe compounds of American suburbia – this still, pond-like horror film becomes an almost dreamlike Never Never Land all thanks to this incredible use of the golden hue. Harking back to legendary filmmakers such as Vincente Minnelli who would use this technique in varied films such as *Meet Me in St.*

Louis (1944) and *Home from the Hill* (1960), Carpenter's masterful handling of color, light, space and movement is all up for showcase here in this opening segment as he directs Donald M. Morgan's crane across the large factory closing in on the film's monster, this impressive and gorgeous Plymouth Fury.

The entire scene is populated by men, and the "women" in this sequence are the cars. These monstrous American machines are all serviced by the men, pampered by them and "cruised" by these oily and grease-stained workers. Christine, however, in her fiery red get up is the only one who chooses not to be objectified or mishandled. She chooses difference and refuses to submit to human bondage – she is her own machine. When a supervisor lifts her hood and inspects her engine, his hand is left in a vulnerable position, however, it is read as though he is peering underneath a young woman's skirt and placing his hand where it shouldn't be. When Christine slams her bonnet down, crushing the supervisor's hand, it is not only her first act of violence, but it is also indicative of whom Christine reflects: a woman who will not be mistreated. The instance she slams her sheet of metal upon the supervisor's hand it kills "Bad to the Bone" and makes way for this poor unfortunate working class Joe to scream in pain. Here in *Christine*, it is primarily men who will fall into the victim category – and ultimately, only male characters die on screen. Also, it is interesting to note that Christine is not the only one being "checked out" by male operators, the way in which her rear view mirror picks up an attendant reflects the possibility that she herself is "cruising" him, and this is a classic testament to this monster car owning choices to be made – it is as if she is already, in her infancy, carefully selecting a "mate". In the case of Christine, her male "owner" will be her plaything, her "lover" and ultimately her victim and the song "Bad to the Bone" (although not from her era) becomes her anthem that transcends time and space. It is an important factor establishing her malevolence and it also dictates that she will go on long after each male "owner/plaything/lover/victim" will drop off.

When a serviceman's fingers come close and tamper with her on the inside – nearing to the engine – this is a somewhat graphic depiction of a conceptualised moment of molestation, so therefore he must pay, and then later in the sequence when a black serviceman "enters" Christine without "consent" and through such neglectful nonchalance pollutes her with his cigar smoke and ash, there will be hell to pay. Throughout the film, Christine is abused at the hands of men, but these men don't live too long soon after. When George Thorogood's lyrics belt out "She could tell right away/I was bad to the bone", we understand the innate evil in Christine, and yet she is also somewhat a monster that might harvest pathos and sympathy – in many ways, she is a woman who wants to be respected and treated well. However, the film pushes it in a more direct monstrous angle, where she becomes a vengeful witch that will manipulate and torment the film's human male protagonist Arnie Cunningham (Keith Gordon) of whom we shall meet in the follow up scene.

With the factory's bell ringing to send the workers home, the head supervisor notices Christine's headlights are still on as well as her radio. When he opens the car door, the dead body of the aforementioned cigar smoking serviceman spills out – his wide dead eyes glaring upward. The scene ends in a grisly moment of shock and horror, with the head supervisor honking Christine's horn to usher his workers back in to help. The build up to this moment is made all the more intense and sinister by the use of magnetic and hypnotic camera movement – the bird's eye view shots, the crane shots, the long tracking shots, the continual movement, all of this contribute to a world at the mercy of machines and paints up a pretty picture of a new kind of movie monster. Christine is empowered by her stance and there is no reasoning with her; she is a monstrous entity ready to kill. Her sister Plymouths are benign, virginal and white, while she is a hypersexual (and violent) red. Christine is stealthy and sensual, glistening with a feminine ease that sends inept servicemen away with their hands wrapped up in bandages, nursing dreadful wounds.

When the factory clock shows 5pm and the work day is complete, Christine makes her first kill, as if suggesting that she "works around the clock", just like Bill Haley and the Comets celebrated the fact that they could (and will) "Rock Around the Clock". This song would also be the hit used for the first season of popular fifties-themed TV sitcom *Happy Days* (1974-1984) that would prove to be a source of inspiration for writer Stephen King, who would call his anti-hero Cunningham in tribute to the Cunningham family on the Gary Marshall produced show – proving that everything inspired is in no doubt connected. Music plays a massive part in *Christine*, and in many ways the film reads like a Greek Chorus themed musical where the songs comment on situation, story or character. The songs that come from Christine act as her "voice", so when the black supervisor turns her radio on and Buddy Holly's "Not Fade Away" comes singing through, the first lyrics we hear are "I'm a gonna tell you how it's gonna be…" which perceptively lets us know that Christine sets up the rules, and that she is in charge.

Carpenter's choice to stress the importance of the black serviceman flicking the ash from his cigar onto Christine's brand new upholstery is made all the more powerful by holding that shot on that suggestive image, and so when the payoff comes (his dead body sprawled out of the car with the cigar still wedged in his mouth) it is somehow expected and yet still shocking. When the supervisor toots Christine's horn, the focus is on the radio which will ultimately make a connective link to 1978, which is the year the rest of the movie is set. Here we understand the importance of music and rock 'n' roll songs in *Christine*, where Stephen King's novel opened every chapter with lyrics from a song about a car or making a reference to a car, here in the film, screenwriter Bill Phillips loads the movie with a musicality and uses each song to make commentary on what is happening or what the Plymouth Fury is "feeling" or "thinking" or trying to communicate. In many ways, the film is similar in structure to Bob Fosse's *Cabaret* (1972) which rejected the integrated songs of the original source material, in favour of placing the songs inside the Kit Kat Klub (albeit for one number performed by a Nazi youth) which made commentary on the situation at hand – namely the rise of Nazism during the beginning of the forties in Berlin.

This entire sequence was inspired by screenwriter Ernest Lehman's recollection of Alfred Hitchcock's idea of a body falling out of the trunk of a newly assembled car. The thought that excited John Carpenter was this notion that a brand new car would be assembled, and that each scenario would show you that this was in fact a new automobile being manufactured and brought to life. However, in the final moment (the gag, if you will), a dead body would be discovered in the boot, which would add an element of the supernatural, the mysterious and the macabre. The question is: How did this body get inside a brand new and newly constructed car? This would launch the inspiration buzzers for Carpenter who sets this sequence (a sequence shot on Fuji while the rest of the film was shot on Kodak to give the scene a softer and more nostalgic quality) up to read like an old EC Comics horror story.

JOHN CARPENTER: (director) There is this elaborate crane shot at the beginning of the film that travels from the fan to the carline and from then on I completely stole an idea from Alfred Hitchcock in this entire sequence. Hitchcock always talked about wanting to film a sequence where you see a car being built and then as you get to the end, you see a body fall out of the hood. So I thought, "You know what, let's do it!" I thought about doing this "birth" sequence where Christine is built and comes to life, and I wanted to do the same kind of thing that Hitchcock always wanted to do. This was my tribute to Hitchcock and one of his great ideas that he talked about. The visual look and the bronze sheen that comes with this sequence came from conversations I had with my Director of Photography Don Morgan. He and I first worked together on a TV movie called *Elvis*, and one of the great things that he did to make the film look old and make certain sequences look kind of old fashioned, was a trick with the lighting where you underexpose it slightly, and this is what we did here with the opening of *Christine*, so it has that sense of yesteryear.

RICHARD KOBRITZ: (producer) The first scene in the picture is the making of Christine which sets up her being born bad. We knew that we wanted this establishing scene from the start. Most of the film was shot in Irwindale, California, but they had found a place outside of there for this opening and it was a real factory that was used to manufacture fences during the war. Much of what you see there was never changed, it was abandoned and they were trying to sell it, and it was huge and cavernous. So you only saw one half of it, while the other half was used to reuse the cars, to paint them, and we had a body shop on the other side of that wire assembly plant.

JOHN CARPENTER: The producer Richard Kobritz came across "Christine" in galleys and he was very excited about it and I went along with him because I needed a job after *The Thing* (1982) failed at the box office. Richard Kobritz and I met on a made for TV movie I did called *Someone's Watching Me!* (1978) which starred Lauren Hutton. There is that photo of me on the set of *Salem's Lot* (1979) with Richard, but we actually met and worked together on the Lauren Hutton picture. He produced that and did an excellent job.

BILL PHILLIPS (screenwriter): Early on in the adaptation, I phoned producer Richard Kobritz to say that the book didn't make it clear whether the "devil" was Roland LeBay or the car itself. Richard called Stephen King, who told him, "Gee… I never thought about that." So we were left with that choice. At the time, MTV was just starting out, and one day in Santa Monica, George Thorogood's "Bad to the Bone" played. My girlfriend Teresa said, "There's your solution." From that moment on, I took the attitude that Christine was just "born bad." Christine was the evil. From there, one could surmise that she had an influence on Roland, but since we cut him from the film anyway, we stuck with Christine being the seat of evil. I didn't plan to make the script dialogue heavy. This was my first feature script. I had written *Summer Solstice* (1981), the last film Henry Fonda (and Myrna Loy) ever acted in. [There was some activity about that, reportedly, when Jane Fonda successfully prevailed on Henry's biographer and took out any mention of *Summer Solstice* so that they could pretend that *On Golden Pond* (1981) was his last film. It wasn't. It was his last feature film, but the propaganda machine was at work. Apparently Peter Fonda strongly disagreed about that censorship.] My agent (also John's agent) was David Gersh. He felt that John and I might collaborate well together, since I supposedly had a skill writing "soft," meaning having likeable characters portrayed in a sort of "non-car chase" way, and John was an expert at writing "hard," being able to provide scares, etc. Since *The Thing* was (unfairly, in my opinion) unpopular when it came out (the same day as *E. T. the Extra-Terrestrial* (1982), as I recall)… Gersh felt we might work well together. And we did. Anyway, because I didn't have a lot of experience with writing film, I didn't have a strong sense of the role of dialogue. Now, more than fifty scripts later, I would do it completely differently. One should always go through a script and rid it of every shred of dialogue not absolutely needed… it helps keep the film more visual. But I do acknowledge that retaining much of Stephen King's dialogue (and inventing some of my own) did contribute to making this film something out of the ordinary. It's not really a scary movie… but it is, I think, a satisfyingly odd movie, and it's one that many people identify with, because it captures how ill-at-ease most of us feel during adolescence. I didn't see the opening as a change of pace away from dialogue necessarily. I think it was primarily visual, and I was aware that this would help us play George's song without a lot of interference or competition from dialogue.

RICHARD KOBRITZ: We had Michael Ochs choose the music and we were shooting somewhere in South Pasadena and we got a phone call and he had to talk to me and over the phone he played me "Bad to the Bone". He told me that he wanted to use it, and I said that would be fine, but it was going to cost quite a bit, but we had to settle on it straight away because Michael Hanselhoff was going to use it in another picture. So he played it for me and I said "Yep, let's buy it!" Then I told John that if he didn't like it we could throw it out, but we did just spend this money on it, but he liked it and it was as if this song was written specifically for this movie.

DONALD M. MORGAN (cinematographer): How I met John Carpenter was really interesting. I was working with Kurt Russell on *Used Cars* (1980), and one day Adrienne Barbeau was on set. She told me that John's next movie which was going to be *Christine* and she asked if I would like to meet John. I said, "Yeah, I would like to meet him!" and she said, "Let me see if I can set that up!" So John came over for lunch one day and told me what the project was. We had a little chit-chat and he never said "You're the cameraman" or "I like you" or anything, he just said, "Nice meeting you." I went back to the set and Adrienne said, "Great! You got the job!"

ROY ARBOGAST (SFX Supervisor): John Carpenter called me in, and we read through the script and the big questions was "How do we make the car do what it is supposed to do?" So the producer Richard Kobritz set up six to eight weeks to go ahead and see what we could do and how we could do it, before they even green lit the picture. I hired a crew and we made moulds on the whole car – the hubcabs, the hoods, the fenders, the mirrors – and we put together a body and took the car parts apart and rebuilt it.

BILL PHILLIPS: The most fun I had writing the script was being able to collaborate with Michael Ochs (brother of the late pro-test folk-singer Phil Ochs). Michael owns (or he did in 1982) the Michael Ochs Archive in Venice, California. I forget how I met him, but Richard and John soon approved my working with him because (unlike most film scripts, where the writer rarely is invited to suggest songs, primarily because they've become so expensive to use) since every chapter in the book is prefaced with a stanza from a rock song, we realized that this was a crucial part of this story. Michael and I identified about a dozen spots where music could go (without stopping the story, the way music in old-fashioned musicals would do). Then we chose about three alternative choices for each of those spots and later ran them by John and Richard, to choose which ones they wanted. Some were retained for their perfect fit with the story, some were dropped because the musical artist didn't want to sell his rights to the movie (I recall Bo Diddley didn't want to license "Who Do You Love?" That turned out fine, because John and Alan Howarth came up with great synthesizer music for the Buddy Repperton death scene.) I would phone Michael (these were the days before email), and say, do you have "such-and-such" I could listen to? He'd respond, "Do you mean the 1953 version done by the Platters or the 1962 version done by..." etc. Then he would traverse his (as I recall) three-story house on the beach in Venice and within a minute drop the needle onto the record and play me the cut. His organization and knowledge was tremendous!

I also recall that despite having over 50,000 albums he knew how to access immediately, he was just beginning to receive copies of CDs, a brand-new medium at the time. By now, most record companies knew about Michael, so they routinely sent him copies of everything they produced, so there would be a library record of it.

KIM GOTTLIEB-WALKER (on set photographer): The factory we created with a mixture of artificial and natural light was beautiful. Barry Bernardino had gathered 18 Plymouth Furies from all over the country for the film and the pristine ones were on that assembly line.

BILL PHILLIPS: I had just finished adapting "Firestarter" (1980), which John really liked but which he walked away from when Universal cut his budget from $27 million down to $15 million. He had the legal right to do this because he had a "pay or play deal", and since they changed the contract, he chose to walk. He bought a Bell-Jet Long Ranger helicopter with the money and took flying lessons. As I recall, he had become fascinated with helicopter flying since working on *The Thing* in Alaska. Anyway, when *Firestarter* (1984) fell apart (our version was much better than what was released... I had taken out all the Six Million Dollar Man-type pyrotechnics that people were then seeing every week on TV... the new version put them all back in), John phoned and asked if I'd like to consider *Christine*. He told me that it was about a killer car, so I first told him I didn't think I'd be interested. All I could think of was *Knight Rider* (1982-1986) and *My Mother the Car* (1965-1966). He asked me to give the book a chance. Just read it. So I said I would, he sent it over, and halfway through I called and said I'd do it. I really liked it and saw that it was head-and-shoulders above other "vehicle" stories at the time.

JOHN CARPENTER: *Firestarter* was the movie that I wish I had done. That would have been great. I had my heart set on directing that film, I just thought the story was excellent and moving and interesting and a lovely tale about a father and daughter. Bill Phillips did a superb job on the script, I mean this script was top notch, as is *Christine*, but I really wish *Firestarter* went ahead. Universal of course changed gears and dropped the project and gave it to someone else, and it was all to do with budgetary reasons. This was such a shame. Bill Phillips is such a great writer and very good at adapting Stephen King's novels, he knows how to condense the material and bring all of the great stuff to the fore. *Firestarter* was a perfect example of this, and I just fell in love with the story. I thought what they did with it was good, but I just wish I got to do it. I wanted to explore this relationship between this girl and her father and how they're both on the run.

RICHARD KOBRITZ: It was coincidental for John to get that phone call to do *Christine* after *Firestarter* got cancelled, and that has to be devastating when a film gets cancelled. You feel like you're about to hit the goal line and do a touchdown and then you find out your film project got cancelled! That is awful. So, you tend to grab something else, and I think that's what John did with *Christine*. And it worked out!

KEITH GORDON ("Arnie Cunningham"): I knew about the silly reviews for *The Thing*, and I knew that John had gone through this really difficult thing, no pun intended, where he was so beat up for *The Thing*, and he was wanting to do something small. At least when he talked about it at the time was the beauty of *Christine* that it was made for Columbia, but it was made like an independent movie. It was by comparison a small budget; it was a negative pickup, so you didn't have the studio riding him nearly as closely as they might otherwise. So I knew that after *The Thing* he was really like, "I want to do something that is less money, and I don't have to worry about what everyone thinks so much."

ADAM DEVLIN (on the songs): This George Thorogood and The Destroyers classic rock number from 1982 opens the film. It's 1957, in the Chrysler automobile factory in Detroit USA, where the production line for the Plymouth Fury is in full swing. The production line is full of pale beige cars except for one, which is red (Christine). "Bad to the Bone" is at the fore of the opening scenes, with George Thororgood's heavy growl and the Destroy-ers' heavy rock thump – it's the perfect choice to open the film. I particularly like the timing/editing of this opening scene, with the camera focusing on Christine, the only car that's different, just as Thorogood gets to the first chorus, with him repeating "Bad to the bone / Bad to the bone / B-B-B-B-Bad / B-B-B-B-Bad / B-B-B-B-Bad / Bad to the bone". Straight up we know there is something menacing going on. A car-worker opens Christine's hood, the sec-ond verse is heard – all about breaking hearts at will and then, as the worker kneels down to check Christine's grill, he puts his hand on the radiator to balance himself and we get Thororgood burst-ing into a repeat chorus – the hood drops and traps the worker's hand. *Christine* was released in 1983 and George Thorogood's "Bad to the Bone" was release the previous year. Opening the film with this song serves two main purposes. Firstly, as a major hit from the previous year it gives the film a contemporary "feel". It is full of machismo and perfectly suits the opening scenes of a car produc-tion line. And despite being a relatively new track, its production style harks back to 1950s "rock 'n' roll", the period the opening scene is set in. It's a clever way to invite the 1980s audience back to the 1950s. The second purpose of this song is through its lyrics. It's full of bravado. The opening line "On the day I was born / The nurses all gathered 'round / And they gazed in wide wonder / At the joy they had found…" ties in beautifully with the image of the car having its final touches applied to it on the production line – as if being "born". It personifies the car. It tells us this car is "different", that this baby is "bad to the bone". It so perfectly tells us exactly what we need to know about this car that it's hard to believe this song wasn't written specifically for this scene, which of course it wasn't.

Christine on the assembly line.

The dead attendant spills out of Christine after ashing his cigar on her upholstery.

Donald M. Morgan overlooks a shot with John Carpenter, during the opening sequence shoot.

Multiple Plymouths were sourced for the shoot.

Producer Richard Kobrtiz and director John Carpenter on set during the prologue.

The attendant cops a slap on the wrist from the malevolent Christine.

"NOT FADE AWAY": Dennis picks up Arnie

Cutting from the urgency of the automobile machinery supervisor honking Christine's horn, we now arrive in the fictional Californian suburb of Rockbridge – a major change of locale from the novel which was set in Pittsburgh, in tribute to Stephen King's friend and sometimes collaborator, horror maestro George A. Romero. The title card also lets us know that times have changed, and we are brought into the late seventies – 1978 – which would make it twenty one years after Christine was born. The music transition is most interesting here as we shift from Buddy Holly's classic "Not Fade Away" with its warm hum and airy nuances making way to an updated version of the number from country and western artist Tanya Tucker who gives the song a grittier and more sexually charged edge. Holly recorded the number in 1957 in New Mexico with his band The Crickets and utilized the Bo Diddley beat for its percussion, having drummer Jerry Allison pound out the beat on a cardboard box. Here in Tucker's version, distorted Fenders would ring out the melody and add to it, while her vocals remain laid back and yet evoke a sense of sensual beckoning. Tucker's greatest hit would be the incredibly moving "Delta Dawn" which would later be covered by Bette Midler on her debut album "The Divine Miss M" (1972) and given an even more theatrical sensibility, and here Tucker's adaptation of Buddy Holly's masterfully composed hit is reborn for a new sound aesthetic.

This musical transition accompanies a large dark blue 1968 Dodge Charger cruising down the leafy suburban street. This is one of director John Carpenter's most treasured and romantically embraced worlds – the American suburb. In *Halloween*, he delivers a poignant and mesmerizing image of small town USA, and what he manages to do so beautifully is power it with a sense of foreboding, ethereal otherworldliness and a quietly nightmarish pulse. Here in *Christine*, Rockbridge is very similar to Haddonfield; a white middle class halcyon tree-lined suburb that is a perfect environment for hushed terror – where a masked madman can stalk boy-crazy babysitters or a car that drives on its own can run down slacker never-do-wells. The Dodge is driven by athletic and handsome jock Dennis Guilder (John Stockwell) who drives down the picturesque street pulling up at his best friend Arnie Cunningham's house. He honks his horn (once again, the sense of urgency and beckoning comes into play) and impatiently mutters "Come on Arnie…" which is a great telling first line – if the entire movie examines Arnie Cunningham's inability to "keep up with his peers", then this throwaway from Dennis is remarkably insightful. Dennis is a good looking self-possessed winner, while his friend Arnie is out of step with his generation, pathetic, nerdish and a loser. Before we are introduced to Arnie, we meet his mother Regina Cunningham (Christine Belford) who from the get go is a domineering figure. Her demeanour, her tone, her attitude and her physical presence is built up and around perpetual annoyance, frustration and seething disdain for a world that doesn't fit into her "schedule" and an embodiment of the "overbearing mother" archetype that sometimes props up in the much more rare male-centric horror. This role of the domineering matriarch in horror stems from a thorough understanding of the same kinds of women in legitimate and pop-psychology, where eternally nagging mothers who fuss over their boys result in said boy becoming either unable to relate to his peers, a fumbling mess with girls, a homosexual or – and more so often in horror films – a psychotic killer.

Arnie Cunningham, on arrival, is established instantly as a pathetic, skittish and atypical geek; he clumsily runs out of his house, spills garbage onto the driveway, forgets to collect his lunch and jolts towards Dennis with a painful nervousness. By the end of this scene, Regina calls out "Slow down", insisting Dennis doesn't speed and this is also incredibly insightful in her role as a character desperate to have her son "slow down" and "not grow up". It also signals the dangers of teen driving which the film embraces as a thematic centrepiece. John Carpenter paints an impressive world of driving teenagers and scrutinizes the importance of the car in the teenage male's life. He also delivers Regina in an acute fashion, fastening her as the forever over protective mother to a boy that will ultimately rebel and suffer.

Another interesting aspect to this establishing scene is the moment where Regina calls out to Arnie that he has forgotten his lunch and that there is "yogurt in there". Yogurt during the late seventies and even more so throughout the health conscious eighties would become a symbol of the burgeoning fitness movement made incredibly popular by everything from Jane Fonda's workout videos to Olivia Newton-John's "Physical" (1981) video clip. This is also another element of controlling Arnie; a way in which Regina can puppeteer her son with the food he puts into his body. Later, the yogurt's symbolic visage will come to be representative of male "fumbling in the dark" and penal malfunction, something that Regina would not even want to think about, after all, she wants Arnie to remain a child ("Try and keep it cold, there's yogurt in there!"). Fumbling and creating chaos and mess is exactly what director Carpenter and screenwriter Bill Phillips weave here in visual terms, with the garbage bag tearing open and spilling onto the driveway being emblematic of Arnie's inability to do a good job and the worrisome fact that this boy is completely out of step with conventional capability.

Regina's complaint about Dennis's car radio is also an indication that she is not only easily irritated but also someone consumed by newsworthy fads and topics that feed into the living rooms of suburban households. She describes the Tanya Tucker version of "Not Fade Away" as "noise pollution", and likens it to Dennis "dumping toxic waste" on her lawn – screenwriter Bill Phillips concocts this character as a woman driven by battling constant and petty inconveniences, something that suburbia is a magical place for. The horror that is born within suburbia – also explored in *Halloween* – can therefore spawn from an extension of banality and innocuousness; for example, Regina's bitterness and irritability can be countered by Christine's eventual rage, fury and bloodthirsty killer instinct. These two female counterparts for Arnie symbolically and tangibly represent oppression at one hand and liberation at the other – but ultimately, a slow death is the result from both. It is only Leigh Cabot (Alexandra Paul) that offers pure salvation, however she is eventually rejected in favour of the vindictive witch that is Christine.

The tree lined streets, the long stretches of asphalt and the rich greens that cinematographer Donald M. Morgan captures with his lens all add to the romance of leafy suburbia, and this unlikely friendship shared between Dennis and Arnie somehow fits in well amidst the neatly groomed lawns and wide driveways. These two boys – who can be read as pseudo-lovers, for their compassion for one another (before Christine enters the picture) is undoubtedly passionate and dedicated – have clearly been friends since they were children, and in Stephen King's thoroughly romantic novel, this is certainly established. Both boys come from very similar backgrounds, and here we see that the Cunningham household is the embodiment of comfortable middle class America and the economically OK baby boomers of the late seventies, with America finally coming out of its oppressive recession.

JOHN CARPENTER: The change of the locale from Pittsburgh, which is where Stephen King sets the novel, to California was set up during the script writing stage of production. I can't truly remember the exact reasoning behind changing the location, however I do strongly believe that Los Angeles has a beautiful picturesque quality to it and that would play well with this film about a car – also, California is a car nation, so it makes sense. The other thing is that Pittsburgh is not the most attractive city in the world, and it's hard to tell this particular story in a big city, I mean a haunted car movie really needs to take place in a semi-isolated place like a small town for it to work.

BILL PHILLIPS: Rockbridge was an invented town, it didn't exist in California. I recall using September 12 superimposed over Dennis' picking up Arnie. That was my wedding anniversary date. No one else in the world cares. A lot of the book features voice over narration by Dennis Guilder and I'm not a fan of narration. Too often in films it's used as a crutch, imposed by studio executives to talk down to the audience and essentially say, "What the filmmaker meant to say but failed to cinematically was…" Look, for example, at the first release of Ridley Scott's *Blade Runner* (1982). It's full of stupid stuff someone imposed on the film, but at the time, Scott didn't have the clout to insist on keeping the narration out. Ten years later, Scott re-released the film in theatres without the narration. It was much better. Granted, there are some movies where a narration works. My favorite is *Days of Heaven* (1978). I tend to like narrations that aren't "voice of God."

KEITH GORDON: I loved *Carrie* (1976) and *The Shining* (1980) and I certainly read some of Stephen King's works, but I wouldn't read everything of his. But of course Stephen was not directly involved with the making of *Christine*, although I did get to speak to him on the phone which was exciting. The novel itself was a hugely successful popular best seller right while we were making the film adaptation which is a very rare thing, and it was extremely hard to get a hold of, so I couldn't read it before getting into the role of Arnie. King was becoming very popular and two other books were being made at the same time we were making *Christine* – *Cujo* (1983) and *The Dead Zone* (1983) – so I was certainly well aware of his growing fan base. I was aware of all this, but not at all focused on it. I always thought of *Christine* as more of a John Carpenter film than a Stephen King adaptation. As far as getting the part of Arnie, my agent called me and told me they were auditioning and I was very excited as I was already a big fan of John Carpenter's. I had never met him but really wanted to work with him, so I got the script and went into the audition with my two looks: the nerdy Arnie look with the glasses and the buttoned up shirt and the cool/crazy Arnie look with a black t-shirt and what not, and the read went well. Then later I went in and shared a scene with John Stockwell who played Dennis Guilder. John was cast first which I thought was odd seeing that Arnie is the central figure of the movie, but I guess Carpenter found John first and saw something he liked so cast him before me.

BILL PHILLIPS: I loved my contributions to Arnie's introduction. The book worked very well, but I had fun with the garbage bag breaking as he was taking out the trash, the yogurt being packed by his mom and later causing him to slip on the floor, the adult word Arnie had tried to use in Scrabble… even the fact that he played

Scrabble. I also thought giving the family a Volvo was perfect, since Volvo (a perfectly good and respectable car) also symbolized to me a slightly overprotective and conventional owner. These tiny details add up. One never wants a detail to be a show-stopper... every element of the script (and the film) should contribute to making the story work. So I just tried to come up with as many elements as I could. Of course, there were many already there from the book. When Kevin Bacon turned them down to play Arnie, I phoned the producer immediately and reported just seeing Keith Gordon in Brian De Palma's *Dressed to Kill* (1980) (where he plays Angie Dickinson's son). I seem to recall that the next day (although my memory may be hazy... maybe it was a few days) they announced signing Keith Gordon to the role. I was very happy mainly because Keith is great and secondarily because traditionally in features (unlike TV) no one listens to the writer. John Carpenter always did. Soon after the film wrapped, I saw Keith on the Venice boardwalk. He gave me his newly-minted business card, white with red blood splotches. It said, "Blood and Guts All Over the Place Productions." Now Keith is a wonderful director.

ELISSA ROSE (on costume design): We first meet the character of Arnie Cunningham taking out the trash, looking like somewhere between a 1950s bookworm and a 1980s geek the likes of Lewis Skolnick (*Revenge of the Nerds* (1984)) or Professor Julius Kelp played by the legendary Jerry Lewis (*The Nutty Professor* (1963)). His costuming is non-assuming and low key, consisting of low cut Converse sneakers, sensible olive coloured trousers co-ordinated with a beige button down shirt, the inside top pocket concealing a plastic pocket protector laden with pens. Completing the cliché is his slicked down hair and thick plastic framed glasses that are later smashed in a confrontation with the greaser bullies and subsequently taped together at the nose piece. The hero garment that develops almost like an emotional barometer to the film's plot is the pale blue Gabardine "Ricky" Jacket.

BILL PHILLIPS: I remember yogurt was often something a health-conscious parent might pack in their kid's lunch, and it also seemed to be something very "uncool" for Arnie to have to bring to school. And of course it was intended all along to be a set-up for Buddy to impale with this switchblade.

ADAM DEVLIN: As the worker who had his hand trapped in Christine's hood is walked off in the previous scene – hand in bandages – another worker comes over and sits in the car. He is smoking a cigar and as he sits, he turns the car radio on, dropping some smouldering ash along the way. The radio starts playing "Not Fade Away" by Buddy Holly. This was first released in 1957, as a B-side to The Cricket's hit single "Oh Boy", which appeared on their album "The 'Chirping' Crickets". The Crickets were a rock 'n' roll band that Buddy Holly founded in the early 1950s. We only get to hear the first two lines of the song – "I'm a-gonna tell you how it's gonna be / You're gonna give your love to me…" We then hear the "knock-off" bell and all the workers leave. The foreman notices something on the production line – a car's headlights are on and its radio is playing. He walks to the car, opens the door and as we hear the lyric "My love a-bigger than a Cadillac / I try to show it and you drive a-me back / Your love for me a-got to be real / For you to know just how I feel…" the cigar smoking man falls out onto the floor, dead – with his cigar is his mouth. The car is Christine. The use of this song for this scene is inspired. Firstly it sets us firmly in 1957 after George Thorogood had suggested it in "Bad to the Bone". Secondly the lyric clearly states that this car is in charge. This car is demanding love and respect. It's a brilliant juxtaposition of song and film. It is as if the car radio is "speaking" for the car. The song then changes into an updated version, sung brilliantly by country star Tanya Tucker and we see a blue "muscle car" with a young man (Dennis) at the wheel. Text on the screen tells us we're now in 1978, and Tucker's version of "Not Fade Away" cuts in with the line "A love for real not fade away". This line, at this point in the film – just as we're meeting Dennis and his blue "muscle car" – tells us this car, like the song, is from that original period but has been "updated". It is basically saying the old can, and should, be renewed.

John Stockwell as Dennis Guilder.

"YOU CARRY YOUR LIFE SAVINGS BETWEEN YOUR LEGS": Dennis and Arnie drive to school

It is worthwhile to note that the first time we see Arnie Cunningham in a car he is being driven by his best friend Dennis. Dennis sits comfortably at the steering wheel of his Dodge, cruising the suburban terrain with great ease and carrying a conversation with his put upon pal that is loaded with sexual content. Arnie wears large oversized Coca-Cola bottle style glasses, and clothes that he swims in – shabby, unkempt and sporting a pencil pocket. All of these physical trappings have since become visual cues that have now become synonymous with nerds and "nerd culture". He sits in the passenger seat completely dwarfed (not so much by size, but by stance) by the athletic and broadly built Dennis. This unlikely pairing is built upon Dennis's worldliness (at least "high school worldliness") and sexual prowess in contextualised narrative comparison to Arnie's awkwardness and virginity. There is also a major sense of allowance in these boys' lives – social allowance which can be summarised in this image of Dennis driving and Arnie sitting by his side. It is a reported matter of fact notion that Dennis is permitted to exist and run his own life (it is interesting to note that his parents are visually missing from the entire film) and that Arnie's choices are made by his parents (most notably Regina, his mother).

The opening to this back and forth conversation sequence has Dennis ask if Arnie and Regina were fighting. Arnie explains that his mother is not happy that he is taking shop as one of his subjects at school. He explains that it "might embarrass her" and this is once again – thanks to the perceptive writing of screenwriter Bill Phillips – an acute commentary on class and status as well as something that makes a vastly important annotative response to Regina's fear of her son being good at something or moving forward. What will be developed and explored in *Christine* is the fact that this pathetic sod Arnie Cunningham is in fact excellent with his hands and excels in auto mechanics. Dennis promotes this character attribute (more explicitly in Stephen King's novel which opens with Dennis narrating the story) and makes a sturdy comment about Arnie's parents' disapproval of taking shop with making note that they won't be complaining when their "stupid Volvo breaks down and you fix it for free."

Breaking this point of conversation, Arnie turns off the radio and this marks the first moment in the film outside of the opening credits that is not scored by rock 'n' roll. We are now entering a world of conversations that are preoccupied with sex, sexual practices, profanity and talk of genitals which seems to dominate a massive chunk of the film's narrative structure. The first conversation outside of musical accompaniment is set to the soft humming of Dennis's Dodge and the "Scrabble talk" opens as an anecdote about spending the night in with parents playing board games but ends with "Fellatio", attributing to the film's obsession with sex and sexual acts. Following this Dennis brings up Arnie's virginity and has a vested interest in wanting him to lose it. He suggests various girls: Gale Justin and Sally Hayes. These girls are dismissed by Arnie (a hairy lip, promiscuity being a turn off) and this annoys Dennis who just wants to help his friend out by ensuring that he moves forward and catches up to his peers ("Now that we're gonna be seniors, I figure it's about time that we got you laid") and this is something that a lot of films from this period would be interested in.

Christine comes out from the teen sex comedy boom which was a massively popular American cinematic institution of the early eighties that included films such as *Porky's* (1981), *Private School* (1983), *Class* (1983), *Screwballs* (1983) and *My Tutor* (1983) to name just a few. Actor John Stockwell would star in one of the best received teen sex comedies and this would come out the same year he would be cast as Dennis in *Christine* – Curtis Hanson's *Losin' It* (1983). Stockwell would later go on to write the teleplay for the excellent made for TV biopic *Breast Men* (1997), which would scrutinize the world of breast implants, making a finely tuned comment on both the sensuous appeal of large breasts and then the health implications for the women that may come later. If *Christine* is obsessed with sex and sensuality, it is also a finely tuned horror story that examines the dangers that come with seduction and carnal conquest

– therefore, what John Carpenter's film does, is marry the frustrated desires of horny young people with potentially dangerous outcomes – something that the zeitgeist of the culture at the time would happily churn out with the slasher trend.

However, Dennis's genuine care for Arnie's happiness goes beyond "getting him laid", it ultimately means to get him involved in the outer circle that exists outside of their intimate friendship, and this buddy-hood is something that pops up again and again in teen-centric cinema, most notably films dedicated to sexual conquest as the core means of narrative function. A film such as Bob Clark's *Porky's* has a group of young boys all trying to lose their virginity but it is actively disinterested in the fragile relationships shared between young boys becoming men, while in *Christine* this is an emotional post. Here it is the one boy whose virginity is a fundamental issue and a tormenting factor that haunts him. Other boys in the film are referred to as virgins (in the following scene, this is established), however their zealous interest in girls and social standing gives them a permissive edge, while Arnie is completely ravaged by the social ills that come with being an outsider. Arnie is out of step, while Dennis is confident and a doer. The scene ends with Arnie miserably confiding in Dennis, saying "I think maybe I'll just beat off", masturbation being the only answer. This closing line goes beyond virginity, it is also an indicative tool that drills into the concept of Arnie being unattractive, something that King's novel truly exaggerates and revels in detail. In the novel, Arnie Cunningham is riddled with pimples, with skin raw and red and oozing puss. Here in the film, actor Keith Gordon – a handsome young actor with strong features – is initially made up to look unremarkable, however, it is Gordon's brilliantly nuanced performance that gives the character his gravitas that makes him conventionally unappealing. In this sense, having physical ugliness as a hindrance to sexual conquest, links the masturbation line to one from Mart Crowley's play and subsequent film adaptation from William Friedkin, *The Boys in the Band* (1970), where the protagonist (facing balding and ageing) quips "Still, it's one thing you can say for masturbation – you certainly don't have to look your best!"

BILL PHILLIPS: Dennis was handed to me completely by Stephen King. My only job was not to blow it. Jock, check. Popular, check. Good-looking, check. Friend of Arnie's, check. Even his subsequent attraction to Leigh was secondary... he wasn't a ladies' man. That would have detracted from Arnie becoming the lothario he eventually does – before his demise. I never had any problem with Dennis and Arnie being friends. In my own high school career, I tended to be (in my small high school) one of the "popular kids." (Class V.P., editor of the yearbook, etc). But I had a "bus-mate," my next door neighbor, who was probably closer to being like Arnie than like Dennis. There was never any awkwardness or embarrassment. I know there are cliques in school, but in my experience, there were always plenty of exceptions, and no one ever faulted you (contrary to some clichéd high school dramas) for befriending people "outside your group." Also, although we never got into this in *Christine*, sometimes parents are friends, and so their kids necessarily hang out together, whether they want to or not.

RICHARD KOBRITZ: *Peyton Place* (1957) meets *Dracula* (1931) was always my analogy in regards to *Salem's Lot*. Stephen King used to view it as the play *Our Town* turning into vampires and I said "No, it's *Peyton Place* turning into vampires". It had kicked around Warner Bros. for a few years, they had owned it and has a number of scripts on it, but they didn't know how to crack it because you can't make a four hour feature, no one is going to sit through it and part of it is the townspeople and how they interact with each other and their hidden secrets and things like that, which make Barlow as well as the James Mason character all the more perfect – they come in, they run an antiques shop, they get to know the people and eventually the vampire kills them. So to me, when I read the book and knew that Warners had two screenplays, I thought, well being the head of the Warners television unit, I convinced the executives to get the project away from the studio and do the piece as a three hour miniseries instead. So we ended up wrestling it from them, and I made changes. I didn't look at the original book as sacrosanct; I thought there were things that you could play with. One of the things was that Barlow in the book was a romantic character; he was like Frank Langella's *Dracula* (1979) or even a George Hamilton – this romantic figure. I changed it to a bloody monster. I didn't want Barlow to speak. I wanted to evoke more Nosferatu than a romantic bloodsucking 1930s Dracula. Paul Monash, the screenwriter, agreed with me on not having Barlow speak, but then we had to give all of his dialogue to the James Mason character and that was hard because we had no idea who we were going to get. However, the president of Warner Bros. happened to be in England and called me and said that he was staying at the same hotel as James Mason and he suggested it to him and then asked me what I thought and I said, "Yes! Let's get him a script". There was no Fed Ex in those days, and I still don't know how we got the script over to him in two or three days, but we did, and that's how we got James Mason who was a consummate professional. We became very good friends, and in fact I wanted to do another picture with him, but unfortunately he died before we got to it – and that film was another Stephen King adaptation, *Apt Pupil* (eventually released in 1998). It was a totally different script to what eventuated, and the boy who we were thinking of casting was perfect, but unfortunately Mason died so that went out the door. Stephen King sent me the manuscript for "Cujo" (1981) and it wasn't that I didn't like it, I just didn't know what I could do with it. I thought it would be tricky to sustain an audience's interest in a film that was mostly one location with a mother and child trapped in a car. I didn't see anything there, I had to be honest with myself and if I didn't see anything fruitful in that, then why waste time on it? If you don't absolutely love the material then don't make it, but also you have to consider, if you love the material that is all well and good, but will anybody else love it? Those are the two questions any producer has to ask. I was not that enthused by "Cujo". Stephen also sent me "It" (1986) and I saw that as a six hour miniseries and I thought 'I cannot be at Warner Bros. television and running and overseeing a six hour miniseries', only because I see a picture about sixty five times from beginning to end, and it's one thing to do it on a two hour movie, but another thing to do it for a four hour miniseries let alone a six hour one. I mean I could never see myself doing something like "The Stand" (1978) for that reason alone. Then, all of a sudden Stephen sent me "Christine"

– and that was it! It was all there! It also celebrated America's love affair with the automobile, which I loved. Gene Kelly, the legendary dancer/director once said to me about Hollywood: "Dress nice and drive a nice car and nobody will care even if you lived in a hovel". And I think that's true, especially in Los Angeles which is obsessed with the notion of having a beautiful set of clothes and a beautiful set of wheels, and that's all that matters. The love America has for cars is the primary reason I went with *Christine*, and the fact that the Arnie character does a one eighty! I mean he is *Caspar Milquetoast* in the beginning and then all of a sudden he is young Elvis midway in the picture that appealed to me immensely. It was also something that really required a real actor not just some pretty boy.

ADAM DEVLIN: As Dennis, with his blue muscle car picks up his nerdy school friend (Arnie), we hear the opening tune of ABBA's "The Name of the Game". This is the first piece of truly contemporary music we hear in the film. With its slow-tempo, throbbing electronic beats, we're very clearly nowhere near the 1950s anymore. We don't get to hear any of the vocals of the song, and we don't need to. Although to those that know the song – it was a top 10 hit in the USA so it would have been widely known – it would have given a subliminal thematic message: something's going on, a game is being played. It is a very inspired and foreboding, albeit subtle, choice for the soundtrack.

Richard Kobritz and Stephen King showcase their flashy "Christine" bomber jackets.

Richard Kobritz on location.

Tobe Hooper, Richard Kobritz and John Carpenter on the set of
Salem's Lot (1979).

"DID YOU SEE THE NEW GIRL?" : Enter Leigh Cabot

In Stephen King's novel, the first voice heard as narrator is Dennis Guilder and he introduces the story as a love triangle – a triangle shared between Arnie Cunningham, Leigh Cabot and the Plymouth Fury, Christine. He also makes a point that Christine came first, and here in John Carpenter's film, this monstrous titular automobile is given an immediate introduction, while her female counterpart – the smart, capable, resourceful and genuinely warm Leigh – is introduced to the film later and with much less fanfare. The sequence that opens her introduction has Carpenter using one of his acutely conditioned and manicured trademark moving camera tricks, where he has his cinematographer Donald M. Morgan cruise down the halls of Rockbridge High School. His lens drills towards Dennis Guilder and Arnie Cunningham tending to their lockers, ready to start their school day. Dennis – the "winner" – is at ease with his locker, taking to books with sturdy strong hands, while Arnie – the "loser" – fumbles with the lock, makes endless attempts at opening the metallic door and remains frustrated and stunted by his inability to control something as mundane as a locker.

The hall is busy and alive with activity. It is host to strolling and chatty students dressed in casual clothes informing us that this is a public high school. Rockbridge seems to be a traditional middle class school – the kind of educational institution that for the most part populated contemporary cinema of the early eighties. These young people are comfortable and without a major social happening (such as war) to fight against. Teens of eighties cinema had new enemies – parents and teachers, and *Christine* is a perfect example of this. Joining Dennis and Arnie is football player Chuck (Marc Poppel) who lunges into Dennis, and playfully tackles him. This roughhousing is part of the "code" for teen boys who buy into the jock ethos and is acceptable and even lauded. It is interesting to note that Chuck completely ignores Arnie, a character who is undeserving of "being one of the boys". Not only is Arnie not able to engage in conversation about high school football, but he is also rendered invisible by the likes of Chuck who is fixed on conversation with Dennis about the sport they both play. Chuck asks Dennis if he is playing the game this year and also enquires about his "gimpy knee" (something that will become a massive issue later in the film), he is met by Dennis boasting that he has to pick up where Chuck and the other boys "fumble", giving us the impression that Dennis is the hero of the game and the quarterback to watch. As Chuck leaves, with an extra playful punch which is reciprocated by Dennis, we meet the beautiful blonde Roseanne (Kelly Preston), who is once again another character who completely ignores Arnie's existence. Roseanne is Dennis's "sometimes girlfriend", and her expression, mannerisms and flirtatious nature ensures us that she is totally smitten by Dennis. When she asks about his ability to "play football", this tiny slice of teen interaction is a moment completely loaded with a sexual charge. She coyly asks "They gonna let you play football this year?" to which Dennis replies "Coach says I'm as good as new", and here in this brief moment, we understand that Roseanne is keen on spending as much time she can with Dennis as humanly possible – she is a cheerleader and he is the star quarterback. While she talks to Dennis, Arnie lingers behind her, mouthing and mimicking her, and instead of being scolded, Dennis darts his eyes at him and grins. Here is a bond between teen boys that exists in secret over the shoulders of teenage girls – something that the film endeavours to examine and then pushes aside once Arnie "meets" Christine. With Arnie behind Roseanne making gooey eyes and biting at her hair, he literally becomes someone in the background ignored by the "beautiful people". Ending with Roseanne flirtatiously spouting an acronym in "TTFN" ("Ta ta for now"), she walks away and is ogled by the boys. Even Arnie is gobsmacked at her beauty and sex appeal, and this sexual charge of girls and women is what fuels John Carpenter's film and is the basis of Stephen King's novel. Teenage boys will become slaves to female sexuality and in *Christine*, this sexuality is materialised in machinery and unhealthy objectiphilia.

Another friend of Dennis's, the horned up Bemis (Douglas Warhit) approaches and joins in watching Roseanne walk away, their eyes fixed on her derrière. He delivers a sleazy observation with "I wouldn't put that in my mouth Dennis, you don't know where it's been!" (crass commentary on cunnilingus) and this is met with Arnie (now finally "visible" to the other student body outside of Dennis) remarking "We know where it hasn't been! It hasn't been with you!" Bemis tells Arnie to "drop dead Cunningham" and this silences the socially frail Arnie who goes back to struggling with his locker. Bemis's comment and Arnie's follow up feed the film's vested interest in boys seeing girls as conquests and soon conversation begins about the "new girl" who he describes as someone who "looks smart" but has "the body of a slut". Bemis's repulsive misogyny bemuses Dennis, who is a character drawn with broad tenderness as later he will comfort Leigh and continually show affection for both her and his best friend Arnie (who will of course become a malevolent misfit), and before he can respond to Bemis we are introduced to this "new girl" and see her through the eyes of Dennis, Bemis and Arnie who watch her like hounds leering at a butcher's window.

Leigh is a stunning and athletic young lady with big billowy auburn brown hair that bounces as she strolls down the hall with Rockbridge High School's principal Mr. Smith (Bruce French). She is on display and walking a line, very similar to the way in which Christine was introduced in the prologue, as a woman on parade, watched and viewed through the perpetually scrutinizing male gaze. The principal also makes mention of Leigh "meeting boys" by joining student activities such as the marching band – more characters, and here one of the adults, casually invested in girls being paired up with boys – to which she replies with a keen interest in working on the school's year book, suggesting a pursuit in journalism, photography or editing (something outside of simply "meeting boys"). When she walks past the boys, she gives them a big beautiful smile, and it is more than likely directed to Dennis who would be the obvious choice in the line-up. However, Bemis insists that the smile was for him, and remarks that he wants to have "deep, meaningful sex" with her; trivialising the role of sex as something as nothing more than a pastime. Bemis is another virgin, but an acceptable one as opposed to Arnie, because he is one that is actively interested in girls and desperate to make an impression on them. In regards to his pursuit of Leigh, Dennis tells Bemis that he has "nothing to lose but your virginity", and the eager horny teen races off after her. Arnie's admiration of Leigh is prevalent here as he considers her "too classy" for Bemis, and eventually the film will match up him and this newfound beauty – but, as the novel suggests from its opening sentence, and as the film moves onto a follow up scene, Christine will be Arnie's first love (and most passionate).

With this sequence ending with Arnie still having trouble with his locker (an overt symbol of his sexual inabilities and control over his domain ("Having trouble with your locker?")) and Dennis managing it for him, and opening it for him (a clear symbol of Dennis being in charge of his sexual prowess and helping the pathetic stunted Arnie), the entirety of the scene is loaded with multi-layered insight into character, theme and narrative potential. It is assumed that someone like Leigh will end up with Dennis, it is reinstated that Arnie is out of touch with the rest of his peers, there is a reference to "Red China" which plays with the political upheaval caused by Cold War influence which would be something that would come into play in multiple films and other art forms during the eighties from action movies such as *Red Dawn* (1984), *Rocky IV* (1985), *Invasion U.S.A.* (1985) and *Top Gun* (1986) through to rock operas on the Broadway and West End stage such as *Chess* (1986). The high school itself as a middle class institution peppered with students and teachers of the late seventies is an environment of sexual charge, archetypal dynamics and plot exposition. The look and feel of the characters tap into a decade divided by hard rock and disco, and a sense of fifties sensibility permeates the air – especially in the aesthetic of characters such as Roseanne, who seems to reflect bubble gum, "let's go to the hub" energy. The film is a tribute to fifties nostalgia and marries the connective tissue of girls and cars as the two most vitally important thing in a teen boy's life. Roseanne is presented as the girlfriend who is on the out and yet still hung up on her beau, while Leigh rolls in as the "new model"; the upgrade, the newfound vision of classic American beauty that, once again, makes a captivating and complicated link to the role of girls and cars.

BILL PHILLIPS: Roseanne was another of those characters I didn't put a lot of thought into. In those cases, your main goal (and theirs) is to capture the moment brilliantly and efficiently so the story can move on. Kelly Preston did a great job doing just that. Alexandra Paul was, of course, beautiful in the leading role of Leigh, the new girl everyone wanted. But Kelly, as Roseanne, was also beautiful. As I recall (in my advanced years) there's an inherent unfairness back in high school where completely attractive people either "make the cut" or don't in terms of popularity. Every time Kelly is on the screen, she is being ignored by the males. Dumb! I do think that one reason *Christine* has become a cult classic is because of the excellent casting done by Karen Rea (and of course, aided and abetted by John and Richard.) Every character is indelible and I think plays an accurate archetype… but not a stereotype. I'm not sure how much of that is brilliance and how much of that is luck – but let's call it brilliance.

ALEXANDRA PAUL ("Leigh Cabot"): I auditioned several times for John Carpenter and the producer, Richard Kobritz. I never met any of the cast until the first day of shooting. I had not yet read a Stephen King novel, because I thought they would be too scary! I am sure horror fans must think I am such a wimp and they'd be right! I am! But once I was cast I read "Christine" right away. I was so impressed with Stephen King's writing, that I read several of his other books soon after. I loved his book of very early short stories, particular the first story, which I think was called "Rage". I then read his book of four novellas, "Different Seasons", which has since become one of my all time favorite books! So now, thanks to being cast in *Christine*, I am a huge fan of Stephen King.

BILL PHILLIPS: I actually liked writing for Alexandra (Leigh). The sad fact is that the rough cut of the film was too long, so thirty minutes had to be cut out. This is a movie about a haunted killer car, so you're not going to cut those sequences. Instead (and this is my fault… I learned this on this film… don't make your script too long), they had to cut what I would call the "soft" scenes that show interpersonal relations. They would have added more dimension to the story, but I don't quarrel with the decisions they made. They had to cut a lot of these because it was too long. You can see some of these outtake scenes on the 25th Anniversary DVD. I hadn't looked at them for about thirty years, and I thought they were pretty good and was sad they aren't in the movie. There were "sensitive" scenes between Arnie and Dennis, Arnie and Leigh, Dennis and Leigh, etc. The person who had the most scenes cut was Leigh. I think about twenty minutes of good stuff was cut of her scenes. Again, I don't quarrel with the cuts chosen to be made, but I'm sorry they were cut. I remember at the premiere, Alexandra didn't know what she was going to find. I didn't talk to her afterwards, but I imagine she was disappointed. Being the "hot" girl everyone wanted to impress was fun to depict. The earliest scene was her being walked in by the principal (Alexandra later commented that her knee socks didn't date well. Ha ha! Oh well. The fashion will come around again.) I remember writing the line about admitting Red China into the U.N. and another student pointing out that this had already been done. The whole point is that everyone was a bit discombobulated by her beauty. I think they all did a good job, and Alexandra did "innocent beauty" very well.

DOUG WARHIT ("Bemis"): Alexandra is the sweetest, nicest and most beautiful person you would ever know. This is the kind of person who would go on game shows and donate all the money to schools, animal charities. I remember seeing her rescue a rat and she took it into a vet to get it rehabilitated. She is just amazing. We hit it off straight away. I have a knack of hitting it off with beautiful girls. It was easy for me. I am still very good friends with Alexandra. I am blessed to know her. Emotionally I wasn't very mature so I had no qualms to say a line like "She has the body of a slut". Today it would be considered very politically incorrect to say things like that. It would have to be rewritten in my opinion. But back then I had no issue with it, it was all about horny teenagers.

ALEXANDRA PAUL: I was always slightly intimidated by John Stockwell, who now is a terrific screenwriter and successful director. Keith is the sweetest man ever, and was amazing as Arnie. Trying to get the right stage of Arnie's metamorphosis in each scene, since we shoot out of order, was an acting challenge, and there was always discussion on how far into the change Arnie was, what he looked like at that time in terms of was his collar up or down, how cool was his hair, etc. I met a very great friend on that set, Doug Warhit. We each went to each other's weddings. Doug played Bemis, one of the boys who taunts Arnie in the beginning of the movie and he has a line about Leigh "Have you seen the new girl? She looks smart but she has the body of a slut". Which I think is hilarious since I actually had the body of a gawky teen. I always thought Kelly Preston (who plays Roseanne, the blonde girl who has a crush on Dennis, John Stockwell's character) was more like Leigh than I was. I also met and fell in love with Bill Ostrander, who played Buddy Reperton, and we dated for a couple years.

RICHARD KOBRITZ: For the first few days of the shoot, Alexandra was a nervous wreck. She wasn't brand new to the business but she was new to the business, and she never realised the weight of the role would be on her shoulders, but by the end of the first week, she was fine. But the first couple of days, she was a nervous young lady.

KEITH GORDON: I had not read much of Stephen King's stuff. Basically, I read the book when I was auditioning. I managed to get a hold of like a pre-publication copy. It was just coming out. I remember that it was a big deal to get a hold of. So I don't know with the dates, exactly how that fell together. And I was really impressed by the writing of it. And I certainly loved *The Shining*. I'm a huge Kubrick fan. I know that there is a split between King and Kubrick on that project. I've since come to appreciate his writing much more. There is stuff that I love that's never actually been done for film that I think could be wonderful. There's an early novella of his called "The Long Walk" (1979) – it's about a future world where kids have to go on this walk. And along in the book, you're kind of like "where is this going?" Then you realise that whoever can't keep up with the walk is killed. It's basically a fascist state controlling people through fear... and trying to survive this insane competition. Someone had sent it to me years ago, and I thought this could be an amazing movie! But King clearly had such an influence. What other writer of our generation has had [influence] way beyond the horror genre in terms of how he's affected socially how people see things.

DOUG WARHIT: I wasn't even important enough to be killed! I was a minor character and all I did was provide a minor irritant to Keith Gordon's character. The role came about through my agent and I read the entire novel over the weekend before the audition. I had a good sense of the material before I went in. I thought the book was excellent and I thought it was better than the movie. I don't want to hurt anyone's feelings, but that was my perspective of it. Stephen King is a great storyteller. Horror is not my genre, but I loved this novel. I did see *Carrie*, and I thought that was excellent. You had someone exceptional like Sissy Spacek playing that role – I couldn't imagine anyone else in that role.

ALEXANDRA PAUL: I auditioned, but I had only done a little bit of work prior. I had starred in one TV movie (*Paper Dolls* (1982)) and had a smaller part in another studio film (*American Nightmare* (1983)), and that was all I had done. I went in and Carpenter likes that I seemed innocent... and I was innocent! The one thing they did tell me was to do something with my hair! I didn't know anything about hair, makeup – that was all just a huge mystery to me. And so, for the final audition, I had asked my roommate, who went to UCLA – and she was always putting mousse in her hair and so I figured she knew something about hair to teach me. So she taught me how to curl my hair, but on the day of the final audition, she had exams, so I did my hair in the curlers and drove to the audition with the curlers in so my hair would look fabulous... and I took them out at the audition. I parked a block away and I'm taking out my curlers and she had forgotten to tell me I needed to dry my hair before I put them in curlers, so my hair was still wet and stick straight and it looked horrible! So, anyway, I got the role, I guess it wasn't really about the hair. Of course, in the movie, my hair is all, like curls and Farrah Fawcett... thank God, I had someone to do my hair!

WILLIAM OSTRANDER: I don't remember when Kelly Preston was cast, but certainly I remember that I thought she was gorgeous! I wanted to ask her out! I never asked out Kelly, but I thought she was beautiful, but then I started dating Alexandra Paul who was extraordinary. We were young. She's an amazing person, and there's some sort of friendship connection that I think that stayed. But it was what it was; we were a couple of young people trying to figure out our way, and when you are out in Los Angeles waiting for the phone to ring, sometimes you have too much time on your hands if you know what I mean. I don't think we stumbled too much with working together because we never actually did any scenes together. We tried to be supportive of one another and sometimes that support was covered in envy, and sometimes it was a matter of being really happy for one another. I think youth was a big part of it.

DOUG WARHIT: During the first scene with the locker, the director John Carpenter was off camera and he was making all these funny faces – pulling these crazy faces at us. I thought, man, how unprofessional can this guy be? But then I realised, way after that, that he was trying to get us to loosen up and have fun, because he is a great director. But back then and in my mind, and at that age, I thought "Why is he doing these things?" He was trying to get a reaction from us. I had never seen a director do that. I also thought I was doing way too much. During the audition I was doing very little, but on set I felt I was doing too much. I thought John could have told me to bring it down a bit. I don't think I'm a great actor and I am not an actor anymore. I really liked watching John Stockwell work – I loved his take on being uncomfortable. He mastered those excruciating looks of discomfort and embarrassment and he made it look real easy. Keith Gordon was a highly experienced actor at that point and completely committed to that character. I think I could have played Keith Gordon's character if I was a better actor. We were basically the same character – it was the same kind of casting. The only thing I remember about Kelly Preston was how beautiful she was. Everyone thought she was absolutely beautiful – and she was.

ALEXANDRA PAUL: That actually was my first day of shooting, and I just remember thinking that line – the actor who is actually my friend Doug, we emailed each other today – Doug Warhit says, which is "She looks smart, but she's got the body of a slut!" is hilarious, and of course I thought was very funny back then! Just because no, not really! They didn't cast the right woman for that! I like the analogy of going down the line and being treated like an object like Christine.

BILL PHILLIPS: Amy Heckerling, another Gersh Agency client at the time, wrote and directed *Fast Times at Ridgemont High* (1982), which was praised for its authenticity. I remember hearing that she brought her script to Beverly Hills High School and had the students go over it for the current vernacular. Years later, I adapted a book about high school girls around Chicago. My youngest son was fifteen then, and I asked him to read it to see if I'd "gotten it right." On two counts, according to him, there were moments I failed: 1) certain things just aren't said from one year to the next. It's a quickly-moving target… teen talk. And 2) I remember getting into a debate with him when he said, "Dad, kids aren't that clever. They don't talk with such wit and efficiency." Of course, he's right, which brings up the whole question of what you're trying to do with the dialogue. In a movie like *His Girl Friday* (1940), the dialogue is crisp, fast, clever, efficient, always entertaining. On the other hand, a writer/director like Wes Anderson intentionally has people talk as incoherently as people often do. There's a philosophical difference to consider. In my opinion, it's less a matter of style and more a matter of what each particular story is trying to say. In *Christine*, I think we were going for authenticity (which is great to work with when you're telling a killer-car story). John would frequently say that in a supernatural story, you want everything else to be completely believable, so the audience will stay with you.

DOUG WARHIT: When I did *Christine*, I was twenty seven. I was not a teenager anymore. *Private School* seemed like a movie where stupid kids did stupid things. No one is writing a book on that movie! That was made via a poll at shopping malls. So people were asked "Should we have Matthew Modine in a movie?" then the votes came through, and it was yes. "Should we have a girl riding a horse topless?" and they took a poll at the mall. So that was made by committee. Unlike *Christine*, which was a film made with an artistic vision, *Private School* was solely made for money.

Doug Warhit (Bemis), John Stockwell (Dennis) and Keith Gordon (Arnie) congregate at the lockers, with news of the new girl Leigh Cabot.

Director John Carpenter with cinematographer Donald M. Morgan shooting the high school locker scene.

Kelly Preston (Roseanne) and Keith Gordon (Arnie) during the
locker scene.

Alexandra Paul makes a beautiful impression in her first movie.

"BUDDY REPPERTON HAS HIS LUNCH": Dennis finds out that Arnie is, once again, being bullied

John Carpenter once again elicits a great tracking shot that opens with a close up of the film's "hero" Dennis Guilder and ends with him walking out of frame to help the film's "anti-hero", Arnie Cunningham. Dennis is sitting outside when a student named Charlie (an uncredited actor) tells him that Buddy Repperton (William Ostrander) has Arnie's lunch. Buddy is clearly established before he is seen, and from Dennis's dedicated response, it is understood that this character is "bad news". This kind of economic character insight is a mark of great writing and a coherent and concise sensibility from screenwriter Bill Phillips: he tells the audience that Arnie is in some kind of trouble and is a victim of bullying, and he also feeds us the notion that other students are used to this (the casual delivery from Charlie) and that Dennis is a true friend who will protect the downtrodden Arnie from the mean blow of the soon-to-be introduced Buddy Repperton.

En route to go and rescue his friend, the painfully sexual Roseanne tries to get Dennis's attention. She springs up as if out of nowhere with a delicate but flirtatious "Hi Dennis" which meets dead silence and no response from her "sometimes boyfriend". Dennis is fixed on helping Arnie, and completely dismissive of Roseanne's beckoning call.

This would be Kelly Preston's first acting role, and she gives the tiny part (a character much more prevalent in Stephen King's novel) an ethereal sensuality that powers every miniscule second she is on screen. In this particular moment on film, she is seen eating an apple as if to evoke some kind of connective literary tissue to the role of Eve in the Garden of Eden, and with her flaxen blonde hair and all-American beauty set amongst the green environs of the Rockbridge High School yard, she is the embodiment of palpable sexual drive and vitality. The naturalist outdoor setting of the high school comes to represent a haven for youth and blossoming sexuality, and in many regards this correlates to two previous John Carpenter works, being *Halloween* and *Elvis*.

In *Halloween*, the only time the exterior of Haddonfield High School is depicted is when we are first introduced to P.J. Soles's character Lynda who is completely preoccupied with sex and in the musical biopic *Elvis*, Kurt Russell as the "king of rock 'n' roll" breaks out into song on the lawn of his old high school, only to gather an admiring gaggle of teenagers (primarily girls) who listen to his bluesy vanilla soul. The pulsating energy of teen sexuality and airy nature lingers not only in these two films, but here in this very brief segue that leads into a pivotal moment in the film which establishes the film's "human villains" who are the bullies of Arnie Cunningham. Much like the mean spirited girls in Brian De Palma's adaptation of Stephen King's *Carrie* (a film also featuring P.J. Soles in yet another unsympathetic teen role) who torment the film's titular "monster", Arnie will be subjected to ridicule and bullying from peers who will get their comeuppance at the hands of supernatural wish fulfilment.

JOHN RICHARD PETERSEN ("High School Student"): I was working at Chicago's O'Hare Airport the summer of 1978 as a cashier at a gift shop. Stephen King's "The Shining" was a paperback for sale there. I bought the book and started reading it on my break... I was hooked. I got home and kept reading, joined the family for dinner then retired to my bedroom to finish the book. I consumed every chapter and was finished with it in 24 hours, as I recall. I have to admit, over the years I have never been a fan of reading fiction. I was always hooked on scripts; comedies, dramas, musicals – looking for parts I could play one day. So, my book collection is 99% scripts. I was doing extensive extra work on the Rod Amateau directed telefilm *High School U.S.A.* (1983) starring Michael J. Fox and Todd Bridges. I believe Michael had been gifted the newly released hardcover book "Christine" for his birthday and was reading it on the set. He talked about how good it was and I bought the book. The background actors always know they are hired to be in the "background" but every day was filled with hope that we might be upgraded to "day player" with a line or reaction. I'm sure there were shots, especially in the hallway, library or football game scene, where I thought for sure I was included in a close up. I think the only scene where I can actually identify myself is when Dennis is walking to the shop to help Arnie at lunch, you can see me with my orange backpack eating lunch. I only worked a few days on *Christine* and I wish I could say they were all remarkable or memorable. Days inside the school were always more comfortable as opposed to spending an entire day in the stands at the football game. My buddy Craig remembered that we got an awful box lunch that day, working in the stands and I can't remember that at all. I'm going to guess that the hallway scene near the beginning of the film and the library scene were likely filmed on the same day.

John Richard Petersen's call sheet.

Director John Carpenter and cinematographer Donald M. Morgan enjoying the shoot.

Kelly Preston and John Richard Petersen behind the scenes.

"WHY DOESN'T IT SAY 'CUNTINGHAM'?": Arnie is bullied by Buddy Repperton and his gang

This entire sequence cements the fact that Arnie Cunningham is a victimised nerd who is bullied by slackers who loiter at the Rockbridge High School garage. Buddy Repperton (William Ostrander) is a good looking and muscular young thug dressed in a tight black t-shirt and fitted dark blue Levis. He also sports Elvis Presley style sideburns and a mane of long shaggy dark brown hair. Buddy seems to be a leftover of a bygone era but evolved enough for a late seventies sensibility – however, it is important to note that he is very much an archetypal throwback to the greasers that would populate gang related teen-centric dramas from the fifties, which would ultimately be the decade that would be significantly and culturally "owned" by teenagers. Movies of that decade would pop up and be marketed at teenage audiences, and nowhere more so than in the horror genre. The lycanthropic venture that chronicles a troubled youth who eventually succumbs to bestial rage, *I Was A Teenage Werewolf* (1957) would be the first film to feature the word "teenage" in the title, and its thematic links to *Christine* can be seen in that both movies deal with a young man's oppressed state leading him into a position of self-possessed violent fury. Arnie Cunningham is an endlessly bullied kid, and therefore this consistent attack lead by the likes of the physically powerful Buddy Repperton will ultimately peddle towards his revenge – however, this wish-fulfilment will come in the guise of a Plymouth Fury.

Buddy's right hand man and more notable "fellow bully" is Moochie (Malcolm Danare), a heavyset lout who spews out vile hatred, while the other two core creeps are Don Vandenberg (Stuart Charno) and Rich (Steven Tash). Buddy taunts Arnie by holding up his lunch and waiting for him to get it, while extending his arms out, gesturing to grab hold of Arnie's genitals. Following up from this, is his play on Arnie's surname by turning "Cunningham" into "Cuntingham". He asks Arnie why his lunch bag is not

clearly marked: "Why doesn't it say 'Cuntingham'?" Later, Buddy
would spit out "cunt face" when his bullying is interrupted, and the
film will bring up the term and its related colloquialisms throughout. The use of the term "cunt" in American cinema during the
period of *Christine's* release would still be considered a jolting turn
of phrase, where films such as *Saturday Night Fever* (1977) would
be scrutinised and edited in varied cuts of the film because of the
word's impact. When John Travolta uses the term in the gritty dis-
co-flavored classic, it is an attack on women who don't fit what he
sees as the "acceptable potential partner", however here in *Christine*,
the term is used as both an emasculating tool as well as a cut throat
attack. Poking fun at Arnie's name rings very similar to an earlier
Stephen King adaptation with Brian De Palma's *Carrie*, where the
principal of Bates High School confuses the titular troubled telekinetic teenager's name with "Cassie". In the musical adaptation,
it is made even more prominent and even given deep thought in
an early soliloquy where Carrie is enraged that no one remembers
her name. Buddy Repperton uses "Cuntingham" to metaphorically
stick the knife in, while Carrie is rendered invisible and meaningless when her principal and whoever else don't know her name.

As far as realised physical threats go with Buddy Repperton, his
knife is drawn and given a number of close-ups, with its glistening
blade catching the wary and terrified eye of Arnie Cunningham.
Here we have the dangerous greaser back from the fifties alive again
in the form of Buddy Repperton, and his Stephen King relative ends
up being a previously concocted slacker in Billy Nolan from *Carrie*,
who would be played by the aforementioned John Travolta. Actor
William Ostrander looks remarkably like Travolta, and this is something that has been discussed before when director John Carpenter
had talked about the character and Ostrander's performance. This
aesthetic linkage does something more profound than be something
to just pass comment on, for what it does is draw these characters
together and makes them "one", similar to the way in which Stephen
King has created Carrie White and Arnie Cunningham (two victimised wallflowers who blossom into monstrous beings hell-bent on
revenge through wish-fulfilment) and sensitive jocks in the guise of
Tommy Ross (who took Carrie to the prom) and Dennis Guilder

(who continually comes to the "rescue" for poor defeated Arnie). Interestingly enough, Dennis doesn't seem to be the only teen who has Arnie's back, the other students show some remote kindness and also seem to be fed up with Buddy's aggressive stunts. One boy insists Buddy put down the knife (an uncredited actor who has one line) while some of the others outside of Repperton's gang seem to be enjoying the bullying going on. Dennis also gets one of them to call upon the shop teacher Mr. Casey (David Spielberg) and they do as he says. Dennis is most certainly Arnie's "knight in shining armour", and because of this, he is also persecuted. In *Christine*, the jocks are not presented as active villains (which would be the case in many teen-centric movie dealing with bullying and put upon geeks, such as *Revenge of the Nerds*), there are certainly Dennis's clique who completely ignore Arnie (as seen in a previous scene), but they don't attack him or put him in physical danger. The human monsters in *Christine* are juvenile delinquents who stray from the path and aren't part of the high school structure – much like Billy Nolan in 1976's *Carrie*, and his dominant girlfriend Chris Hargensen (Nancy Allen) who is banned from going to her own prom and therefore symbolically cast out of a social construct. Also, the bullies in *Christine* are solely male and small in number, compared to the victimisers in *Carrie* who are all female – but have males at their beckoning call to join in on the bullying that goes on. Plus the mean Bates High School sorority attack on mass in the early sequence where Carrie White is physically assaulted by her whole class in the locker room, whereas Arnie Cunningham is lynched by four cruel teen boys who seem to be alien from the rest of the student body.

Buddy holds up Arnie's lunch like dangling a treat for a dog, and then when he stabs the bag, the yogurt that Arnie's mother Regina mentioned earlier, spills out, oozing onto the cold gas stained floor of the school garage. Here is some terrific sexual imagery, where the yogurt is presented as semen pathetically dribbling onto sterile grounds. Matching the "fumbling with his locker", Arnie is then pushed over and slips into the yogurt, soiling himself and turning into a gooey mess. It is necessary to note, that before taking on the lead in John Carpenter's film, actor Keith Gordon would have a small but vital role in Bob Fosse's autobiographical grim masterpiece *All That Jazz* (1979), where he would play a "young" Joe Gideon (as played as an adult by Roy Scheider) and would appear in a flashback sequence where he is about to go onstage to do a tap dance act before being sexually molested by hardened showgirls. Upon going onstage dancing, the entire seedy audience would laugh in hysterics at his soiled crotch, marked with fresh semen. As an extension on this theme, lyrically connecting characters in *Christine* is something that screenwriter Bill Phillips excels in, where he has both Buddy Repperton and Regina Cunningham as characters who hold up Arnie's lunch as a form of oppression. Regina presents a sturdy obstacle that will never negotiate or give way to moving forward while Buddy stands for physical threats, violence, danger and ruthless torment. Both are stunting figures in Arnie's life, and both taunt him with something that is meant to be nourishing – his lunch.

Adding insult to injury to Arnie slipping on the yogurt, Buddy crushes his glasses that have fallen off the poor sod, and director John Carpenter has his cinematographer Donald M. Morgan capture Buddy in a great low angle image, which emphasises his power, authority, strength, bravado and most of all, menace. Buddy grins down at Arnie and towers over him like a gigantic ogre, and some semi-homoeroticism permeates the sequence. The scene somewhat reads a lot like the rape sequence in *Deliverance* (1972), where worldly "sophisticated" men are stripped of their humanity by "uncivilised mountain people". The "pretty boy" Dennis has his crotch squeezed by the slob Moochie (a quiet link to the very sensual Jon Voight having his mouth admired by one of the snivelling hillbillies in *Deliverance*) and this evokes a notion of the "ugly and repressed" taking it out on the "beautiful and free", which is something that horror films regularly make comment of. Moochie's grip of Dennis's genitals also paints a disturbing picture of sexual violence and the concept of male to male rape, which is seldom detailed in film, however when depicted (*Midnight Express* (1978), *The Rape of Richard Beck* (1985) et al.) is a harrowing examination of what it "means to be a man" and what it "means to be rendered effeminate". Masculinity is continually at the forefront of these films dealing with male sexual victimisation, and although *Christine* uses this as a bullet point to aspects of bullying, it is still intelligently commenting on the role of maleness, stoicism, defence and integrity. Arnie comes to represent the terrified victim, while Dennis is the hero who is turned into a secondary victim, and one who has empowering affectations literally crushed. Dennis also provides Arnie with a platform to somewhat stand up to Buddy Repperton – the handsome jock calls out Buddy's use of his switch blade as "chicken shit" to which Arnie agrees in one fleeting moment of wavering courage. This enforces the instant desire for Arnie to follow Dennis's lead, whereas Dennis resorts to endlessly protecting Arnie from the face of adversity, which is a grinning slacker who wields a sharp blade. The final image of this sequence has Arnie staring at Dennis longingly – waiting for a command, waiting for reassurance. At the end of the altercation, Dennis, with his shirt soiled and ruffled, looks defeated and even in John Stockwell's measured and thoughtful performance you can tell that it's been a long battle having to protect and defend Arnie all through their young lives.

What seems to be the most characteristically painful aspect to Arnie being bullied is that locale. Arnie is "good with his hands" and good at auto mechanics which is something brought up in Stephen King's novel and also established as the film moves forward, and to have him victimised and attacked in the place where he would most prosper and grow is even more an insult to his attack. Buddy and the bullies seem to "live" there too, and they are all car-obsessed – their clothes stained with grease and oil – so ironically, they could somehow relate to Arnie, who has a way with engines, fuel gages, fenders and the like.

Enter Mr. Casey, the shop teacher, who comes in to end this ugly attack on Arnie. Mr. Casey's mannerisms and coping methods embody the quiet rage that teachers learn to have to control in films dealing with wayward teens. In films like *Christine*, teachers have to claim their own over rebellious and dangerous students and sometimes they are forced to lash out. Motion pictures of the time such as the aforementioned *Fame, Class of 1984* (1982), *Stand and Deliver* (1988) and many more, pitted well-meaning teachers against their angry students and here in John Carpenter's film, Mr.

Casey is one of them. In a scene reminiscent of the much referred to *Carrie*, Mr. Casey rough handles Buddy Repperton and shakes fear into him, much like Ms. Collins (Betty Buckley) the physical education teacher rattles and slaps the bitchy Chris Hargensen. Mr. Casey also ignores Buddy's youth and student status by forcing adulthood upon him with the threat of police intervention while the angst ridden Buddy threatens Mr. Casey and refers to his balding marking a culturally significant spout about the youthful generation up against the authority figures who struggle to keep their authoritarian position. Buddy's threats close with a violent promise to Arnie: "You're gonna wish you were never born!" This final vocal attack drills Arnie's genuine self-loathing and his eventual rendering into invisibility when he loses himself to Christine, and the seriousness of this entire scene pounds the motion into what would ultimately be the counter-catalyst, to the follow up sequence where Arnie will meet his "genie in the lamp". Buddy's rage is completely palpable and deadly and he is instantly set up as the focal point "bad guy", akin to classic evil doers in Westerns such as Lee Marvin in *The Man Who Shot Liberty Valance* (1962). With John Carpenter being a long standing Western fan, the maestro paints this altercation scene like a showdown in a saloon from some of his all-time favorites such as *Rio Bravo* (1959). The gun slinging is replaced with knife fights and agro roughhousing between students (and intercepting teachers) and the film lends itself to that dramatic tradition of long lasting violent rivalries between bullies and put upon nerds, with the eventual result of having the nerds claiming revenge. The sequence also clearly establishes the characters that will be Christine's victims – if she is the "supernatural monster" of the piece, and these bullies as the "human nasties", then she will make them pay.

The way the entire sequence is shot also explores deep rooted ideas and concepts. All the close ups used are there to give a sense of urgency and building terror, and while it is not traditionally set up like a fight scene in the classic sense (with wide open shots and compositions that showcase actors roughing it up), it does bring attention to such isolated activity forcing us the audience to nervously not know where things are going. Actor John Stockwell had an issue with it being a "close up fight", but this was a particular style that Carpenter designed and had Donald M. Morgan work on. Editor Marion Rothman uses her skills of precision and cutting elegance to finesse such a fight sequence and the lack of stunt people in use aid her decision making as to where to cut and where to throw to.

JOHN CARPENTER: I composed the fight between the bullies and John Stockwell and Keith Gordon in a series of close-ups. You never get a wide angle on any of the action, so the idea is that there is an uncomfortable closeness or claustrophobia to the fight. I guess it adds to the tension if the action is all depicted at close range. The same idea came later when I have Alexandra Paul choking in the car – I just shot these two sequences in close-ups to add to the frenzy.

RICHARD KOBRITZ: I do like the fact that the film came out at the same time as other movies dealing with troubled young boys, but at the time I never thought of that. I think our timing was apropos, but we never measured it that way, at least I didn't. Good stories are the reason I dive into a project and Stephen King was new and fresh in those days. Not to say that he isn't now, but he has done three books a year sometimes, and all of a sudden, sometimes, the bag of tricks is not as new and as inspired as it has been in the past and this is because he has riffed on this kind of material before. I think the best two Stephen King adaptations are *Misery* (1990) and *Carrie*.

KEITH GORDON: I had been working in New York in theatre and film, and I certainly knew John Carpenter's work and was a fan and was excited at the idea of meeting him. I went in and I auditioned, and the reading seemed to go well. I came back a couple days later and did it again and they taped it and that was the last I heard for a while. And then not that long afterwards I got a call saying they wanted me to do it. It was thrilling, I loved the idea of working with Carpenter and it seemed like an amazing role. But it was funny because as an actor you're just out there trying to get work. You never know when things are going to happen. You do auditions and you think they are great and you never hear again and you don't get the job. And you do auditions and you think you sucked and you do get the job, so it's a very strange process. But I was very, very happy and very excited.

WILLIAM OSTRANDER ("Buddy Repperton"): I hadn't read the book, but because it's John Carpenter and Stephen King, you go "Okay"! In 1983 and around that time in the early eighties, there were a lot of films being made that went across the system in Hollywood which was evolving, but in the late seventies it was more of a studio system. There was a different kind of acting world then, but you could tell by the way you did movies. When John Travolta made the switch from television into movies, it opened doors for everybody, but there were still a class of actors that were doing B movies. But nobody was really a "serious actor" or hoped for a career where you really had to consider doing different kinds of films. There was a sort of snobbery to doing a horror film but then you think "it's John Carpenter and Stephen King", which means it will get a hell of a lot of attention. I didn't know much about the project, but I think at that time there were certain expectations of the genre that you had to let go of. John Carpenter also did a picture of Elvis Presley. He did a great job with that. He and Kurt Russell did that together. So I I liked that and I knew of his reputation because of *Halloween*. I did another film with the casting director Karen Rea, and she said, "I think you will be perfect as Buddy Repperton. I'd like to give you the script and take it home, and then you can come back and read to John Carpenter". So I thought "that's swell!" So I take the script home and I seem to fit the reputation of what the description was in the script for the character. Buddy Repperton was tall with broad shoulders, with long hair, and originally he was described with his hair being flicked back in a ponytail and he had a mean, stupid-looking face. She said I was perfect for that! Ha! William Forsythe was up for the part too and I auditioned with the feel that Buddy Repperton should intimidate some of the others trying out for the role.

BILL PHILLIPS: After John and my introduction, I first wrote *Sea Story* for him about three people crossing the Atlantic from Provincetown, Massachusetts to Corryvreckan, Scotland, to retrieve a sunken galleon's buried treasure from the base of that whirlpool… the second largest in the world behind The Maelstrom, but Edgar Allan Poe had already used that one. The film was deemed "too expensive", probably because so much of it was shot on water, which often eats up a film budget. Then came *Firestarter*. The first draft had been written by Bill Lancaster. I did the second, then John walked. Then came *Christine*. The script was written very fast. I think sixty days elapsed between starting to write and starting to shoot. Practically unheard of these days. I phoned him or met with him whenever I would depart from the story in the book. For example, we discussed why to get rid of Roland LeBay, how I wanted to kill Moochie and Buddy, etc. I think he was preoccupied with the thousands of other details a director needs to attend to during the time I was writing, but he was always available and responsive, and as I recall, he usually agreed with me (for better or worse.) Richard Kobritz, the producer, asked me to go through it and add more swear words. In those days, a "hard R" rating made the most money in Hollywood (now I think it's PG-13). He pointed out that high school boys in particular liked to swear to show their "manhood." So I obliged. Later, the NY Times called *Christine* the most foul-mouthed film in the history of the English language. A few months later, however, Brian De Palma's *Scarface* (1983) came out, in which the F word was used more than two hundred times. So I was off the hook. My mother, ever-loyal, pointed out one day in Dodger Stadium that the guys sitting in front of us used language much worse than I had in the film.

WILLIAM OSTRANDER: The scene that we auditioned for was for the scene in the shop. William Forsythe was involved and grabbed hold of the actor standing in for Arnie and slammed him on John Carpenter's desk and John was like "We don't need that". I didn't audition with Keith Gordon, but John Stockwell and I were all at the same agency at that time. I was from the Midwest, from Indiana. That's where I got my union card and that was for *Fire* *and Ice* (1983) which I did voice work for the character of Taro and that was fun to do. Before that, I did a couple of non-union films, and one was with Joey Travolta and that was my first picture. A week later I was in Hollywood. Early in my career people thought I looked like John Travolta.

KEITH GORDON: I'm thrilled that Bill Ostrander did the role of Buddy because I think he was wonderful. He was also a really nice guy! I don't know how much John was actively thinking about it, but he put together a cast full of pretty decent human beings, and I think that's a great thing. Sometimes, especially younger actors will play bullies or play tough that can cross over into some of them needing to act that way in the world. Bill is not that way at all. Bill is like a really sweet, cool guy who could play a horrible son of a bitch but didn't bring that energy to the set, and I was grateful for that because it is always a drag when you get around somebody who feels like, "Well I'm playing an asshole, so I'm going to be an asshole!"

WILLIAM OSTRANDER: In the shop, when the guy tells me to go to the office, and I punch that metal door, that was improvised. I punched that metal door at that point, that was not in the script of course, and it was meant to make Buddy more menacing. I think that was where John wanted us to go. They wanted somebody to be more of a threat and not able to keep his cool. In that scene in the shop, I calculated that we probably did it a hundred and eighty times that day. John did at least three takes on everything: there was the practice for lighting and then there was the run through practice, and then we would do one, and most of the time John said, "We got one. Now let's do one for the bank!" So it was almost always three to four takes, sometimes six takes. So in that scene, for example, where I'm talking to the shop teacher, and he says, "Empty your pockets, or I'm going to…" or something like that and I say, "Yeah, try it, and I'll knock you through the wall, you fuck!" I was doing the off-camera work for actor playing the teacher. I came forward to say "You little bald fuck!" and I threw my head forward and what happened was my head came into view of the shot they were doing of the shop teacher. So John liked that take, so he just decided to add my overlapping stuff, and part of the dialogue was as if it was always scripted that way. One of the constant comments that I get when we do autograph shows is people telling me their age when they first saw the film. So now, I often ask people how old they were when they first saw it. I would say that overall the people who are the most affected by the movie were either in junior high school, about to become high schoolers, when the movie came out. One of the things that they responded to, at least with me, was how afraid they were of going to high school and being terrorised by a Buddy Repperton. I think that one of the reasons for that is that scene or a part of the scene, and the movie itself showed real archetypes, real high school archetypes. David Spielberg is part of that. David didn't come in as the big bully teacher who's going to take control. I tried and maybe with John's direction as well and Bill's script, it didn't become completely teacher versus student. We still behaved, I feel, within realistic boundaries that you would have seen in 1978. My character didn't try attacking the shop teacher; he came in and shook me by the shirt and I just accepted it. You didn't just punch the teacher! I think that there are temptations sometimes with actors that play scenes because you're in the heat of the moment or maybe because your vanity wants to stand out or something like that. David played that scene in such a way that kept us within the boundaries of what really could have been a real situation in a shop class, in a high school in America. David did a great job and we all tried to stay true to that instead of exaggerating the truth. I think that is what makes the film what it is today. I don't think it is the horror part of the film, yes, that is part of it. My experience from autograph shows, the most responsive people to the character of Buddy Repperton, at least, were those who felt in junior high school or high school, they were recognising real character types, real archetypes in their lives.

RICHARD KOBRITZ: The script never originally had so much profanity in it. What you got were a lot of these young actors trying to play with nasty dialogue and it always takes a really good actor to do it. The easy thing to do when you're making this kind of a picture is use the F word and I think you can use that three times before you get an R rating. We were R rated, but I think we overused the profanity in retrospect. It wasn't about getting a hard R rating and I really believe that you lose the power of words when you throw in so many F's and so forth here and there. The bad guys especially constantly use the F word and to me it is just not creative. You are blunting the overall effect by overexposing it too much. We knew that the characters we had in our film were far more interesting and better than a lot of teenage characters of that time. We had to keep it that way. We could have had the car doing more evil things, but that would be repetitive. I mean how many people can she run over? I mean she does it in flames, she does it in the garage, she does it in the alley way when she kills Moochie – so if we kept her killing everyone it would lose its effectiveness, so in many ways it's like the overuse of the F word. It loses its power when it's overused.

MALCOLM DANARE ("Moochie"): "Cunt" is a naughty word. You do not want to call anyone that, especially a woman. There was a lot of swearing in that movie. And it's funny because in *Heaven Help Us* (1985) there is a lot of swearing in that film too, by Kevin Dillon. I'm blown away when I think back now at all the swearing. And it's funny because I found my original script to *Christine* –and collectors will offer you crazy money for a script. It is unbelievable! I will never give it up! I will probably give it to my friend Bill Gibson so that he can put it in his *Christine* museum. It is just crazy what people want from this film.

WILLIAM OSTRANDER: The screenwriter wrote a pretty risqué bunch of expletives. It was laced with a lot of profanity that you typically did not hear in film. No one uses the word "cunt" in a film! Even today, nobody uses the word "cunt" in a film very often. Maybe in English or Australian films, but not American films. So calling him "cunt face" was really stepping into an attacking area and stepping all over the values of good taste. I certainly appreciated the script and I was real surprised by the dialogue. Even today, I enjoy it, I sign autographs using all the best lines! People love it! They love "cunt face" or "Cuntingham" or "You're gonna wish you were never fucking born!" People love that and wear that on T-shirts or have it on posters, or whatever. So, today, the expletives and language actually are something that people like about my character. In fact, at one autograph show, people would come up to me and tell me that he and his buddies have all the Buddy Repperton comments they commonly use. You know, "cunt face" is now part of their repertoire.

MALCOLM DANARE: I had already done two films before *Christine*, *The Lords of Discipline* (1983) and *Flashdance* (1983). Back in the early 1980s they still had a thing called "the studio system". I was under contract by Paramount to do three films for them. My first one was *The Lords of Discipline*. My second was *Flashdance*, and then I was offered a really interesting film called *Police Academy* (1984), but then another script came around called *Christine*, and I thought to myself, "Wow! It's John Carpenter and Stephen King!" You cannot go wrong in that type of horror realm! Everybody knew who John Carpenter was from *Halloween* and I was a huge fan of *The Thing*. I broke my contract with Paramount to do *Christine*. I had no idea who the character was, but I knew that I was auditioning for the role of "Moochie". They basically said, "Hey, look. We want you to do the role, but what you need to do is come in and do a thing called 'a mix and match'." I was the first one of the bad guys to be cast! I auditioned with William Forsythe, who was going to be the original Buddy Repperton, believe it or not. Then they brought Andrew McCarthy in to audition for the role that Keith Gordon obviously got playing the role of Arnie. So we were doing all these different mixing and matching in the auditions, and there was this one audition that we did, and Keith Gordon wasn't around at that point yet. With William Forsythe we do the shop scene, where Buddy Repperton and Moochie get in trouble, and they fix a knife into the lunch bag. Bill Forsythe took Andrew McCarthy and flipped him onto John Carpenter's desk! This was in the audition, and literally, John Carpenter was absolutely in shock. He couldn't believe what had just happened. Anyway, that was really the only mixing and matching that I did as Moochie, and the next thing they said was, "You're playing the role of Moochie." The first scene that we ever really did was that shop scene when we actually started filming the movie.

WILLIAM OSTRANDER: The fight scene was easy for me. All I had to do was stand there, accept the punch and turn and fall into some boxes. For me, it was pretty easy. I was involved in martial arts, so I never really thought twice about that part of it. I wasn't a part of them teaching John about punching or any of that kind of stuff. I simply had to take a hit and fall into some boxes. One of the things that was important to me was that his character wasn't suddenly beaten up by John Stockwell's character. If the shop teacher hadn't come in, I would like to believe, that my character at least would give John Stockwell a severe beating! When you watch the scene there are the master shots and each one of the characters gets covered for their lines and there are multiple characters in each. One shot for the shop teacher, for myself and for Keith and John and Malcolm. So, all of the different shots added up to a lot of takes. The yogurt was put into a paper bag, and I think they had put it into a plastic bag. It wasn't like a yogurt cup or something like that. So the knife went in and made a mess pretty easily.

MALCOLM DANARE: The audition was insane; I mean, he literally flipped Andrew McCarthy. It would be like if I were to meet someone for the first time, pick them up and throw them down on the ground! But he was doing it in the audition, and that is what he did on John Carpenter's desk. Extremely intense and extremely uncalled for on Bill's part. I'm friends with Bill, so I know him pretty well, but back then we were twenty-year-old kids wanting to get the role. I was literally the first guy out of the four bad guys in the Buddy Repperton gang. I am going to assume I was the first one cast because I had already known that I was slated to do the film, but I didn't meet any of the bad guys because they weren't in any of the auditions with me. I was auditioning with other people, so maybe they were mixing and matching with other people. But I know that I was pretty much cast early on in the process. At that point, I think Keith Gordon's biggest film up until that point had been *Dressed to Kill*. So at that point, I really didn't know Keith. I heard that Kevin Bacon was supposed to do the role of Arnie Cunningham. I never met Kevin during that period, I know Kevin pretty well because I was supposed to do another film many years later called *Flatliners* (1990). All the actors back then knew each other, like Kevin Bacon, Andrew McCarthy, Kevin Dillon, Charlie Sheen, Emilio Estevez. We were the young kids of our time in the 1980s. Eric Stoltz was pretty close to getting the role of Arnie, too, if I am not mistaken. It was really interesting. I knew that Carpenter wanted me to really take a lot of chances with Keith Gordon. He wanted us to really pick on him, in the rehearsals. So during the rehearsals, Carpenter says to me, "I just want you to really make this guy uncomfortable." And I said, "Fine, man. I'll go there, I'll do it", and Steven says, "Oh, Malcolm, I don't know if I am going to do it." I said, "Fine. It's rehearsals." Whatever we do in the take is going to be the take. I'm really giving it to Keith Gordon, at that point. And I had never met Keith, and he, as an actor, knew what was going on and knew what I was doing, but he was uncomfortable. At one point before we started shooting the whole big shop scene, he went over to Carpenter and said, "I'm really uncomfortable with Malcolm doing what he is doing, in the rehearsals." So Carpenter, before we even started shooting, called me over and he said, "Keith is really uncomfortable with what you are doing to him during the rehearsals. I want you to do it more now, during the take." With Bill Ostrander and I, the main bad guys in the film, we went a little overboard with it, but that is what Carpenter wanted.

WILLIAM OSTRANDER: In America today, there are very few places where young men can establish their independence, beat their chest and display their manhood if you will – and that is in their cars. Also on top of that, is the reason girls should like them and all that. Cars are one of those ways it can be done where you can assert yourself, and your taste and your strength. It's pretty characteristic of Buddy Repperton to have a vehicle that is representative of himself – that is the image that he wanted to project. I think for Keith too; he wanted to project an image of who he wants to be or who he thinks he is. In the case of my character, he may have known a little bit of mechanics; he may have been someone who liked working on cars or maybe found that to be a career later on if he finished high school. I think it is a very natural thing in today's world that boys used cars to have that threshold experience to establishing who they want to be perceived as.

MALCOLM DANARE: We had to figure out a way that I was going to injure John Stockwell. That is a pretty good grab, so they thought okay, let's put something in there, in the crotch of his pants. It just wasn't comfortable for him. So someone said, "Why don't we just get a sock and stick it in there?" I had to grab John from behind and grab him from the crotch and do the whole thing, and it worked perfectly. It wasn't a multiple take thing, but we probably got it done in six, seven, eight takes – just to make it look vicious.

STEVEN TASH ("Rich Cholony"): I had recently been living in NYC and after my studies with Stella Adler (Marlon Brando and Robert DeNiro's teacher), I followed some friends back out to L.A., my home town. I started doing theater, my first love. In fact, I was a lead actor in a play called *Album*. It was the West Coast premiere of a play that was done in New York first, and in the same play and role there was Keith Gordon. Agents would approach me after seeing certain plays I was in but I had no interest in turning what I loved into a commercial endeavor, at least not so quickly. Lonny Chapman, a great character actor (he worked with James Dean) and theater director who ran the Group Repertory Theater in L.A. that I and Sean Penn and a big group of talented actors were in, told me to go meet with his agents. He said jump and I did. While waiting in their Beverly Hills offices the amazing Ray Milland (from films like *The Lost Weekend* (1945)) sat next to me, also waiting to see his agent. It felt like I was in the right place. Almost right away I was getting out and auditioning, and quickly had a few call backs for *Christine*. They were looking to group the mischievous friends from the film, matching actors together in different groupings. What I recall at the final audition was the producer, Richard Kobritz, leaning over to John Carpenter and nodding in my direction saying, *him, with the wild hair.*

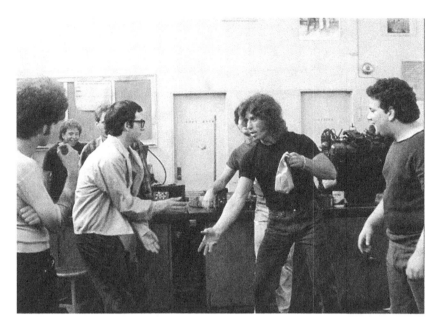

The fight in the garage begins.

Staging the fight.

John Carpenter directs John Stockwell in how to punch William Ostrander.

As Dennis, John Stockwell throws a punch. Something that actor would struggle with.

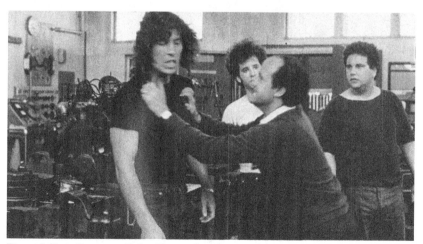

David Spielberg as Mr. Casey has enough with the thugs that terrorize Arnie Cunningham.

William Ostrander in a publicity still as Buddy Repperton.

The bullies pose for a publicity still: Steven Tash (Rich), William Ostrander (Buddy) and Malcolm Danare (Moochie).

Director John Carpenter would decide to use close-ups throughout the confrontation sequence between Arnie and the bullies.

"HER NAME'S CHRISTINE": Arnie meets (and falls in love with) Christine

Before Arnie Cunningham catches a glimpse of Christine – and before this fateful "meeting" turns into obsessive infatuation – each sequence in the film sets up Arnie as an oppressed loser. Upon his initial introduction he is berated by his mother in front of his best friend, then his virginity is scrutinised by the well-meaning Dennis Guilder. After that he is rendered invisible by his peers and then finally brutally attacked by Buddy Repperton and his fellow thugs. However, the character arc will slowly develop and Arnie will eventually shift from insignificant dweeb to a cocky agitator.

The drive back home for Dennis and Arnie involves quiet talk of the bullies not being suspended and having their actions going ultimately unpunished. Clearly at Rockbridge High School, these parasitic slackers ride above the rules and dodge bullets by persistently being a threat. Severing such conversation is an excitable Arnie who jolts in his seat and spots someone or something off a nearby road. He calls out to Dennis "Stop the car, Dennis! Stop the car!" and then "I want to look at her!" Here there is a suggestion that Arnie has seen a beautiful girl that has pricked his attention, but instead it is a rundown, completely dishevelled Plymouth Fury that is coated with dirt and grime and looks like its best days are far behind it. This is the car from the opening prologue, and "she" is completely "not herself": a wreckage of machinery, totalled and ready for the scrapheap. But Arnie doesn't see this uselessness in her, instead he has an instant attraction to her and from here on in, his passionate infatuation with this car will take centre stage as the film's primal character driven horror.

Christine is a trashed Plymouth Fury and certainly no longer that gorgeous car from the opening and Dennis quickly asserts his disdain for her: "It's a piece of shit, Arnie." Dennis refers to Christine as an "it", while Arnie gives her a gender straight away with "She could be fixed up"; commenting on the potentially beautiful

Christine he says "She could be really tough". The pronoun of "she" being prescribed to a car is not a new thing at the time of the film's release, cars were often read and interpreted as women or girls, and in film history, a lot of cars (and other forms of transportation such as ships and trains) would have women's names. Arnie touches the defeated car with gentle care and tenderness, as if touching a teenage girl on his first date. His hands delicately caress her door frame and steering wheel and he is immediately protective over her, even up against Dennis who remains anti-Christine.

Entering the scene and coming out of seemingly nowhere is George LeBay (Roberts Blossom), a creepy old character straight from the horror comics of the fifties as seen in the EC publications. He is filthy, unsettling in appearance and with his back in a fitted brace – resembling some kind of bizarre turn of the century corset – he looks as though he is a character who harbours a dark and torturous past. A superb character actor, Blossom would make a startling impression in *Deranged* (1974), a film based on the life of real life serial killer Ed Gein, and here, in this small supporting role, he is sublimely well-suited as someone who knows the truth about the supernatural Christine, but just wants to rid himself of her to move on. While Dennis's reluctance and suspicion about both Christine and LeBay acts as an extension of protecting Arnie from "undesirables", the car's name is mentioned for the first time: "Her name's Christine", to which Arnie responds smiling, "I like that". Following this introduction of teenage boy and dismantled car, George LeBay provides some exposition regarding Christine's past. He regales a story about his brother Roland who was the car's previous owner and talks of the smell of a brand new vehicle that he links to "the smell of pussy" (more of the film's inherent and vested interest in female genitalia and more importantly the linkage to automobiles). "Roland went through hell and back with Christine", George explains, but the awful truth behind what really happened is not divulged, instead that comes up later in Blossom's second and final scene.

Arnie's glasses (busted up by Buddy Repperton) are now taped up together which evokes more cliché nerd characteristics in the history of the archetype, and in a sense his broken demeanour matches

Christine's. In the film, screenwriter Bill Phillips would be actively interested in the concept of the "ugly duckling" story trope where two characters – a boy and his car – would grow beautiful and self-possessed together, making a massive transformation from damaged goods to in control powerhouses.

During the entire scene, Dennis scolds Arnie for even considering buying this burnt out car, but Arnie explains that saving all summer for college has leant its way to this fateful meeting of Christine, this classic American muscle car that he wishes to purchase. She is sold for $250.00, and George LeBay happily obliges to such a raw deal. A lot of incredibly intricate elements and story pulses are introduced in this quick but vital catalyst: it is learnt that Christine is twenty years old and Arnie is excited by this, her meter reads at a high point (ninety three thousand miles) but this doesn't deter Arnie or influence his decision in buying her, and Dennis talks about Arnie as a "stupid kid" to George while the hardened old cretin calls the young football jock a "shitter". Throughout these elements we see Arnie's love for something that is an "antique" and in need to be repaired and "loved", the truth behind Dennis's threshold in regards to caring for Arnie and George LeBay's absolute disregard for human interaction and empathy and his pulsating misanthropy. Also, the insult "shitter" will be a commonly used turn of phrase throughout the movie (as it was in the novel) and used to describe those who are mean spirited, a nuisance or simply get in the way.

As previously mentioned, this scene is the catalyst that propels the rest of the film. It establishes the incurable and eventually sick and twisted "romance" shared between Arnie and Christine but here in its early development, it sets up their union as something promising and even healthful. This is the first time we see Arnie genuinely happy and excited about something, and what eventuates is the result of Christine being Arnie's "genie in the lamp" as owing her (and being possessed by her in return) contributes to his dramatic transformation that winds up destructive and evil. Christine's potential is what Arnie sees as "beautiful" and this drive (which is borderline sexual) is something George LeBay has seen before. As much as he quickly wants to rid himself of Christine,

LeBay is reminded of his brother when he watches Arnie "fall in love/lust" with Christine. In small bouts of information given by George LeBay we learn that it was 1957 when his brother Roland bought Christine. In Stephen King's novel, Roland's rotting corpse would appear in the backseat of Christine, talking to Arnie and influencing him as an entity and a spirit guide. The model used for the film would be different and not feature a backseat, therefore this would not be utilized in the film, but more so, director John Carpenter wanted a cleaner and more direct approach. Instead of using the decaying ghost of Ronald LeBay as an evil instigator, the true malevolence and sinister energy would come from Christine herself. This would prove to be a much smarter choice as Christine is the monster of the film, a monstrous machine hell-bent on having her man and discarding him when the time comes.

During the closing moments of this scene while Arnie makes his payment of $250.00 to buy Christine, Dennis warns him, saying "It's your funeral, man", which in turn is a sad prediction of things to come. Although Arnie sees Christine as a beautiful woman who needs love and attention, Dennis struggles to remain loyal to Arnie's need to be respected and nurtured. In this three-handed scene with Christine as the centrepiece (something that she will continue to feature as for the rest of the film), Roland's death is mentioned, but not elaborated upon until later – in essence, this catalyst that ushers in the beginning of the second act, is only a "half story", where hidden truths shall be revealed as Christine goes from "ugly duckling" to glamorous vengeful witch.

JOHN CARPENTER: When I get asked what attracted me to directing *Christine*, my answer is always this: I needed a job! I had seen killer car movies before and most of them weren't great, so I thought "OK, let me try my hand at this!" However, when I got the treatment and read up on Stephen King's idea of the previous owner being inside the car and being a decaying apparition talking to the current owner, the teenage owner Arnie, I was not impressed and not happy with that aspect at all. I didn't like the decomposing ghost sitting in the backseat, I didn't care for that at all. I decided from the beginning, as soon as I got the job to direct this film, to make the car the central figure, and to have the car possessed by an unknown force and got rid of the ghost of her previous owner straight away. So therefore, the car herself would then take control of Arnie and possess him. It was purely about doing a job and making this film all about a killer car, or a haunted car. In retrospect, maybe it might have worked to have the old owner's decaying ghost in the backseat, but who knows?

KEITH GORDON: John had a very relaxed sensibility in the way he directed and was on set. This was something that I very much enjoyed, he had a playful, fun manner to him and there were many practical jokes on set. He also used the same crew people over and over again on each movie so that was great because there was a sense of community on the set. Brian [De Palma] was a lot more serious. Now I learnt a lot from Brian in regards to filmmaking, but with John it was far more jovial and not so intense. I mean John would grab a mic and hide it for the day! He had a playful nature that had a means to an end in that it would keep the energy levels up for the cast and crew and keep them on their toes while also having fun! Brian was more like, you're here to work and do the work. But both are very good directors and both are superb with their actors. Brian loved to rehearse his cast, whereas John would be more keen on chatting about character. John and I spent hours together talking about Arnie; what should he look like? What kind of kid was he? What was his relationship like with Christine? What would the transformation in Arnie be like? What would change and what would stay the same? Brian would do far more takes than John. He would say, "Ok cut, now play it angry. OK cut, now play it sad. OK cut...", Brian wanted a whole range of emotions from each scene whereas John would do a couple of takes, but if he got what he liked than he would move on. Also both directors are so distinct in their visual style and tone, Brian's shots are far more complex and there is usually constant movement while John has an amazing eye for composition – he is such a wonderful classicist, he loved the films of John Ford, Howard Hawks; he was a very straightforward director, where Brian would spend a whole day setting up one shot. You tended to cover more ground with John and because *Christine* was made up of so many shooting locations. John's films are gorgeous to look at, there is a lot of attention to light and composition but Brian is all about movement with a highly stylized European visual sensibility which is almost baroque, where John treated every film like a Western.

JOHN CARPENTER: There were several cars and because it was a Plymouth Fury we had to find them and cherry them out and they looked incredible, but some of them didn't run very well and some of them were just finely tuned racing cars – we had a variation from the transportation department. But they all looked so gorgeous. By the end of the movie I was asked if I wanted one, and I said "Oh just hang on to it", but yes, I should have taken it! I drive a Cadillac, I love the Cadillac, that is my car of choice. But I know nothing about cars and I didn't spend any time researching cars, I was lucky because everything was there written for me!

RICHARD KOBRITZ: Stephen King takes the relationship a young man has with his car and twists it and makes it perverse. Los Angeles and California has an obsession with the automobile, like nowhere else in the United States, and everybody is judged by the car they drive. Here, Stephen King takes that and creates this nerd who buys a car that he fixes up and soon enough the car takes over, it takes possession over its owner. Was Arnie inherently bad? No, not at all. Was the car born bad? Yes. And that was the option we took. We went for the notion that the car was born bad versus what King had in his novel where the car's initial owner Roland LeBay would possess the car and his ghost would run the gamut. John Carpenter, Bill Phillips and I were in my office going over the script and I asked a question "Is the car inherently bad or is it infested by the ghost of the first owner?" and none of us had an answer. So I called up Stephen King and I told him about our dilemma and he said quite simply, "I dunno, I never thought about that. Do what you want!" To see a spooky ghost in the backseat spurning Arnie on was just not good, it wasn't a good idea and John and Bill agreed.

BILL PHILLIPS: Remember that in 1982, there was not the slew of books on the subject of archetypes, etc that there is now, so I was never conscious of working from any formula. I still don't like formulas for anything... except one: I agree that a movie has to "start" by page 10 or 15. By "start", I mean that the audience needs to know what ride they're on. I don't remember being conscious of that when I wrote *Christine*, but since then, fifty scripts later, I'm always careful to accomplish that one formulaic thing. I sometimes get forty pages into a rough draft before the "START" comes... so then my job is to cut 25-30 pages from that, so that people don't get antsy and wonder what it is they're supposed to be watching. I remember when my oldest son was very young, we went to *Superman* (1978) with Brando in it... and it was a full hour before Superman made an appearance. That wouldn't happen today.

MARION ROTHMAN (editor): Working any one of these films was individual and unlike the others. I was available and an agent arranged a meeting. I had not read the book. I wasn't a fan of horror movies but knew of John Carpenter's reputation. I watched *The Thing* prior to the interview. John was a pleasure to work with and for. He designs scenes and is a pleasure to edit. He was open and appreciative and easy. A nice human being.

VIRGINIA KATZ (assistant editor): In the early films I worked on like *Summer Wishes, Winter Dreams* (1973) and *Let's Scare Jessica to Death* (1971), I was just starting out in the business. *Summer Wishes, Winter Dreams* was edited by my father, Sid Katz. By the time I moved to L.A. and started working with Marion Rothman I was much more experienced. The job came along because I was Marion's assistant. By then we had worked together for years. I began my career in NYC as an apprentice to my father. He was a fantastic teacher and taught me the ins and outs of being an assistant. From my first day in the cutting room I knew I had found my niche. I loved puzzles as a child and editing is like a big one! Putting the pieces together to tell the whole story.

DONALD M. MORGAN: Well, by the time the editing was going on, I didn't have much to do with that. I know that Marion Rothman was very co-operative with everybody. I liked her very much, but I didn't have much to do with her. It's pretty much I shoot it, they cut it. But Richard was really a good producer. I really liked working with him. He was one of the ones that I think was one of the driving forces for us to go up to the ranch and do all those inserts. I don't know what the conversation was, or whether John promoted it, but they built the set that they needed more stuff of the car coming back alive. He was very supportive.

KIM GOTTLIEB-WALKER: A good set photographer is working constantly – shooting rehearsals, the scenes themselves, the prep for special effects, cast and crew interacting, guests visiting, creating photographic props, sometimes helping with continuity. I make sure to introduce myself to everyone, to let them know I am there to cover all of their photographic needs and requests. Everyone gets used to me being there all the time with the camera and everyone is happy to have their work documented. Occasionally, if the light is good just off the set, actors will pose for me, to get a still that really represents the essence of the film, like bad Arnie kneeling in front of pristine Christine, or Roberts Blossom holding the key. Kodak had just come out with an ultra high speed color negative film, and I used it for the first time on *Christine*. It was a god-send for shooting those dark night time scenes, like the alley pursuit, where there was action but no light. I was amazed at the results.

BILL GIBSON (Christine Car Club president/collector): I believe Christine, the car, captured my heart from the book and the film just sealed the deal. It just keeps growing from there. Like a lot of others out there, it is really an easy movie to relate to. I think we all at times feel like we are in Arnie's (Keith Gordon's) shoes, not feeling like we belong, different, trying to fit in and find ourselves. The awkwardness and growing pains of our teenage years! And of course the fantasy of a car that can repair itself is a big plus! Cars do basically become part of the family. A lot of great memories as a child growing up driving with dad in the old Corvair convertible, sitting behind the wheel, with dad's help of course. I believe the film solidified the saving of not only the '57 and '58 Plymouths but also the early Forward Look cars. They are seen and viewed as works of art. The curves, style, meticulous attention to detail and overall pre-sentation have made them a staple point in our automotive history.

ROY ARBOGAST: We had around six weeks to pick the cars and have them all ready for the show. It was not a green lit picture when we got the script. But that was the fun part, because we were all wondering if we were going to make the movie at all! My team and I were wondering if this would actually come to fruition, because we had to get the cars to work. I know back then we were a special effects group that were so busy that we were doing pictures back to back – and if I ever had a choice, I would always go back to working with John Carpenter. The number of cars that sticks in my head is twenty seven. We were building this car out in the country and they would take out the good ones and make them look great and we would take out the old ones and fix them up. All of the dressing of the decrepit Christine was done by Daniel Lomino who was the head of the art department. He had her look all run down for the backyard. The special effects union was all about the car doing the things that it had to do that were supernatural in theme – and so all the inserts and interior shots were us.

A vision of beauty: Even in such disarray, Christine seduces Arnie Cunningham from the moment he spots her.

George LeBay sells the smitten Arnie the beaten up Plymouth
Fury while Dennis watches in disbelief.

Roberts Blossom as George LeBay.

John Carpenter directed Keith Gordon on the first meeting of Christine.

The deal is made.

Arnie Cunningham (Keith Gordon) smitten by Christine.

"YOU ARE NOT KEEPING ANY CAR AT THIS HOUSE":
Regina puts her foot down

Regina Cunningham's seething rage is at a boiling point here in this kitchen scene. Director John Carpenter shoots this domestic scenario with calculated blocking, as if he were staging a play. Regina is seen in a dominant stable position and she stands with her back away from the kitchen sink, smoking a cigarette – as if rejecting the domestic trappings of housework in favour of holding court. Michael Cunningham (Robert Darnell) stands in a submissive position of the kitchen (in the shadows of a doorway) and he keeps his gestures and mannerisms at bay to Regina's unspoken "command". Michael is ineffectual and dominated by Regina, and in many ways, the film plays with gender roles the same way fifties classic *Rebel Without a Cause* (1955) does having Jim Backus seen in an apron and on his knees, with the angst-ridden James Dean forcing him to "man up" to the domineering and cold Ann Doran. Eventually, Christine will lend itself to visual cues from that teen-centric melodrama with Arnie Cunningham's costuming making a transition from dowdy geek to cool James Dean-like panther (most notably with the red jacket that actor Keith Gordon will soon wear in tribute to Dean's in *Rebel Without a Cause*).

Regina stands firmly against the idea of her son owning a car and this is completely to do with him gaining any form of independence, or any representation of liberation from her clutches. She masks her disdain with the meaningless and superficial "You could have consulted with us", but even in "consultation" there would only be one answer. Regina's oppressive nature over her son is however tested in this sequence where Arnie shows aspects of fighting back. Standing at polar opposite to Regina is not her son however, it is Dennis, who is Arnie's guardian angel – even exhausted by protecting his poor defenceless friend against his harridan mother. Dennis is seen drinking milk which is more a comment on Regina, who not only emasculates her son, but renders all boys as children – even sexually active jocks such as Dennis.

When Arnie cusses at his situation (not being allowed to own a car), his father Michael reacts but is hushed by the furious Regina, who cuts her husband off and takes over. Michael's expression is incredibly telling; he drops his head in submission to his wife and remains in the darkness of the corner of her kitchen. There is some wonderfully inspired dialogue that follows where Arnie expresses his quiet frustrations about being embarrassing to his mother and avoiding this being the case. He even makes mention of her bridge club, which would be a stable cliché amongst middle-class families countering their dreary existences with dead pastimes such as a card game. The stoic, stern and perpetually angry Regina is masterfully played by Christine Belford and as her foil, Keith Gordon excels at pushing the downtrodden kid who finally bites back and will not stay defeated. This kind of back and forth is measured and nuanced and is most certainly a perfect example of films dealing with sons trying to break free from domestic oppression up against their mothers who are desperate to keep them as little boys.

The film will omit a scene that depicts Regina in a sensitive and sympathetic light where she watches Arnie (now heavily under the influence of Christine) sleep, and sobs to herself, completely aware that she is losing her son. However, cutting this scene keeps Regina angry, unsympathetic and possibly deserving of death (after all, this is a revenge fuelled horror film), but this will not be the case in Carpenter's vision. The staging is once again reminiscent of a Western with Regina at one point, Arnie at the other, Dennis in front of him and completely in direct polar opposition to her and the impotent Michael remaining in shadows. There is one moment where Michael does cross over to catch a glimpse at Christine through the window, shaking his head in a disapproving manner. Christine is the new enemy here – a burden on the Cunningham household.

Regina once again mentions Arnie's age ("You're seventeen years old") and this cements Arnie's inability to have Christine "all on his own". He falls back into the trap of being dominated because he ultimately needs his parents' permission to register Christine but in his newfound defiance and fighting back, he sees this as a tiny obstacle. When he reels off a list of school clubs that Regina forced him into (college courses, chess club etc), he clearly states his frustrated desire to speak, feel, act and control on his own. Regina closes the argument with a cold: "You are not keeping any car at this house". This kills Arnie's zeal to keep nagging and his ventures out, removing himself from the shackles of Regina's grip and starting upon his own independence. Here in *Christine*, cars are most clearly a symbol of liberation from the suffocating domestic and also a mark of growing up – something that truly terrifies Regina.

JOHN CARPENTER: Keith Gordon was a dream! He is a very smart guy and an excellent actor. I mean I didn't have to do much with him, he just knew what he was doing and did all of his research on his own and just brought with him this tremendous amount of energy and dedication to this role. He has since become a director and an excellent one at that – so yes, Keith is a very smart guy. A film guy. He knows movies very well. He was the kind of actor who would come up to you after a few takes and ask "Can I give you something else? Should we play it this way? Are you sure you don't want me to do it again?" I loved working with him, he is just excellent. A few years ago we had a reunion for *Christine* at this horror convention, so it was great to see him again, and Alexandra and John, and also John is another director too!

BILL PHILLIPS: I frankly didn't have a strong feeling about Regina Cunningham. Sure, Arnie needed controlling parents, and because of how he later treated his father, the mother had to be stronger. As I recall, I must have gotten most of who she is from the book. I think I came up with the "What you're doing is toxic waste" line she utters to Dennis when she first appears… but to me she was more what I call an "integumentary character." She had to be there, but she wasn't a main character. I think Christine Belford did a great job with the part, but I take no pride of authorship here. She was an actor doing what actors do best. She embodied the part. Remember that the part was written based on the book. The casting came later, so I really didn't know who was going to play Regina. I didn't know her or of her, but I do think she was perfect in the part.

I love the dynamic between Regina and Michael – she clearly heads the house, while Michael seems ineffectual and rather incompetent in his role as a parent. I think this balance of power in that marriage was already in the book. I don't remember making a significant contribution to that. Michael had to be weaker so Regina could be stronger, and vice versa.

DONALD M. MORGAN: I never handled either TV movies or theatrical movies differently. I pretty much photograph stuff. But I just love doing "moody" stuff and John Carpenter, of course, really likes "moody" stuff! So I fell in love with the guy! He liked what I liked so we had a good relationship. I didn't really do too much different in any of the movies. I copped a lot of flack in the early days from people in television thinking everything should be bright, and yet I got nominated for an Emmy for John's *Elvis*. I was nominated nine times and won five Emmys for television movies. They were all dark and moody where they needed to be!

Keith Gordon as the oppressed Arnie Cunningham.

A family portrait of the Cunninghams: Keith Gordon (Arnie Cunningham), Christine Belford (Regina Cunningham) and Robert Darnell (Michael Cunningham).

"I KNOW A CREEP WHEN I SEE ONE":
Darnell sets up the rules

In this swift establishing pre-sequence where Arnie Cunningham drives Christine down a dark street, heading towards the decrepit and foreboding Darnell's garage, the film lends itself to classicist Gothic literature or cinema. It is as though Arnie is entering an old world; a world in wreckage – an America that is forgotten and detached from "modernisms" that we have become privy to in the first few scenes of the film (ABBA on the radio, yogurt, a reference to communist Russia et al). Much like the carriage that takes Jonathan Harker to Dracula's castle, here we have the film's anti-hero, the dweeb Arnie Cunningham taking his newly purchased run down Plymouth Fury into a refuge that will hopefully be the place of her restoration. The image of Arnie driving the spluttering Christine over to Darnell's private garage summarises the desperation of a boy in love with his new car and in need to get her "tough" again. Escorted by Dennis who drives his car with ease and without stalling, the moment before Arnie drives Christine into Darnell's is preceded by Dennis having to honk his horn to have the door rise, because Christine's honker doesn't work (more of her inabilities in her ravaged state).

Christine enters Darnell's and thus enters a new home. Here is a soiled and forgotten place with its overhanging sign and crotchety garage door lifting up exposing a world of auto mechanics at their most primal and at the service to men from a bygone era – painted by oil, grease and hardened lives. The look of the run down trash heap that is Christine unsteadily cruising through the spacious garage confuses Will Darnell (Robert Prosky) and he is instantly agitated by how this vehicle fumes up the place. He scolds Arnie straight away (yet another adult antagonist) telling him to turn the car off "before we all choke to death!" – and in this line we get a sense of what is a foreshadowing of what is to come, as eventually Darnell will choke to death inside a burnt out Christine.

Darnell is a broadly written and performed character with an incurable potty mouth. Actor Robert Prosky has loads of fun given the opportunity to constantly throw out profanity that is incredibly engaging and entertaining, as well as threatening. Like an Edward G. Robinson for the eighties, Prosky's Darnell is a leftover of the forties, a dishevelled mess who is clouded by disdain and a deep rooted misanthropy. Darnell's mention of the "son of a bitch" who had a car like Christine implies that that may have been in fact the now dead Roland LeBay (her previous owner), and this is treated as a subtlety in the script because it makes way for more talk that links Christine to the human anatomy. Darnell refers to her as a "mechanical asshole" – countering earlier connective linkage between car and vagina, and this cements the continual adage that Christine is somewhat "human"; an insight that director John Carpenter plays with throughout his direction and something that actor Keith Gordon as Christine's "kept man" revels in performing.

Darnell also barks out some rules, one of which is "no smoking", and this makes a smart connection to Regina earlier who is seen smoking in her kitchen, holding court. Dennis makes the point of the "men over there are smoking" (other "work stiffs" playing cards and chain smoking), to which Darnell doesn't even acknowledge. Instead, he turns his hatred towards the perceptive and protective Dennis to the fragile Arnie, and Darnell's disdain for the nerd is summarised by "I know a creep when I see one." Darnell's rules go on: he won't "take shit from kids", and especially "not from rich ass snot nosed kids" (which comments on the classism explored in the film) and he will not tolerate being interrupted and for these kids to "not get smart". This is all laid out and founded in an ignored hypocrisy of the older generation and within this sequence the teenager versus adult authority: here, Darnell, a character outside of middle class trappings who is a self-described "working stiff" comes face to face with a child of the baby boomer generation who has things "easy", and this kind of confrontation is a standpoint in the importance of class resentment that permeates *Christine*.

Robert Prosky would have the distinction of being an actor who seemed to "start off late" in film and television, seeing that his first screen credit would be for the made for TV movie *They've Killed*

President Lincoln! (1971), when he was forty one years of age. However, upon looking at Prosky and getting a sense of his acting style, he seems to legitimately be a performer of the hardened Golden Age of Hollywood. He would tread the boards and impress *Christine*'s casting director Karen Rea in the workshop production of the play *Glengarry Glen Ross* before it would make its Broadway premiere in 1984, and it was there that Rea contacted producer Richard Kobritz and insisted they cast him in the role of Darnell. Prosky would work on varied films released the same year as *Christine* in solid character parts such as *The Keep* and *The Lords of Discipline* (both 1983). Prosky seems to take great pleasure in not only delivering the lion's share on verbal violence, but he also cleverly loads the character with nuanced utter disdain for the young. When Darnell assumes that Dennis talked Arnie into buying Christine, we get the sense that this dishevelled garage operator has no hope for the human race – in his eyes, even someone's "best friend" will coax their pal into signing over their life.

Darnell's garage itself is just as bleak as its owner's outlook on life. It is an extension of World War II and hidden away in the compounds of Californian suburbia. It is home to grease monkeys who have lost hope and seek refuge from a world that has no space for them. Darnell is the one mechanic given a fleshed out purpose and voice, and he is presented as yet another adult bully – outside of Regina – who manipulates and berates Arnie Cunningham. Eventually Arnie will come into contact with Detective Rudolph Junkins (Harry Dean Stanton) when the film calls for police intervention, however, Junkins will be an adult figure that is not so much a bully, but more so a man doing his job and questioning the nonchalant anti-hero, however, Darnell remains an antagonist who sits alongside Regina as an oppressive malice, heavy and overstated. But something changes in Darnell in the coming sequence, where this gruff menace somewhat sees something in Arnie's work ethic that is admirable and even worthy of support. Unlike Regina, who remains cold and detached, Darnell eventually respects Arnie, and communicates this in the best way he can.

Throughout this introductory scene however, Arnie is still lacking confidence and lets himself be grilled by the sweaty oafish Darnell.

Arnie's heads remains lowered even until the closing shot, while Dennis remains headstrong and sternly upright as the eternal protector and defender of his troubled friend. Dennis also calls out the smoking mechanics after Darnell talks about the rule of "no smoking" and even flips the bird to the irritated garage owner. It is interesting to note that Darnell doesn't seem to attack Dennis (besides a snide "shut your pie hole"), but instead plants all his attacks upon Arnie, who takes it in his stride – it is yet another bully that will pick at him; something that he has since grown accustomed to. Darnell snarls at Dennis "you're trying to protect your buddy", and even with this acute observation (as it is the first time a character has verbally acknowledged Dennis's love for Arnie) the grisly senior mechanic is set up as someone who could be a possible victim later down the track. All of this biting subtext is pinned by visual brilliance as director John Carpenter blocks the scene with Christine taking to her parking position that will become a focal point through the film. Carpenter pans his camera and drives it towards that position later down in the piece when Arnie discovers his "woman" "mutilated and beaten", sending him into a fiery rage. Here, Christine is an "ugly duckling", readily awaiting her restoration/makeover (much like Carrie White coming out of her ill-fitted skirts and slipping into a silk pale pink prom dress) while Darnell becomes an extension to George LeBay, but also a polar opposite as one man has sold Christine (ridding this demonic car from his ownership) while the other has Christine as a live-in tenant.

KEITH GORDON: I think Prosky relished swearing in the film. He was truly a great character actor. I think truly Prosky loved playing people that were nothing like him than anything else. He was really a very soft-spoken, thoughtful guy. Very intelligent, kind of intellectual. So I think playing this guy with that voice – that "Fuck you!" – was a blast for him because he was nothing like that. He was just this complete 180 from the real man. So I have the feeling that the more profane and weird and mean, I think the more fun he was having, and I think that was true for Roberts Blossom. I think for a character part of the fun of it is you throw away your own persona, and you just secure into this other person that you get to be for a little bit; it's nothing like you, and that's the fun of it. Prosky seemed to really love that! He was amazing! If you sat with him and chatted with him – mirrored nothing of Darnell in that man. They had zero in common. He was this erudite, thoughtful, funny, but witty in this urbane way. Just watching him transform into this other being was great!

RICHARD KOBRITZ: Roberts Blossom was amazing and Robert Prosky was great. We were doing some casting in New York and the casting director said to me "Have you seen this guy Robert Prosky in *Glengarry Glen Ross*?" and I said "No" and she said "Well, you better get a ticket". I went to see it and I called John up – and he was in California – and I said "We have Darnell!"

BILL PHILLIPS: Most of Darnell was supplied by Stephen King. I remember going to the set and Robert Prosky pointed out to me that there were certain off-color things King had included in the book that I had left out of the script. I must have double-checked with John first, but I put things back in for Prosky to say because he wanted to be even more colorful. For example, he remembered King having written something about "… putting the toilet paper on the spools… shit like that." It was fun to go back and rediscover little gems like that. Remember that this adaptation was done very quickly, so it was great to have invitations to go back to the source material and look again. That didn't happen much. When I went to USC film school, one of my best professors was Jerry Lewis. He taught directing. And he had an expression, "You can't polish a turd." I unabashedly stole this line and gave it to Darnell. It just fit his character.

RICHARD KOBRITZ: I knew the president of Columbia and he knew that I knew Stephen King. We were having lunch one day and he said to me, "I hear there's a new Stephen King book coming out, and I hear it's really good and I think somebody's bought it. Do you know who it is?" I said, "Yeah! Me!" I thought he was gonna die at the table! Now the film was a negative pick up, meaning once they agreed on a budget they would fund the budget through a bank and we would operate independently shipping them the dailies and then showing them a rough cut with John Carpenter having final cut.

KIM GOTTLIEB-WALKER: The very first feature I ever worked on was so bad, it was never released, as far as I know... but Debra Hill was the script supervisor on it... and that's how we met. Later, when she had co-written and was producing *Halloween*, she remembered those crew members she had enjoyed working with, including me and the whole camera crew, and asked us to shoot *Halloween*. She had told John about my career as a rock photographer and he approved. I became part of their team for five films – *Halloween*, *The Fog* (1980), *Halloween II* (1981), *Escape from New York* (1981), and *Christine*. *Christine* had a bigger budget, bigger cast and crew, but John was still just as well organized, knew exactly what he needed, shot by shot, still communicated with his crew beautifully, so everyone knew exactly what to do and was still absolutely wonderful to work with – good humored and appreciative of every person on his set. I think Dean Cundey had already committed to shooting another project, so we had a new Director of Photography, Don Morgan, who fit in perfectly with his cheerful machismo and talent.

DONALD M. MORGAN: There were the producers and John Carpenter and myself, and we went out to this building that we would use for the garage and we said, "This would really work!" When we got there, they were tearing the roof off part of it. We said, "What are you doing?" They said, "We're tearing it down!" And we were like "We're gonna use it for the movie!" Their response was "Well, that's not our fault... not our problem." And they just kept tearing stuff off the roof. And the guy got on the phone real quick and all of a sudden they stopped it because we really wanted that building. But if they had gone another day, then it would have been too late, or at least it would have been ripped up pretty bad. We got there just in the nick of time!

BILL GIBSON: Around twenty-four cars were used for the film and two are in museums right now. This car was built from parts from multiple cars used in the film back in 1983. Ed Sandlin Sr. worked for John Carpenter (one of the sound guys). His son Ed Sandlin Jr., late teens/early 20s during the time, wanted one of the cars but they were not able to get one from the studio lot when filming was complete. So they did the next best thing by finding a '58 that was in desperate need of restoration that an owner did not sell to the studio (thankfully as she most likely would have ended up being destroyed like most of the others). Ed Jr. and his best friend Richard took her to Bill and Ed's junkyard and had as many parts as they wanted to choose from to Frankenstein her back together. The irony is I recently found out that this vehicle has an actual manufacturing date of 31 October 1957! Halloween! Stephen King didn't even script that!

ROY ARBOGAST: John Carpenter was the nicest guy I ever worked for. He would send a script that he would write and was very considerate about the budget at all times. I mean most of John's pictures were low budget and he understood that and so therefore we would work it out within our restrictions. He was great and brilliant and he always let me know that if we ran ourselves into a corner he would sharpen his pencil and rewrite certain scenes so the SFX department could work it out. He would give us total control on the look of the effects – his production meetings were very short, we never beat anything to death, we just got into it and discussed it swiftly. He was just a great director and visionary. For *Christine* it was completely a family vibe. John never put up with grumpy people or nasty people or negative people. There was one moment on *Christine* where someone was fed up and tired and irritable, and John called us all in to the office and said "If we can't have fun, then let's do something else!" That's how he was. He wanted the mood on the set to be light and fun. John was amazing. He could fly a helicopter, write a script and direct a film – just incredible.

Robert Prosky (Will Darnell) grills Arnie (Keith
Gordon) while Dennis (John Stockwell) looks on.

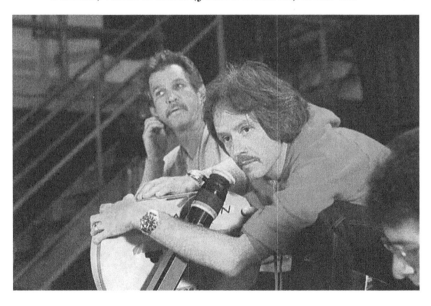

John Carpenter and Donald M. Morgan on location in what would become the Darnell garage.

John Carpenter: master of horror.

"AS I WALK ALONG, I WONDER A-WHAT WENT WRONG WITH OUR LOVE":
Dennis tells Arnie that he isn't ugly

Christine is a film about relationships. It examines romantic unity, obsession, the struggle to break out of an oppressed state and most fundamentally it is about companionship – both nurturing and damaging. In the case of Arnie Cunningham and his multiple connections with other characters throughout the film (including the most pivotal and monstrous being his "romance" with Christine), this tragic figure's most nourishing and deep relationship is shared with his long time best friend and confidant Dennis Guilder. In many regards, *Christine* reads much like many Westerns of previous decades, where the most meaningful and rich relationships are those shared between men taking on the wild frontier. Bringing this closer to home – and also queering the text – Arnie and Dennis's relationship reminds us of James Dean and Sal Mineo in *Rebel Without a Cause*, where the permission to love between young men is certainly strained, but there nonetheless. This sequence, where Dennis and Arnie share a quiet moment of what truly is a masked (or closeted) sexual interchange and exchange, runs parallel with the scene in *Rebel Without a Cause* where the confident and sexually free James Dean hands over his jacket to the repressed and lonely (and also queer) Sal Mineo.

The scene opens with Dennis driving Arnie home late at night, and here there is a wonderful play on the idea of the romantic date ending badly – with the boy driving the girl home after something has interrupted their potential consummation. This kind of sequence is commonplace in many teen-centric films (most notably those of the fifties, which *Christine* is a direct homage to) and what makes it remarkably fresh is the beautifully played homoeroticism of the scene. Dennis and Arnie's relationship is definitely a borderline romantic one; Dennis is popular with the girls and a self-possessed winner, and Arnie looks up to that and admires that. Here is a young man – good looking, athletic and in charge – that Arnie can quietly look up to and possibly (and secretly) fall in love with. On the other hand, Dennis seems to embrace being the protector and strong arm for Arnie to cling on to, so there is a compassionate design in the young jock's make-up that brings him to the defence and solidarity he shares with his less fortunate friend.

In the earliest moments of this film, the mateship and union of boys is something thoughtfully examined, and this is a secret world of boys outside the complications and charge of understanding girls. There are multiple conversations that involve girls with the female sex painted up as a mystical Shangri-La that needs to be conquered and owned, however, the intimacy lies within the interaction of boys in their hormone fuelled back and forths. Ultimately, Arnie's need to be loved goes beyond "getting laid" as Dennis had suggested in an earlier scene, he needs to feel that warmth of acceptance, and thus far, the only character to provide that is Dennis himself.

With Dennis pulling up outside Arnie's house, the scene is lit romantically, it remains quiet, it is a scene "done in secret" – there is a palpable sense of longing during this serene exchange, and here at this "end of the road" there seems to be a moment where all the chaos and madness of finding hope has come to an end. This intimate moment shared between jock and nerd stems from a long line of "buddy movies" where two men finally accept their friendship as genuinely fulfilling and much more than falling into the trappings of prescribed masculinity: endless police partner films would engage in a shock intimacy, and comedy films would play off the "fag-panic" but within that draw attention to the genuine love shared between characters. Here, in *Christine*, it is not at all the case of "we love each other but we're not faggots", instead it is "we love each other, but we don't *love* each other" and also "let's not even discuss it". The turning point in this moment is where Dennis assures Arnie that he isn't ugly – this brilliant piece of writing summarises Dennis's macho love for this best friend. If ugliness is used as a point of expression for loneliness, ostracism, alienation, despair and hopelessness in Arnie, then Dennis has tried to vanquish all of those feelings in one tender piece of dialogue. Arnie precedes this (and ignites Dennis to champion Arnie's non-ugliness) by explaining that Christine is something "just as ugly as he is" but "someone" who "can be saved". Arnie sees his own insecurities living in that wreck of a car, and if he can fix her up ("she can be tough") then in a sense he can live vicariously through her and become beautiful too. After Dennis tells Arnie that he isn't "ugly", he then half-jokes "queer, maybe, but not ugly" and this is the moment that sums up the fag-panic that permeates any film or book that deals with male companionship that is not sexual. Dennis is calling out the subtext by naming it and therefore dismissing any real thoughts or feelings that may in fact be truthful to what it is he is referring to. If "queer" is called out, then it will not truly exist – it will be outed and treated as throwaway, but if things were left unsaid and a topic of someone's looks was the foundation of conversation alone in a dark car, then possible "fag-panic" may incur. The notion of a good looking popular teen boy telling his best friend that he is not ugly is a testament to not only male friendship but also an insight into male aesthetics and the appreciation of such things, which is clearly something that can lead into homoerotic charged dialogue or queer fear. During this period in film, the term "faggot" would be used relentlessly – primarily in teenage comedies – and it would be an insult that would go beyond persecuting homosexuals. In a film such as *Teen Wolf* (1985) when a stressed out Michael J. Fox confides in his best friend that he is a werewolf, his friend is relieved because he initially thought he was going to tell him he was a "fag". Later into the decade in *Bill and Ted's Excellent Adventure* (1989) the two leads deeply care about each other, but when they catch themselves hugging they both pull back and call out "fag" – this is not the case here in *Christine* which is far more sensitive and intelligent in dealing with male mateship, however, it does employ the Dennis character to call out "Arnie's possibility of being queer" as an aside to mask profound feelings.

Of course, as in all teen-centric horror movies and other genres included, there is a monstrous entity that will interrupt the romantic union shared in the darkness of quiet cars parked out in suburban terrain and here it is presented as Arnie's oppressive parents. They stand as shadowy figures in the distance watching their son with great scrutiny as he farewells his best friend, interrupting the quiet conversation and once again becoming the domineering adults that pepper the film. Here at this point in the film, they somehow feature as literal monstrous beings, both foreboding and menacing, with their faces not clearly seen and backlit; they become the angry mob, ready to lynch the "different".

The scene ends with Bonnie Raitt's version of Del Shannon's "Runaway" – here, once again, a contemporary variant of a classic rock 'n' roll song plays in Dennis's car harking back to the cover of Buddy Holly's "Not Fade Away" earlier. Dennis Guilder is a "modern character" but still haunted by the fifties and this is something that will catch up with him when he has to come head to head with the demonic Christine. Raitt's soulful singing of Del Shannon's lyrics is mournful and also sexually charged; she manages to convey a sense of desperation and desire all at the same time, and once again, the song is used to make acute commentary on character, plot and theme. Dennis is about to lose his best friend, and Raitt's treatment of "Runaway" embodies his feelings – feelings that he would never outwardly express in fear of being called a "faggot". The lyrics sing:

> As I walk along, I wonder
> A-what went wrong with our love
> A love that was so strong…

Dennis drives into the night with those lyrics ringing something honest and eye-opening; here is a nice young man who genuinely loves his best friend, and as Bonnie Raitt echoes Del Shannon's sentiment, it is an accepted fact that their "love has gone wrong" and it was most certainly "a love that was so strong". Christine has won the heart of Arnie Cunningham, and she will completely control it, manipulate it and destroy it as the film moves forward. It is interesting to note that this is ultimately the second last scene where Arnie is "himself" and it is the last scene where he shares the camaraderie and tenderness with Dennis. From here on in, Arnie will transform and evolve into someone else – all thanks to the influence of the malevolent Christine.

"What is it about that car?", asks Dennis, and it is clear that his mind has not changed about this run down Plymouth Fury being more trouble than she is worth. This is way before Dennis comes to realise that Christine is a mystical force that empowers Arnie but also transforms him for the worse, ultimately he sees this car as a problem, but being a good friend and someone who loves Arnie, allows for him to take on such a huge task in repairing her. Arnie in clear defeatist terms sighs "You better find yourself another charity besides me and Christine", and here he suggests that the car is an appendage, an extension of how pathetic he is, which leads into the lovely exchange about ugliness and how Christine can be saved from such a curse – but Arnie might not. With the scene looking as though it could end with the duo kissing, this is the turning point for both these two boys – one will become possessed and the other will sit back and watch that happen, until it is time to act.

Christine not only scrutinizes male to male relations, but it intelligently draws into gender and gender politics. This entire sequence occurs before Leigh Cabot becomes an instrumental player and cuts a divide between Arnie and Dennis, propelling this scene with the passionate belief system that boys will be best friends and share the most intimate of feelings (primarily unspoken, but delivered in varied senses) before the intervention of girls will distance them. Here in this film, Leigh (a human female) will only represent romantic unity as a fabricated façade for Arnie whose true love remains the machine that is Christine. With this scene fading to black (the first time editor Marion Rothman will use this storytelling device), and as aforementioned, we see the end of Arnie as we know him and will soon be introduced to a slightly altered version of the boy and eventually to someone completely unrecognizable. We also see Dennis losing his best friend to the power of Christine, and being consumed by darkness, as it falls unto him as he drives into the night with Bonnie Raitt's modern take on a rock 'n' roll favorite that has haunting undertones and melancholia embedded within the foundation of its chord progression. Interestingly enough, another Stephen King adaptation will use the song in its original form (Del Shannon's hit) in *Children of the Corn* (1984) which would have it played as the adults (Linda Hamilton and Peter Horton) find the children resisting the child cult playing in an empty house. In *Christine*, the next chapter is about to begin.

BILL PHILLIPS: There are scenes between the two that were cut out of the film because it was running too long, and you would have seen more of this sensitivity between them. At one point (and as I recall, this was in the book, but I'm not positive) Dennis comforts Arnie in the car by giving him a hug just as two fifteen-year-old girls walk by and looked disgusted because they think they're seeing a homosexual display of affections. There was a joke that these two guys would be misunderstood at that moment. It was never intended that they were actually homosexual. Of course, I don't know about King, but I personally wasn't as "evolved" on that subject (most guys weren't in 1982, when I wrote this) as I am now. I accept that perfectly now, although I didn't not accept it then. I just didn't think about it.

KEITH GORDON: There are two love triangles in this film: the one between Arnie, Leigh and Christine and the one between Arnie, Dennis and Christine. The thing about teenage years is that as we grow up, we tend to form very strong bonds with members of the same sex. And for most teenagers a lot of sexual confusion is a huge part of their life. I definitely think that connection between Arnie and Dennis exists. Arnie sees him as a handsome, successful winner who gets all the girls and is a football hero on campus and there is this kind of adoration and for Dennis he sees Arnie as someone to protect and love. Their relationship is absolutely at the heart of the film and Christine seduces Arnie away from him. Dennis gives Arnie some of what Christine gives him, but ultimately Christine gives him more to the point where it becomes unhealthy. It's juicy brilliant stuff. Leigh is the idealized love object, the normal representation of healthy romance whereas Christine is the depraved idea of love. Arnie never gets a chance to know Leigh to the depths he knows Dennis, so the love affair between the two boys is extremely palpable and the heart of the film.

BILL PHILLIPS: I was aware that Stephen King had given his Arnie character a terrible case of acne and that it was very unlikely that we would present that onscreen. It's just too off-putting to have an audience want to see, and it's also a credibility problem to have it clear up too quickly. The whole idea of Arnie being unattractive was merely so he could become more attractive as he fixed up Christine. Sort of a "Portrait of Dorian Gray" phenomenon. I remember being aware of that at the time I was writing.

KEITH GORDON: We played a lot in rehearsal time and not just as in rehearsing the scenes, we would talk about character and what the manifestations would be like in Arnie's transitioning. One of the main things I worked on was changing my voice. I wanted to make sure it changed at least an octave and a half during the course of the film. The nerdy Arnie is very high, nasal and reflects his high strung nature and by the end of the movie he has a low, deep voice which is threatening and mean. And this was the same thing with my body language. From the get go, John Carpenter and I wanted to set up how far Arnie's craziness would go. What I really wanted to do with this role is find the core of his polar opposite of what was going on at the time, in other words, I wanted to find the evil seed in nerdy Arnie and the moments of vulnerability in sinister Arnie. As an actor, you really need to try and find the contradictions in what you're playing. I find that Arnie is such a tragic, sad figure. There was a scene that was ultimately cut from the film where I have a major breakdown and fall into John Stockwell's arms and John Carpenter just thought it was far too intense. He said that it had to go because it was far too risky. But it was a great exercise; this was ultimately what Arnie was about – a lonely, sad, miserable hurt kid who is oppressed by his unsympathetic parents, he lives in the shadow of the good looking popular Dennis and is forever in a rut.

ADAM DEVLIN: Although Bonnie Raitt had released several albums during the early/mid 1970s, her first hit single was her cover of Del Shannon's 1961 hit "Runaway", lifted from her 1977 album "Sweet Forgiveness". Following a scene where Dennis and Arnie return to Arnie's home after he has purchased an old, broken down 1957 Plymouth Fury – "Christine" – Dennis drives off, looking back in his rear-view mirror at Arnie arguing with his parents. He turns his radio on and we hear the opening verse of Bonnie Raitt's cover of "Runaway" – "As I walk along, I wonder / A-what

went wrong with our love / A love that was so strong…"The choice
of this song works on several levels. It references the relationship
between Arnie, who Dennis just dropped off to his angry parents.
It also hints at the relationship between Dennis (the jock) and
Arnie (the nerd). It draws out a curiosity as to what is happening to
the relationship between these two young men. It's a bold choice to
include this song at this point in the film. In fact, this scene to me
has a hint of homoeroticism to it. At this point in the film, we want
to know more about these two characters – and the choice of this
song helps to anchor that curiosity in us.

CLEMENTINE BASTOW (on gender): Dismissed in over-
views of Carpenter's work as a "director for hire" movie, it's true
he did take the job as, well, a job, but there are nuances in *Christine* that mark it as more than just simple card-punching. As I've
grown older and returned to the film over the past two decades, I've
discovered there's much more to love in *Christine* than the simple
pleasures of its expertly tuned thrills, though I'm never sure which
reading of the film is the one I want to settle on. Each time I watch
it I discover something new to love. As Roger Ebert said in his
review upon the film's release, apparently possessed by the spirit of
Groucho Marx, "I've seen a lot of movies where the teenage guy
parks in a car with the girl he loves. This is the first one where he
parks with a girl in the car he loves." *Christine* is *American Graffiti* (1973) if Ron Howard was going steady with his '58 Chevy
Impala instead of Cindy Williams. But *Christine* is more than just
a romance between a boy and his car. Carpenter's disgust at Rea-
ganomics and capitalism is clear in *They Live* (1988), but there are
feminist qualities to much of his work that receive far less attention (unless you, too, see *The Thing* as an analogy for the destructive
power of patriarchy). A feminist reading of *Christine* is, to my eye
at least, the most obvious one. Why else does Carpenter shoot the
car's slow crawl down that Detroit assembly line like a woman running the gauntlet along a street full of ogling harassers? Scores of
sweaty, unpleasant men give Christine the "not bad…" treatment;
one even huffs and puffs like an onlooker in an Art Frahm pin-up.
As a quality control worker stalks Christine, his eyes on her rear end,

we see him framed in her rear view mirror, as though she's looking over her shoulder in a dark alley. Far from the microaggressions and assaults many women have endured, too terrified to move, however, Christine is quick to seek revenge: as soon as he "lifts her skirt" to look under her hood, she snaps her bonnet down, crushing his arm. A similar fate awaits another worker, who dares to smoke a cigar in her front seat. Freud may or may not have said "Sometimes a cigar is just a cigar", but there's no denying the phallic implications of that non-consensual ashing on Christine's upholstery. If there's one clue to Carpenter's politics in *Christine*, it comes courtesy of his score. The record track-listing, released in 1990, reveals that the movement that accompanies Buddy Repperton and his fellow "Shitters'" attack of Christine is called "The Rape". It shouldn't be a surprise, since the Shitters' destruction of Christine is filmed with an uncomfortably unflinching gaze, the high school boys whooping and hollering like they've been transported to the set of *The Accused* (1988), but Carpenter's choice of wording for his score makes it explicit. ("The Rape" is also foreshadowed in the earlier fight scene where he knifes Arnie's yogurt, the dairy snack –packed by mom – symbolic of everything Buddy hates.) This, coupled with Arnie's transformation from dweeb to cool dude to terrifying masculine monster, points to *Christine*'s being a cautionary tale about the destructive power of toxic masculinity. Arnie's best friend Dennis might be the quarterback, but he's a sensitive guy. "You're not ugly, Arnie," he says, tears in his eyes. But when he follows that up with "Queer, maybe, but not ugly", it doesn't feel like playful joshing or meanness – the two boys are comfortable showing they care about, maybe even love each other. (It's a cruel irony that Carpenter's interest in exploring male friendships has often been decried as "sexist".) Turning Arnie into the ultimate alpha male is perhaps Christine's most startling act of feminist revenge, then. As enjoyable as it is seeing Buddy and co meet increasingly gruesome ends, inventing "Kill All Rapists" sparkle GIF feminism before the inventors of Tumblr were even born, *Christine* is more than just a revenge flick. In helping Arnie become what we'd now pathologise as "a successful pick-up artist", the avenging automobile says "You want to see all that masculinity can be? Ok, I'll show you". The

Arnie we and Dennis meet on New Years Eve is obsessed with "pussy", disgusted by emotions, and sees love as a destructive force: he represents the worst of contemporary masculinity, its ultimate end-point. He chides the sensitive Dennis for not cracking open enough cold ones, and makes the quarterback cry as he plunges into oncoming traffic. Faced with the possibility of being either "queer" or "in love" (or both), Arnie would rather die (but not before giving Christine's vulval Plymouth hood ornament one last rub). There are counter-arguments to all of this, of course, which is the beauty of film and the beauty of a film like *Christine*, and most of those counter-arguments would have to do with Christine's lust for female blood as well as that of her oppressors, especially the smart, capable Leigh. But if you'd like to hear my counter-counter argument, which centres on how groups of feminist women often cut each other down when they're meant to be dismantling patriarchy, you'll have to buy me a six-pack of Southern Cross beer and meet me on the highway at midnight.

KEITH GORDON: Originally there was a scene where I had a big breakdown and fall into Dennis's arms. Well it was very intense to shoot because whenever you have a weeping, crying, screaming breakdown, it's intense! I mean, as an actor, you are trying to bring yourself to the reality of that as much as you can so it was intense to go through. I was disappointed when it was cut because it was like this big acting moment, but I also really respected and understood. John told me, he warned me. He said, "In editing, it was too serious. It was suddenly a Bergman movie and not a movie about this car", and even then I got it. I don't remember the exact moment when John told me about it, but I think he said, "Maybe I let you go the wrong direction with it." I think he got so caught up in the fact that I brought all those emotions and I had tears running down my face and snot running out of my nose, and I think he got caught up in it and I got caught up in it, and it was really good in a vacuum, but it didn't fit the movie. That was another big lesson for me as a director later on because you can have these scenes – and I relearn this lesson all the time – you shouldn't be on a movie set and have a scene that is very emotional or on the other hand very funny. That doesn't mean it is going to work that well in the movie. I've been on so many movie sets, as an actor, and later as a director with my own stuff or on a TV show where people on the set have tears in their eyes, the toughest crew guy is sniffling, and that doesn't mean it is going to be a great scene in the context of the piece. That's a big lesson! It's very easy to be seduced by what things feel like on a set, but often, they really have nothing to do with each other. To reference a non-Carpenter film, but when I went to the set on *Dressed to Kill*, and they were shooting the scene where Angie gets killed in the elevator, I thought it was the dopiest thing I had ever seen! "Oh my God. This is not going to be scary at all! It's silly. The special effects look terrible, and it's not scary" and it was a huge lesson for me to see that scene put together and really think it is a fucking genius scene! But being there watching it being shot, little piece by little piece, all I saw was how phoney and silly it looked. The experience on a movie set is just not necessarily what the experience is going to be on film. So often the scenes that might have somebody's best performance... I've cut things out of my own movies where some of the best things we did – the acting or the best shot, but if it doesn't work in the movie, it's not really the best. So that was a big lesson! It was a little painful but it made sense when he said it.

"JUST PROMISE ME DARLING, YOUR LOVE IN RETURN": Arnie works on Christine

A title card reads: October 9th. Indicating that some time has passed, and we bear witness to the dedicated and determined Arnie Cunningham, now wet with fresh grease and oil and sporting a white t-shirt and jeans, looking more confident and at ease with himself. He is also without his glasses – the first time ever – and his face bears slight maturity from when we last saw him. He collects car parts from Darnell's scrap heap and tends to his Plymouth Fury Christine who sits there waiting, forcing such zealous worship from her "chosen man". Actor Keith Gordon would go on the record in saying that he championed the fact that the role of Arnie Cunningham required both a transitional arc from dweeb to "cool cat" and that the film called for a pseudo-sexual relationship with his car – this scene showcases the beginning of both.

Watching Arnie take to the machinery of Christine with swift measures and detail is Darnell who is standing by his associate Pepper Boyd (Richard Collier). Both aged raggedy men look on at Arnie and admire his capability and expertise in auto mechanics (something that Regina Cunningham had repressed and not allowed). Pepper remarks, "The boy does have good hands", which is greeted by Darnell's cynical "Bad taste in cars". As much as Darnell has a newfound admiration of Arnie and his work ethic, he is still suspicious about Christine herself, and sees her as a liability and not an asset. However, Darnell summons Arnie and makes him an offer. Arnie without his glasses and as aforementioned sporting a liberating white t-shirt that is fitted and "more grown up" and jeans, looks like a greaser from the fifties – even his hair is starting to take shape into such a mould, but his mannerisms are still at a quiver, flinching at Darnell's spewing off profanity and orders. What the old curmudgeon offers is a trade: if Arnie does odd jobs around his garage, he will help him out in restoring the wreck Christine. He explains to Arnie that he can raid his junk pile and may even throw in some bucks to help him along the way. Humorously, screenwriter Bill Phillips has Arnie come across as too proud to accept such help and says "I'll think about it" which infuriates Darnell who barks out "Well don't think about it too long or I'll throw ya out on ya fuckin' ass!" His anger defuses his sentiment and he waddles off into the dark recesses of the film – only to have one more scene where he is seduced and killed by Christine.

Arnie exhales and looks upon his new love. Solemnly walking over to her he opens the car door and steps inside. A beautiful image of Christine head on sits at centre frame and as John Carpenter has his camera close in on her, he once again sets up a visual cue that will come into play later down the track where Christine (raped and beaten by Buddy Repperton and his gang) will soon resurrect and reshape in front of her man Arnie. But here, the soon-to-be restored Christine cradles Arnie, who sits in the driver's seat, switches on her radio and nestles upon her inviting steering wheel. The song that plays is Johnny Ace's "Pledging My Love" which sings:

> *Forever my darling, our love will be true*
> *Always and forever, I'll love just you*

Christine's voice is articulated by the songs that come through her speakers. Here, she pledges her undying and eternal love for Arnie. The song was written by Ferdinand Washington and Don Robey and published in 1954 (three years before the birth of Christine), and recorded by Johnny Ace who had died the same year from a self-inflicted gunshot wound. Also, this sentient Plymouth Fury would not be the only car from eighties cinema that would sing out this haunting and melancholy song. In Robert Zemeckis' *Back to the Future* (1985), Lea Thompson and Michael J. Fox are caught in an awkward situation with the song playing over a sequence set in the halcyon fifties which has a future son of a young woman romantically chased by his own mother. Just as perverse and disturbing is what eventuates with Arnie Cunningham and his car, however, in this scene – an early sequence, where things are not yet sinister or malevolent – we feel for the put upon Arnie and we welcome this place of refuge, far from a cruel and unfeeling world.

Here, Arnie is comforted by Christine, nursed by her warmth and caressed by her protective shield. He massages her steering wheel as if he were fondling the breasts of a girlfriend, and he places his tired and exhausted head upon it the way a husband would relax with his wife after a long day at the office. Christine is ultimately Arnie's new lover and she is a "woman" who will love him no matter what and will do anything for him no matter how extreme things get.

BILL PHILLIPS: America's love affair with automobiles is of course a well-known phenomenon… and I think teenage boys epitomize that, partly because they're just beginning to grow into adulthood, or pre-adulthood, and this represents their best bet for independence. I don't think that I personally contributed to this argument at all. I just took what was in the book and did my best to put it in the movie, where it would fit.

JOHN CARPENTER: There wasn't much directing of Keith, I really have to say. He was just so smart and so intuitive and he just knew exactly what to do. A lot of it was in Bill Phillips' script as well, the whole idea that this car was a beautiful and deadly woman. Keith played out each scene as though he were talking to a beautiful woman, and was completely obsessed and dedicated to this seductive woman. I really directed from a purely technical sense when I worked with Keith – it was primarily about where do I place the camera in this scene? Where do I open the scene? Where does this end?

KEITH GORDON: I would lay my head on the steering wheel and John would say, "It's like you're laying your head on a woman's shoulder." And that was definitely part of the dialogue about the making of it. We've all been there in our lives; we've all been pulled away from positive, healthy relationships with positive, healthy people into darker, destructive relationships with people who are destructive and possessive, and so Christine was the ultimate version of that! She was so possessive, she was killing off anyone around me and ultimately killed me. It really is a pretty good analogy for bad relationships! But I remember talking about that with John and that was definitely on his mind. And again, we didn't want to lay it on too heavy but it's there, always in the seams.

BILL PHILLIPS: That admiration Darnell has for Arnie's work with his hands was already in the book, as I recall. He's talking to Pepper and agrees, "Great hands. Bad taste in cars."

KEITH GORDON: I honestly feel that *Christine* truly is about relationships. The desperate need people have for them and how they can turn ugly. What I love about it is its examination of how much one gives up their personality, character and soul once they're in a relationship which is completely about possession. There is always a domineering partner in a relationship and when I was shooting *Christine* I was in one with a much older woman who because she was older and more experienced was dominant and the aggressor, which was perfect for this role and perfect for my character's relationship with this car. I feel that this film really is different from other possession movies in that it is about possession in the form of a relationship. I always treated the union between Arnie and Christine as a highly sexual one; look at the way I touch her steering wheel in parts, or more explicitly the V of her grill, which is totally a vaginal image, with my blood stained hand. Amazing stuff! Also, I think that people are slaves to their things – their homes, their possessions, their work and yes, to their cars!

RICHARD KOBRITZ: There was certainly some readings and back and forths and John met with the actors and talked them through the scenes, but a good casting director can lead you in the right direction and a bad one can lead you astray. I think the cast we assembled were either young and hungry or old and experienced and the combination worked very well for us.

BILL PHILLIPS: I always told myself while adapting it that it was a story about your possessions possessing you. And that's certainly there. But when it comes right down to it, as much as I try to dress it up, it's really a killer car movie. Perhaps an attempt to make it more than that pays off and might contribute to why it's a cult movie today. Yes, it's a killer car movie, but with universal truths and pain we all recognize.

ADAM DEVLIN: Arnie is working on Christine, rebuilding her and following a conversation with the garage owner we see Arnie go and sit behind Christine's steering wheel. As he does this, we hear Johnny Ace's "Pledging My Love". Arnie slowly leans forward and "hugs" the steering wheel and his left hand moves up and onto the dash as he slowly "caresses" it. As he does this we hear the first verse of "Pledging My Love" – "Forever my darling our love will be true / Always and forever I'll love just you / Just promise me darling your love in return / May this fire in my soul dear forever burn / My heart's at your command dear". We don't know if this song is playing on Christine's radio or not – so we're not sure if this is Christine's pledge of love to Arnie, or Arnie's pledge of love to Christine. It could in fact be both, but what is clear is that this scene is showing us a budding "loving" relationship between Arnie and Christine – his car – is forming. That the song we're hearing is from the 1950s – the era Christine is from – and that Arnie is cuddling and caressing Christine tends to indicate that this may well be a representation of the love both Arnie and Christine have for each other. It's a brilliant piece of cinema.

KEITH GORDON: A lot of it was not surprising because a number of those cues were in the script. I wish I remember which was which. A lot of that music had been written into it or added into it. Again, I don't know which was Bill Phillips and which was John on revised pages, but I do know that a certain number of those tracks are not like, "Oh, my God! How did they think of that?" I was around a little bit when John was recording his music, and I think they had some of the other music they were working on mixing in. So I don't think when I saw the film, there was a lot of being taken off guard by what was in there. So it didn't have that effect. I love the music, and obviously, it's an incredibly big part in the voice of the film. "Harlem Nocturne" – that was one I don't think I had ever heard before I saw the finished film, and I ended up using that in *The Singing Detective* (2003) because it was a great piece of music that I had never heard before *Christine*. For *The Singing Detective*, we needed a piece of music, again from that era. I ended up stealing it because it was something I liked so much. A lot of the cues that were on the car radio were written in ahead of time if I am remembering correctly. We might have even played a couple of them on the set a couple of times. I'm not as sure of this as I wish I was. Different cars had different musical voices, and also just part of a way to again playing with the fact that it is a film that takes place in two periods simultaneously. It is taking place in 1978, but Christine is carrying her own temporal field around with her, and in her universe, it's 1957. There's also a musicality to the sound design in that. What's interesting is the song ends, but there's a rhythmic nature which makes sense because both in real life there is a rhythm. But there is also if you listen to it, there's a rhythm in that sound that almost takes the place of music in terms of creating a sense of forward motion to it. It's a really interesting piece of sound design, too. I even listen to it. I remember thinking at the time that it is not just a bunch of random sounds. John is such a musician, and I have a feeling that was very carefully constructed to create the music of this creation in a way.

Robert Prosky as Darnell secretly admires Arnie's (Keith Gordon) talents as a mechanic.

"DO YOU LIKE MUSIC?": Dennis asks Leigh out dancing

In a scene that could very well read out of a teen-sex comedy of the period, Dennis Guilder and his two friends Chuck and Bemis sit together at the Rockbridge High School library ogling the lovely Leigh Cabot. Leigh is studying, deep in thought, and she motions her pencil towards her mouth taking in all the text her eyes soak up. One of the boys makes a crude remark along the lines of "to be that pencil" and from this moment (which is fundamentally an extension of the earlier scene where Leigh Cabot is introduced), there is a playoff that entirely encapsulates the character as desire personified – a girl who is the object of lust, every boy's fantasy and the one trophy above all else. However, as the film moves forward, it is discovered that Leigh is more than eye-candy to salivating boys: she is resourceful, more than capable, intelligent, steadfast, compassionate, reasonable and above all else, a girl who understands anguish and in turn sympathises with those who feel such devastating and crushing torments. Adding to the boys' lust for Leigh in the library is a comment that implies male sexual devices such as an erection: "Just don't tip the table over" which acts not only as a gag but also as an indication that Chuck admires the "bigness" of Dennis – Dennis being the "big man on campus".

Dennis finally gets the nerve to go over to Leigh and ask her out. He walks towards her then straight past her and collects a book from a nearby shelf. The book that he grabs is actually a jacketless copy of Stephen King's novel of "Christine", which is a nice touch by the art department on the film. Dennis and Leigh's conversation is a perfect example of economic dialogue – it is small talk but loaded with information and also a clear indication into character, tone and theme. He asks her "Do you like music?" and follows it up with "What about dancing?" He then continues with cutting to the chase and asking her out; a date to occur "After the game" which is a pivotal insight where the true meaning of life for teenage boys is the "game" and everything else comes afterwards. In

American cinema and culture, football is religion and girls can wait
– this is hinted at in *Christine*. However, it fails for Dennis as Leigh
explains that "she has a date" and although it is of course unclear as
to who the lucky fellow is, as the film progresses and we get to the
"game" in question, we see that it is in fact a changed Arnie. It is
also important to note that this "game" will change Dennis's position of power too – rendering him with a broken leg.

Before approaching Leigh, Dennis ignores Roseanne, with her
gorgeous smile beaming in his direction and her head coaxed in
a flirtatious manner, beckoning for him to come and sit with her.
Sadly, this is a fleeting moment for Roseanne who still believes
that she may still be attractive to her sometime boyfriend, but here
in this scene she is completely ignored and rendered invisible. In
a deleted scene, Dennis would make mention of Roseanne who
was one of the many people to sign his cast when he is laid up in
hospital with a broken leg, but from here on in, Roseanne will be
relegated and seen as the "old model" (speaking in terms of cars)
with Leigh being the new and improved "just in" sex machine. The
tracking shot of Dennis walking towards Leigh, catching Roseanne's disappointment that he isn't stopping to talk to her and in
turn, Leigh not paying attention to him is an excellent example of
John Carpenter's dedication to story and how characters fill the
emotional pull of a scene without saying too much. The high school
library is supposedly a place of learning but an environment still
charged with sexual energy and this scene brims of such horniness.

When Leigh turns Dennis down, he turns back to his friends
who eagerly want him to succeed – a hint at vicarious living and
the unspoken hidden rules of teen boys – but Dennis has been
turned down and therefore has "let the team down"; he even loses
a bet made with the perpetually horned up Bemis. Adding to such
insult is the librarian herself (played by Jan Burrell) as an old harridan watching and protecting moral codes – an extension to a film
populated by oppressive adults. Buying into the notion that the "old
world" is "dull" and stifling, Leigh agrees that history and/or studying history is boring, and when she talks with Dennis (albeit however briefly) they refer to dancing which during the period of the
film's setting (the late seventies) would more than possibly be the

world of disco – a new form of musical style and culture trying to breathe within the compounds of a film so invested in rock 'n 'roll of a bygone era. Leigh's comment at the end of the film "I hate rock 'n' roll" in many ways correlates to her disinterest in history and the past. When she voices her fear of Christine, she refers to the car "always playing those old songs", and this is more of her innate fear of an era she had nothing to do with, but is haunting her.

Dennis failing to win a date with Leigh questions his status as high school stud, and this contradicts Bemis's earlier reference to Dennis as "studly", while Leigh Cabot as played by the earthy and very beautiful Alexandra Paul is open, aware, a girl who can make choices and someone who will begin to start speaking up. Kelly Preston's Roseanne is also traditionally beautiful but it is a beauty in contrast – yes she is still fresh, gorgeous and open much like Paul's Leigh, but she does remain "voiceless" and rendered invisible as the film moves on. She will only have one more scene, where once again she is plotted as a character in love with someone who seems to have forgotten her.

JOHN CARPENTER: Alexandra Paul was just beautiful. She impressed me so much. She came in to read for us and she blew us away. She hadn't done any acting before, she was a model, but she had this incredible innate quality that was just gorgeous, simply gorgeous. I just really fell in love with her, I thought she was great.

RICHARD KOBRITZ: Kelly Preston didn't have any more to do than what you see her do in the film. There was another girl signed on before her, she was also blonde and they almost looked alike, but she had a chance to appear in a pilot and she had the deal – so she hadn't worked yet and we let her go. So I said to my casting director "Find me another blonde!" because I didn't want her to be another brunette because she was going to be playing off against the already cast Alexandra Paul who was of course a brunette. So we got Kelly Powsisz – as she was known at the time – and she came over and was full of energy and we cast her. After she finished the film, she called up and asked us to change her name because she had changer her professional name, and we said "Sure!" and from then on she was "Kelly Preston". It was a small part and she did fine by it, but we never thought more of it or less of it.

ALEXANDRA PAUL: I read the book mostly for just background, but because some things were changed, I worked from the script; plus I'm from New England anyway. So I know King is from New England. The film is in California. The book, I think is in New England. So, I didn't work off the book. I remember being very impressed with the book because it really brought to life that world, but I was working on a film based on it, so I really needed to concentrate on the actual script. I was very serious about the studying part and learning my lines and learn my character but overall there was a real insecurity that "I'm not supposed to be here" so… it took me a while as an actor to get over it.

Kelly Preston as cheerleader Roseanne becomes the girl ignored.

Alexandra Paul as Leigh Cabot about to be asked out.

Doug Warhit, John Stockwell and Mark Poppel behind the scenes.

CALL SHEET

POLAR FILM CORPORATION

THURSDAY

Day JUNE 2 8 3
28th

Day out of 44

Producer RICHARD KOBRITZ	Crew Call: 7AM
Director JOHN CARPENTER	Shooting Call 8:00 AM
Title "CHRISTINE"	Location VERDUGO HIGH SCHOOL 10626 PLAINVIEW, TUJUNGA.

SET # SET	SCENES	CAST	D/N	PAGES	LOCATION
INT. HIGH SCHOOL Study Hall DENNIS TRIES TO GET A DATE.	35	2, 13, 14, 15, 25.	D	24/8	VERDUG HIGH SCH 10626 PLAI VIEW, TUJU
				TOT 24/8	

CAST & DAY PLAYERS	PART OF	MAKE-UP/LEAVE	SET CALL	REMARKS
1. KEITH GORDON	ARNIE	HOLD		
2. JOHN STOCKWELL	DENNIS	7A	8A	
3. ALEXANDRA PAUL	LEIGH	7A	8A	RepT. TO LOCATI
5. HARRY DEAN STANTON	JUNKINS	HOLD		
8. WILLIAM OSTRANDER	BUDDY	HOLD		
9. MALCOLM DANARE	MOOCHIE	HOLD		
10. STEVE TASH	RICH	HOLD		
11. STUART CHARNO	DON VANDENBERG	HOLD		
12. MARC POPPEL	CHUCK JENKINS	7A	8A	REPT. TO LOCATION
14. KELLY PALZIS	ROSEANNE	7A	8A	Rept. TO LOCATI
15. DOUG WARHIT	HARRY BEMIS	7A	8A	
25. JAN BURRELL (SU)	MRS. ROY	7A	8A	
	(SU) NEW			

ATMOSPHERE AND STAND-INS	SPECIAL INSTRUCTIONS
-3 STAND-INS - WAY, WRIGHT, FORTE	7AM REPORT TO LOCATION
-2 JOCKS	730A Rept. TO LOCATION
-30 STUDENTS (MALE/FEMALE)	

	ADVANCE SHOOTING NOTES			
SHOOTING DATE	SET NO.	SET NAME	LOCATION	SCENE NO.
JUNE 3rd fri	D	INT. - HOSP, 707, Room, Corrid, / Sun Rm.	Vet Hosp. 16111 Plummer st Building #2 3rd Floor.	60, 61, 87, 88 116 SEPULVEDA # 891-7911
JUNE 6th MON	N	EXT. DRIVE-IN THEATRE	Pickwick DRIVE-IN	TBA
JUNE 7th TUES	N	EXT. HIGHWAY EXIT RAMP EXT. STREET NEAR FACTORY	MISSION RD + HUNTINGTON DR. E DST LA. 100 HRU 103.	
JUNE 8th WED 9th THUR	N	EXT. FACTORY	R.B +WCORP 104 THRU 115 44610 WORTH AVE TO COMP. E. LOS ANGELES	

1ST ASSISTANT DIRECTOR: LARRY FRANCO	PRODUCTION MANAGER: ROBERT DOUDELL
2ND ASSISTANT DIRECTOR: JACK PHILBRICK	ASSOCIATE PRODUCER: BARRY BERNARDI
DGA TRAINEE : CONNIE GARCIA-SINGER	

The callsheet for the library scene as given to extra John Richard Petersen.

"HEY MAN, NO GLASSES, YOU'RE LOOKING GOOD":
Arnie breaks a date with Dennis

Somewhat alluding to the fact that this may mirror the earlier scene where Dennis and Arnie are in Dennis's car together and having their intimate and profoundly meaningful interaction interrupted by the Cunningham parentals, here is a complete inversion of such a scene. Dennis pulls up in the Cunningham driveway (something that he has done multiple times in the film) to pick up Arnie to go out to the movies. From a gender/sexuality perspective and reading, it is interesting to see that after failing to land a date with Leigh Cabot, Dennis goes back to Arnie who is ultimately the "safe bet" and the loner who will always be there for him. But the narrative is shifting and Christine's supernatural influence is taking form. Arnie breaks the date and even more poignant than that is the fact that Arnie is coming into his own and will slowly not need Dennis anymore.

Stepping out of the shadows, Arnie's walk and demeanour has changed. Here is a new, and frighteningly different boy. In the background we hear Regina Cunningham's anger, continuing to berate her son, but Arnie's change in appearance seems to have a new attitude to go along with it as he shrugs her off with "Get off my back!" The opening of the scene has Regina and her husband berating Arnie, but it is quickly dismissed with Arnie becoming defiant and his own man. Later in this very telling sequence, Regina voices her concern about her son but she also mentions Christine in the same breath: "Ever since he bought that car he's been obsessed with it." The exposition delivered by Regina about the previous owner dying in Christine is a necessary backstory, and screenwriter Bill Phillips delivers this with swift elegance. Christine Belford spins this piece of important information with frailty and masterful wrist wringing as she mentions signing the registration papers and upon doing that uncovering the truth about George LeBay's death. When asked by Dennis if Arnie knows about any of this, she cries out "Arnie doesn't know anything anymore" – a loaded line to end the scene.

Upon seeing Arnie, Dennis comments on his appearance. Arnie is no longer wearing glasses ("Hey man, no glasses, you're looking good"), he wears a shirt opened up revealing a tight black t-shirt, fitted grey jeans and his hair is also different. The fifties is seeping in and his attitude and body language have severely altered – a self-possessed and in charge teen, not taking "shit" from parents or well-meaning friends. Arnie also states that he has Darnell's car which suggests he no longer needs rides from Dennis – that his independence (which comes through the restoration of Christine) is truly on its way.

With Regina being concerned that his plans with Dennis are cancelled, Dennis mentions not seeing him much anymore which adds to her anguish. Here, in this pond-like sequence, there is a brief glimpse of Regina's pain at the thought of losing her son to Christine. In a deleted scene, Regina would quietly open Arnie's bedroom door to find him sleeping, and she would weep over her boy completely oblivious to the heartache he would have to deal with day by day. She would also look over his sleeping body as a quiet, restful young man, not tormented or troubled, but pure and fresh to a cruel unfeeling world. When she barks "Arnold Cunningham you are going to find yourself with no friends at all if you keep treating people this way", she is now clambering for him to embrace personal interactions with people (like Dennis) rather than keeping himself locked away and in deep solace with an automobile. Regina now wishes to accept Arnie's social life as long as it has nothing to do with Christine. By the end of the scene, both Regina and Dennis watch Arnie disappear into the night – they are on their way to losing someone they loved (albeit in two varied ways).

JOHN CARPENTER: I really loved Christine Belford as the mom. All of the character actors were brilliant. I read them and cast. Robert Prosky was just terrific and such a nice man. A really nice man. Harry Dean Stanton I knew and had worked with him before on *Escape from New York*, and I had cast him as the cop. But

Christine Belford was fabulous, I really liked her, I loved her work. She could play older and do it so well.

BILL PHILLIPS: My rule of thumb is to say as little as possible about anything. Audiences are smart. When you're plotting a mystery, for example, you might find ten different places to posit a handgun. Then, when the first draft is finished, you can read the whole thing and decide better which eight of those to delete. I don't remember specifically choosing what to use with Regina, but I'm sure whatever was used was sufficient… and probably in the roughest of drafts, she repeated herself. Audiences don't need to be spoon fed constantly.

MARION ROTHMAN: As far as follow up movies I worked with John Carpenter on, *Starman* (1984) was shot principally on location. I remained at the studio cutting. That meant watching dailies without John. He would send comments or we talked on the phone. The film came together very nicely. Also John likes to do his own scores. I'm not a fan of synthesizers and pushed him to hire a composer. I can't remember who won! *Memoirs of an Invisible Man* (1992) relied heavily on visual effects which made for a long post-production schedule. My career before *Christine* started with an interest in theatre, directing. I studied a BA at UCLA Theatre Arts, started a summer theatre in Guerneville, CA and then lived in Europe for two years. I returned and bluffed my way into secretarial job at 20th Century Fox. Then I sat in on George Stevens' *The Diary of Ann Frank* (1959) editing, taking notes for three sets of editors. I promoted myself to apprentice editor and progressed from there.

VIRGINIA KATZ: I had read many Stephen King novels but not "Christine" and all I knew about the movie initially was that John Carpenter was directing it. I knew the story. Working with John was terrific. He would always ask my opinion which, as an assistant and that didn't often happen with other directors. I think John is a great director. He knows exactly what he wants. I mean, he got emotion from a car! His timing and expertise with the camera are impeccable.

BILL PHILLIPS: Usually when I plot out a transitional arc of any character, I just make a chart… so although I don't specifically remember doing this, I probably made such a chart and filled it in with gradual steps for a transition from "loser" to cool Elvis-type guy.

KIM GOTTLIEB-WALKER: A still photographer is essential, on even the lowest budget indie film. He or she documents the history of the production, as well as providing essential material for the press kit, promotion, magazine and newspaper reviews and articles, film festival, etc. It is extremely difficult to promote a film without that unique material, both on and off screen. And moments like "the director working with the actors" is a treasured part of film history, not preserved in any other way.

Christine Belford as Regina Cunningham.

"NO SHITTER EVER CAME BETWEEN HIM AND CHRISTINE": Dennis confronts George LeBay

John Carpenter is not only an incredible story teller and film director, he is also an accomplished musician and composer and his eerie music (with co-writing credit shared by the super talented Alan Howarth) manages to prop up this scene and lead into the next scene with elegant articulation. It guides a POV shot as we return to George LeBay's dishevelled "headquarters" and see through the eyes of Dennis Guilder, who is eager to find out more about this mysterious car his best friend has recently bought and since become obsessed by. "No shitter ever came between him and Christine, if they did… watch out!" warns LeBay, who then extends upon on what Regina Cunningham had mentioned in the previous scene – he refers to disjointed and creepy stories about his brother's death. This all adds up to a magnetic and classic horror trope build up to how the scene finally is resolved: the closing line of the scene has Dennis fretfully ask "What do you mean came back?" This is in reference to the Plymouth Fury reconstructing itself and returning for more carnage. LeBay's expression says it all, there is no need for screenwriter Bill Phillips to add any more exposition, because from here on in, Christine herself will come to life and lead the story on her own terms, with all the human co-stars as pawns to serve her and to be given a serving to.

In this two-hander scene shared between the middle class young Dennis and the working class elderly LeBay, the shambles is being packed up for sale. LeBay is leaving for good it seems; running away from a haunted past. Now that he has rid himself of Christine, he feels the need to leave Rockbridge. LeBay links Arnie Cunningham's instant love for Christine to his brother's and from this recalls his death and also the demise of his wife Rita and their five year old daughter Alma – both of whom died in Christine of monoxide poisoning. As an observational aside, the surname of LeBay that writer Stephen King penned conjures tonal similarities to the infamous Anton LaVey – the head of the Church of Satan who would make a splash among Hollywood circles during the sixties and seventies, and it is interesting to note that he would act as a consultant on a previous supernatural vehicle horror film *The Car* (1977) which would also feature a quote from him pre-credits. Satanic inferences do not pepper *Christine* at all, this is certainly not a religious horror film, it is a film about possession but not about the devil. LeBay goes on: "The only thing my brother ever loved in his life was that car" and this is the crux of men (and boys) who fall under the spell of Christine: they are completely consumed by her, used by her and obey her every demand. George LeBay's brother is not painted as a sympathetic victim, he is referred to as someone who was in love with a car, and not his wife or child. George made his brother give the car away "for decency" after the fact that Rita and Alma died as a result of owning this Plymouth, however the car came back and killed him – the car being something not to be reckoned with, once again, harking back to the concept of Christine being a vengeful witch; a monstrous harpy who will not take the backseat.

The way this scene plays out is solid and meaningful backstory set amidst a dishevelled home (number plates decorating the shed etc) which is an expansion on the recurring theme of class and disenfranchisement. Here we are in the world of "white trash" and how this subcultural element of poor white people has a vast connection to cars and how mechanics are one of the only means of making a living. However, within such cold environs, there is an element of humanity. The brothers LeBay seem to be estranged. Separated by the advent of Christine – much like Dennis and Arnie will come to understand. But here in this tiny back and forth, it is understood that George was fond of Rita and Alma, and as the last straw in a noble act of defending deceased mother and daughter and their honour is by ridding the family of the malevolent muscle car. George survives the film, however his existence is purely a shambolic one (as reflected in his homestead) and this is the case because of the influence of Christine.

BILL PHILLIPS: George, Roland's brother, was given a lot of his memorable energy by Roberts Blossom, who played him so well. One of King's words I often felt funny writing was "shitter." It just wasn't ever part of my vocabulary. In fact, I still don't know if it's part of anyone's vocabulary – but Blossom certainly made it work for me. The story of getting rid of Roland LeBay is true. I had seen *An American Werewolf in London* (1981) the year before, and it seemed to me (and when I phoned John, he agreed) that we didn't want to do exactly the same thing they had done with Griffin Dunne in that film. (The film was excellent, but we didn't want to copy it.) Besides, it complicated the story greatly by promoting Roland as the Evil One… when we were still trying to decide whether it was Christine, the car, who was evil – or Roland. By losing Roland, and thanks to George Thorogood's "Bad to the Bone", we had our answer. As much as "shitter" seemed like a foreign phrase to me, I realized that it was so much a part of the book that it simply couldn't be left out. I don't recall any lines to leave out… although I think if I encountered the word "groovy," I wouldn't use it.

RICHARD KOBRITZ: John Carpenter had written a script for *Someone's Watching Me!* and it was in the feature department and nothing was happening with it. They weren't going to make it. I said "Let's make the thing" and they said "Well he's signed on as a director" and at that time I don't think John was in the Director's Guild and he may have been working as an independent. So I met with the executives and said "Let's make this movie" and we went from there, and John was very easy, and very smart and very articulate, and there is no flamboyance to him, it's all real. I was quite impressed by him and we kept the friendship going in between the two pictures. We tried to develop something else that didn't work out, we couldn't break the story on something, so to speak and finally when I got *Christine*, I thought to myself "Who am I gonna get to direct it?" and so I called John up! It was one of those crazy phone calls where he just had *Firestarter* cancelled on him, so he was more than willing. So we talked on the phone and I told him that I just bought a book off Stephen King which I think is really great and he asked what's it called and I told him it was "Christine", and he asked what it was about and I told him that it was about a car, and he said "Is it any good?" and I said "It's really good" so that made his mind up and he said "OK, let's do it!" It was that quick. I mean there were contracts and red tape to follow, but as far as him committing, that's how fast it was.

"YOU KEEP A-KNOCKIN' BUT YOU CAN'T COME IN":
Dennis tries to enter Christine

Dennis Guilder sneaks into Darnell's garage via a gap in an out-fold window. Here is the first time Dennis looks like a shadowy figure, almost threatening in appearance until the light hits him and we, the audience, see that it is our hero doing some investigative work in order to save his friend. The use of Little Richard's "Keep A-Knockin'" is an inspired touch here, once again, the songs that spill out of the radio acting as Christine's "voice". Recorded on 16 January 1957, "Keep A-Knockin'" was a massive hit for Little Richard, the song hits a vital nerve in the thematic elements of the film (it will be used once again during the "gang rape" sequence) and will also celebrate the connective tissue shared between muscle cars and rock 'n' roll history. Little Richard himself would be a flamboyant queer artist who came from a background of appropriating songs that stemmed from the backwaters of the South and originally conceived by many black gay musicians and drag artists who were forerunners in the civil rights and then eventual gay rights movement. The fact that this song is performed by a black man and yet the "voice" for a female machine is an interesting consideration that bleeds together the sociological struggles of outsiders finding a well suited mask be it drag or *objectophilia*.

Christine (thanks to Little Richard) will not allow Dennis inside because she will not submit, and therefore her warning about "coming in" as per the lyric from the song, summarises her rejection of the young jock. Funnily enough, this would be Dennis's second rejection from a female in the film, and as the next scene renders him thematically "impotent", there will be no pursuit of the opposite sex for the duration of the film. However, Leigh, who will become dedicated to destroying Christine, will summon the help of Dennis and eventually grow close to him. However, in this short scene shared between Dennis and Christine, the Plymouth Fury has her work cut out for her with Arnie Cunningham, therefore, Dennis is not invited "in". In Christine's "eyes", the world is purely hers and Arnie's and "no shitter will come between them". Dennis is not permitted to enter their union and therefore he is left outside, endlessly trying to pry into the car, with the door handle staying firmly shut.

Dennis peers inside and spots her car meter and it reads over eighty thousand miles – this is a car that has driven a lot through the years. A source of inspiration upon writing the novel, Stephen King had the idea of "what if a car's meter went backwards, as if it was reclaiming time spent on the road?" and this is the seed that grew into what would be one of his bestsellers of the early eighties.

The beautiful image of Christine head on – the monster taking a breather, ready to kill – is a stunning composition and it is married well with Dennis being utterly stupefied that she is already in such great condition and that Arnie has done such a great job on restoring a banged up fifties model. Christine is beautiful and will become even more beautiful in the follow up scene, where she will glide into the sunkissed arena, watching Dennis play his little "game of football". Dennis attempting to open Christine's door is a sign of him wanting to examine her – to see what the appeal is and also what makes her so threatening to not only him but Regina Cunningham, but the blasting of Little Richard's screeching terrifies him and he bolts out of the garage and into the night.

JOHN CARPENTER: John Stockwell didn't give a shit how I directed! He was there to do a job. Keith may have asked a few questions here and there about my approach to certain scenes, because he was invested in learning about camera and the technical side of making of a film, as well as creative input. They were there to do their thing, to act.

BILL PHILLIPS: It was strange trying to imbue an inanimate object with evil. Later, I had a meeting with Dino De Laurentiis, where we discussed my adapting another Stephen King work – a short story called "The Mangler", about a laundry machine that "walked" down the street and killed people. I passed. I didn't want to become the "strange inanimate object-killer adapter."

RICHARD KOBRITZ: The lack of success on *The Thing* contributed to John not being able to do *Firestarter* for Universal. *The Thing* had come out at the same time as *E.T. the Extra-Terrestrial* and that went through the roof, it was a massive hit. But *The Thing* – which is now a very popular and much loved cult film – did not do well on its original release, so Universal cancelled *Firestarter* on him. This is a very normal method of operation, they felt that they were burnt and they weren't going to risk it a second time around. Now audiences will stand in line for ages to see *The Thing* because audience's opinions change.

JOHN CARPENTER: I wish I could say the choice of excellent rock 'n' roll songs was my genius, but we hired a guy who was an expert who came in with a list of songs from the era and he felt that they were appropriate, and we thought they were great and fit well. This was also the first time that a movie used "Bad to the Bone", which I loved. Rock 'n' roll should be scary and destructive, but it isn't really, it is essentially benign, and as far as my own scoring on it I just wanted to fill in what was necessary and not to have a plan. I scored it so the music would feed into what characters were feeling or doing or saying, when the songs ceased to play.

WILLIAM C. CARRUTH (music editor): Most of the music was already chosen by John Carpenter and Alan Howarth. John and Alan would add guitar chords and I would cut them in where we needed them to sweeten our music tracks. We would spend days in Alan Howarth's studio at his house just recording different sounds that John would play on the two or three different guitars that we would use as musical SFX to sweeten our music tracks. As far as the editor Marion Rothman goes, I worked with her on a lot of films as her assistant, co-editor and music editor. I'm a third generation film editor as my father was a music editor; his name was Richard Carruth and I learned my craft from him starting at age seven. He worked on classics such as *Gentlemen Prefer Blondes* (1953), *How to Marry a Millionaire* (1953), *River of No Return* (1954) and many more. I think I was nine when I started getting a hold of the work. Music editing comes natural to me and I've worked on masterpiece films like *Porgy and Bess* (1959), *West Side Story* (1961), *Man of La Mancha* (1972) and *Cabaret*. When you need to make a music cut you find the spot where everything else fits and you make it there for it to really work.

ROY ARBOGAST: The radio was controlled by big heavy switches and we cranked them up and down as the radio would turn on and turn off. Everything was controlled off camera. I never saw the Plymouth as a big muscle car; I just saw it as a nice fast car. I drove a Corvette as a kid, so it was fun to be around a different kind of car and it commanded such attention on screen. When you're on a film set, especially a big SFX film like this one, there is no time to get to know actors like John Stockwell, we are there to do the job. So for that scene it would have been me in control to the switchboard to get the radio on and then off. The entire film was a pretty hard shoot as it called for a lot of mechanical work, but John Carpenter made it incredibly warm and fun.

ADAM DEVLIN: Following a scene where Dennis learns that Christine's previous owner died of carbon monoxide poisoning, he returns to the man who sold Christine to Arnie. There he learns that not only did the previous owner die in Christine but that Christine was also "involved" in the death of his wife and daughter. Dennis breaks into the garage where Arnie is rebuilding Christine and tries to open the locked front door. It won't open so he thumps the door. As he does this, "You Keep A-Knockin'" by Little Richard comes on Christine's radio – "Keep a knockin' but you can't come in / Keep a knockin' but you can't come in / Keep a knockin' but you can't come in / Come back tomorrow night and try it again / You said, you love me and you can't come in". This is an inspired choice and an amazing piece of storytelling. It is here that we're left in no doubt that the car radio is "talking" for Christine; the radio is essentially Christine's voice. And the message could not be clearer – NO, you are not getting into this car! The choice of Little Richard, who's most acclaimed and popular period was the 1950s leaves us with no doubt that this is "the voice" of Christine – who was built in 1957, the very year "Keep A-Knockin'" was a major hit for Little Richard. Dennis quickly escapes out the window from which he entered and Christine is left alone – just the way she likes it! This song is used again later in the film. As Christine is being vandalised by some thugs the radio starts playing this song, only this time it fails to deter the vandals. This is a clever re-use of the song as it shows us that although Christine clearly has some powers over what happens to her, she is still essentially "just a car" and no match for a group of vandals hell-bent on destroying her. This time around, they do "come in".

"I KNOW WHERE HE KEEPS IT": Christine makes an appearance and Dennis is knocked to the ground

Following the scene where Dennis is rejected by Christine, we enter a world where he dominates and succeeds – the realm of American football. Opening with a terrific image of three girls walking across the sidelines, with their seventies feathered hair bouncing in the air, it is a perfect and yet discreet summary of the era painted in John Carpenter's film. Audiences would become accustomed to films made in the early eighties and yet set in the late seventies and this would be one of those – and as much as critics may feel certain visual cues may have not changed so drastically, fashion experts and essayists would: the Farrah Fawcett hairstyle (made popular by the television series *Charlie's Angels* (1976-1981)) would be a go-to doo for many teen girls during the late seventies. These extras play off that aesthetic perfectly well. Also, in many regards the girls could easily be in a rock 'n' roll band à la The Runaways, which is another counterpoint to the make-up of *Christine*: a film about rock 'n' roll and the great trajectory of rock music from the songs Christine plays to musicians like The Runaways, but also it is a film about the current trend of disco (as later hinted at in the drive-in scene). However here at the football game, musical subcultures take the backseat, as we are involved in the almost bloated and all-too masculine world of jocks.

Although girls populate the scene as spectators, this is a scene dominated by maleness, so when Christine rolls in looking absolutely stunning with a sheen, shiny fenders, her vibrant red looking like the most sensual of lipsticks worn by any teen beauty, the feminine mystique pierces the skin of machismo and masculinity and dominates the scene. Christine has made her entrance and it is a dynamic, mesmerising one. She is every femme fatale from every Film Noir of the forties and her command for attention is vital. As the game moves forward, we notice Roseanne – the bubbly blonde forever relegated to the sidelines – in her cheerleader garb bounc-

ing up and down and thrusting her pom-poms with great vigour.
She is clearly there for Dennis, and for Dennis to notice her, but
once again, completely ignored as his focus remains on the game,
and then shifts to Christine and what Christine delivers: Arnie
Cunningham, his best friend now completely "changed" with the
new girl Leigh Cabot on his arm.

This scene is incredibly important thematically and in a narrative
sense: it will mark the last time we see Roseanne, it will establish
the fact Buddy Repperton and his pals know where Christine is
"kept", Dennis Guilder will be forever changed physically and the
change in Arnie will be permanent and increasingly sick. Having
the bullies at the football game is an interesting choice from screenwriter Bill Phillips and in many regards it would make no sense
(why would slackers be keen on watching "do gooders" play their
little game?). However actor William Ostrander who plays Buddy
created a backstory for the character, where he always thought that
Buddy would be the ultimate in athletes. Here is this muscular and
strong young man completely cut out for football, living vicariously
through the game played by the more socially acceptable young
men headed by Dennis Guilder. Upon Christine's arrival, Buddy
asks "Isn't that Cuntingham's car?" to which his friend Moochie
replies "I know where he keeps it." Perfect economic dialogue that
establishes the fact that these thugs know where Arnie keeps his
beloved Christine. Much like Dennis, the bullies are all completely
in awe of Christine and bewitched by her presence when she pulls
up in the car lot by the football field.

As the eerie John Carpenter/Alan Howarth score takes hold of
the final moments of the scene, we watch Dennis watch Christine
and two things begin to happen internally: Dennis is shocked at the
majesty of this once beaten down Plymouth and in complete disbelief that his friend had restored her to such immaculate perfection
and also the surprising disbelief in seeing his once nerdy, pathetic
friend kissing the beautiful new girl in town. Within these realisa-
tions, Dennis is perplexed by his friend Arnie and also a sense of
jealousy can be argued to come into the fore. The romantic triangle
has more sides than three – this involves Arnie, Leigh, Dennis and
Christine. With his gaze fixed on Arnie (now sporting classic fifties

style clothes and looking sharp) who steps out of Christine with Leigh by his side, Dennis is knocked to the ground and damaged.

The camera circles the knocked down Dennis as he spits out his mouthguard and writhes in pain on the green grassy field. The image of the football congregation – students and the like circling Dennis – floods the beautifully composed scene, and Arnie and Leigh make their way to join such a tribute, leaving Christine alone, watching from the distance, her windshield under lit and featuring a spark of sunlight (her burning intelligence) and looking ominous and foreboding – judging and longing for more carnage. She is a vindictive femme fatale, and Dennis is now the man injured and made "impotent" much like many men tormented and tortured by the femme fatales of many great Noirs. Eventually Dennis will end up on crutches harkening back to that wonderful opening image during the credits sequence of *Double Indemnity* (1944) where Fred McMurray hobbles along – the man who lost everything because of a deadly dame in the way of Barbara Stanwyck. Much like Stanwyck and other women in Noir (Jean Simmons in *Angel Face* (1953), Rita Hayworth in *Gilda* (1946), Veronica Lake in *This Gun For Hire* (1942) and so forth), Christine's power comes from a combination of beauty, elegance, other worldly sophistication and desire. She is a vibrant red, made all the more vivid here through John Carpenter's lens, and now that she has been completely restored, she can take control as the vengeful witch that she is. Her beauty in comparison to Arnie Cunningham's newfound beauty, self-confidence and self-possession is undeniable – as she has come into pristine sex appeal, Arnie has also lost his glasses, his dumpy attitude and has emerged confident. Also, his connection to Leigh is thanks to the ownership of Christine; he has "found himself" through this sentient car. It is interesting to note, that perhaps this connection with Leigh has happened earlier as she mentions in the library scene that she had a date earlier planned (rejecting the handsome all-American jock Dennis in favour for the nerdy Arnie).

JOHN CARPENTER: As far as capturing the aesthetic of 1978 when we were making a film in 1983, it was all very, very weird! It was very strange. I mean nothing had really changed! I went over this with my art department and initially I asked them "What can we do to make this look as though it's a few years ago?" and they looked at me and we all decided that there was really nothing to change! I mean, not much had changed within the period of 1978 to 1983, this was such a short section of time between. So we didn't really worry about it for too long, and what we decided on early was to have a title card tell the audience that "OK, this is 1978!" That was pretty much all we did.

KEITH GORDON: I actually love the football sequence. I think that is a particularly beautifully done series of images, and the way football going through the air. I think that is an underappreciated sequence; I guess people don't talk about it as much because it is not as action packed. That's one of the scenes every time I see the film I still smile, it's just really effective. That was really among other things the reveal of Arnie phase two. Even more shocking is there's that car. It's the first time you really get to look at it and go, "Okay". But the whole way the football stuff is shot is really creative and really interesting and really gives the injury real impact! We've all seen a million sports teams/sports movies where someone gets hurt. I felt like they somehow really captured the physical impact of getting really hurt. There's a lot of good structure in the storytelling, and that goes back to King's novel and Bill's script. They're really good storytellers. I think there was a nice cumulative effect of a lot of good choices being made from the source material on forward.

ALEXANDRA PAUL: I remember when Bill Ostrander – who played Buddy – and I started dating. It was June 1st, and it was during the football sequence. I just remember a bunch of us talking, and then I think I put my hand on his knee. I think that was it. We were outside, on the steps of the honey wagon. That's how I remember it, but gosh, memory can be totally false to how he remembers it. That's the only thing I remember of our interactions. I don't remember anything else on the set before we started dating. I guess he asked me out, maybe that day. We started dating during the filming.

WILLIAM OSTRANDER: I always thought that Buddy Repperton went to the football match because secretly he would love to be able to play. I feel that he would have been an incredible football player. He was an athlete, but unlike John Stockwell's character, he would use his physical strength and power for all the wrong reasons. I also think he was there hoping that someone like Stockwell would get hurt! And he did! So he liked that.

ALEXANDRA PAUL: Kelly Preston and I were only in one scene together, and she was in that football scene. She played a cheerleader. We did shoot a few days together. She's a lovely woman, and her character, she's a sweet young woman, too. She's not that snotty, teenaged trope. She's not that; she's a nice girl: pretty and successful socially and all that. The new girl comes into town and all the boys just go "Whoop!" and their eyesight just goes from Kelly right to the new girl because she's basically strange.

JOHN RICHARD PETERSEN: The football game was filmed outside the Calabasas High School and interiors were done at the Van Nuys High School. I do remember, as with most shoots, an exterior of one school would be used with the interior being filmed at another school or on a soundstage. Kelly Palzis on the set was so very pretty and came across as sweet, kind and "approachable" and was the only actor I had a photo taken with on that set, the day of the hallway/library scene shoot. For years I always wondered whatever happened to that lovely young lady... until I came across an article on Kelly Preston. I was stunned to discover I had a photo with Mrs. John Travolta. Unfortunately, that photo together was our only interaction.

ALEXANDRA PAUL: I think the film is all about love! Isn't that what everything is about in the end? Yes, *Christine* is about loves – the first love of a girl, of a dream. There is the friendship between Arnie and Dennis, the fraught relationship Arnie has with his parents, the car that saves him because restoring her gives his life meaning and he is so empowered that the new girl in school falls for him. I think every movie has to have love in it. Someone once told me that life is made up of one choice: To live in love or to live in fear: trying to get love, and our fear of not getting it, in this sense movies reflect life! Also, I never hated that car, even though I have a line in the movie where I say "I hate this car". I was pretty much in awe of her, in awe of all twenty one incarnations of her. It was movie magic how they made the movie, in my opinion. When I was a kid, though, I had two recurring dreams. One was me hiding behind a rock in our front garden in Connecticut, at night, while a pair of headlights comes down the road towards me. In the dream, I am always scared. I think that was Christine.

BILL PHILLIPS: "I know where he keeps it" is my daughter's favourite line from that film. It's become such a family saying, if we're looking for something, that when I saw Malcolm Danare (who played Moochie) recently, I asked him to autograph a photo of himself being crushed by the car, with the phrase, "I know where he keeps it." Strange Christmas present.

MALCOLM DANARE: I became really good friends with Steven Tash and Kelly Preston who at the time was Kelly Palzis, in the film. So Kelly and I became really good friends. John Stockwell and I became pretty good friends. Bill kept more to himself because he actually ended up dating Alexandra Paul. When we got to all these different scenes, we all played really well together. I didn't really hang out with Keith. The bad guys stuck to ourselves. Stuart Charno was awesome too. I actually really like Stuart and keep in touch with him every once in a while.

KEITH GORDON: The cars used were just beautiful. I believe they found twenty four of them across the country in various states of repair and disrepair. That particular model there were not many of them. I mean, it was not a big production line, so the fact that they took even twenty four. It was a huge deal; they had to take ads in newspapers. If I remember correctly, I think seven of those became totally cannibalised to use as parts, essentially. There were seventeen functional Christine's at the maximum that could be used for different things. You had a couple built to go at very high speed and were really kind of suped-up! You had others that were designed to take impact and not get crushed too easily – they had reinforcement built into the frame. There were some that looked the most perfect, that all the parts were just in the best shape, and so they were the ones you used when you wanted her to look amazing. We were shooting in this giant closed up factory or warehouse out in the middle of nowhere at the edges of California. That was where they built the old sets for Darnell's garage but also at the very beginning where they kept all the Christine's. I will say walking into a room with like seventeen of those cars all lined up next to each other was pretty cool! I hope there are some pictures somewhere! But there was just like this row of red, white Fury's just sitting there was pretty amazing! A lot of them didn't survive the film, and a lot of them were destroyed in the course of the making of the film, so at the end of it, I think there were only like two left. One was part of some contest that the studio did where you could win a Christine, and the other was put in storage. I think there were others that were half beat up where they saved bits of. I think there were only two left that were left unmolested when all was said and done. Again, these are going off memories that are a bit old, so I wouldn't swear to my numbers.

ALEXANDRA PAUL: I would say given that the film was shot in 1983 and I was nineteen, I don't remember what my interpretation was then, but I do see it as a lot about the power of a woman over a man. That's not Leigh's power as much as it is Christine's power, especially over a teenaged young man. Her ultimate power in a way that is very different from the bullies that are exemplified by the characters. So the kind of power they weld is very different than the kind of power Christine wields and then, of course, Leigh then wields, too, ultimately over all the guys in the high school.

ALAN HOWARTH (co-composer): Well, I think in terms of, in the beginning, it was really the underscore of the action of what was happening, and so many of the scenes have sort of long, drone underscores with just a little bit of theme. And that is just how John saw the music for the movie, in that the actors were acting in such a way that there was a lot of contemplation, there was a lot of thinking about. The only times that we did any action cue was when Christine was chasing somebody. There's one that I've gotten lots of positive comments about, during the football game. We called it "The Football Run" that somehow seems to resonate with people too. Again that was another action moment. Otherwise, it's the real Christine relationship with Arnie is those songs, and it is all spelt out that way.

LISA RAE BARTOLOMEI (on sound design): In this scene, sound design and score elements come together to create a visceral and internalised experience of Dennis's injury in the football game. We open at a high school football game with only the natural sounds of crowds cheering and the violent, striking blows of body slamming brutally against body. We hear a kick drum deep in the mix, almost like a heartbeat, creating a sense of foreboding that presages the arrival of Christine with its engine like tempo. When Christine arrives in frame, the drums switch to a more snare like sound (presumably from the school band) and the rustling of the cheering pom-poms in the crowd. While convincingly sitting as part of the crowd's atmospheric sound these drums almost smoky jazz beats hint at Arnie's transformation from nerd into cool guy through his relationship with Christine. As we zoom in on Dennis's face playing the next pass we see him notice Arnie kissing the new girl Leigh. The atmospheric crowd sounds almost totally fade out of the mix at this point and are replaced with a haunting slightly dissonant harpsichord like synth melody. This music transports us right into Dennis's shock and confusion around Arnie's new "cool" persona and his winning of the trophy girl despite Dennis's position as the Alpha Male on account of his status in the school hierarchy as a football hero. This inner monologue through music comes crashing back to reality as we hear the mighty thud of Dennis's body rammed to the ground. The deep resonant tones of the synth sounds reverberate on one chord amplifying the intensity of this visceral, body blow sound and the crowd returns, cheering in the carnality of the moment. We are horrifyingly thrown back to reality. We then focus in on Christine as the score again dominates the aural landscape. We hear a high-pitched drone sound that throughout the film consistently appears in moments when Christine reveals her supernatural powers. Did Christine somehow cause Dennis's accident? The clues in the scoring and sound design firmly point to yes.

ELISSA ROSE: As the love affair with Christine ignites at Darnell's Auto, Arnie subtly sheds his nerdy skin and attire. He becomes cocky and self-assured, firstly ditching the glasses, his t-shirts changing from white to black, become darker with the simultaneous darkening of his psyche, are worn underneath Chambre shirts unbuttoned to the chest. Christine's creeping possessive hold on Arnie is further revealed when he attends his best friend's football game wearing head to toe black, hair undone and a shirt the replica hue of Christine's duco – crimson red.

The bullies of the piece posing for the camera in this publicity still – William Ostrander (Buddy Repperton), Steven Tash (Rich Cholony) and Stuart Charno (Don Vandenberg).

John Carpenter, Keith Gordon and Alexandra Paul on the high
school football field.

Behind the scenes at the football field.

Behind the scenes at the football field.

"PART OF BEING A PARENT IS TRYING TO KILL YOUR KIDS": Arnie visits Dennis in hospital

Upon the release of *Christine*, film critics responded to one line of dialogue that seemed to resonate and glow with a heavy undercurrent that seemed to embody the attitudes of teens during the early eighties in both a cinematic landscape as well as a sociological one. By the end of this scene which is set in a hospital room – where the banged up Dennis Guilder lies in bed with his neck in a brace, being paid a visit by his "evolving" and "changed" best friend Arnie Cunningham – we hear the film's anti-hero turn to his damaged pal with: "Has it ever occurred to you, that part of being a parent is trying to kill your kids?" This profound question hit a nerve with film theorists scrutinising teen-centric cinema of the period, and what screenwriter Bill Phillips does here with such inspired writing is illuminate the notion that young people of this period have one direct enemy that refuses them to grow, develop and break away – their parents.

Horror films during the early eighties would predominantly feature four kinds of cinematic representations of parents: the "mama bear", the patriarch who would embody "the sins of the father" model, the completely absentee parent and the parental unit somehow attached to the film's core threat. The "mama bear" would be prominent in horror during the early eighties (Jo Beth Williams in *Poltergeist* (1982), Barbara Hershey in *The Entity* (1982), Dee Wallace in *Cujo*) and they would be empowered women at odds with the forces of evil that jeopardize the safety of both their children and themselves. However, it can be argued that in their protection of their brood there could be a subtle underlying factor to ensure their children would be safe from the world à la Mother Gothel's over protection of Rapunzel and therefore, their undying love may be suffocating and obsessive. The "sinful" father would pop up in droves as well (James Brolin in *The Amityville Horror* (1979), Jack Nicholson in *The Shining*) who would actively try and kill the youngsters would ultimately be protected by their traumatised mothers, and the slasher film – which would be the most vitally important subgenre of horror of the early eighties – would feature teens predominantly free from parental observation (*Friday the 13th* (1980), *The Burning* (1981) et al) or feature mothers and fathers somehow connected to the featured movie "monster" (*Mortuary* (1983), *A Nightmare on Elm Street* (1984)). Here in *Christine*, Arnie Cunningham – now cocksure, confident and self-possessed, but also unnerving in his demeanour, creepy and unsettling – throws this line at Dennis with quiet burning intelligence and definite insight into truth behind such a sentiment. While *Halloween III: Season of the Witch* (1982) has a corporate body try and kill children across America, here in this film about a haunted car, the parental figures are there to stunt the growth of their teenage son – and instead of Arnie's angst being benign and frustrated as it was early in the piece, it is now something internalised and to be fought against. Arnie mentions that if they don't let him keep Christine, then he would quit high school. This startles Dennis, who now understands his best friend's absolute obsession with this car.

Beautifully performed by both Keith Gordon and John Stockwell, the scene moves swiftly in conversation that ultimately serves the transition in Arnie's character. Presenting Dennis with a large book of dirty limericks, Arnie listens to Dennis's painful accident and the fact that he may have been paralysed, but doesn't seem to respond in any kind of sympathetic way. Instead the conversation shifts to talk about his newfound relationship with Leigh Cabot which then quickly changes to talk about Christine and how she upsets his parents. "They just don't want me to grow up, coz then they'd have to face getting old", says Arnie, and this may be true in his case. It is also a response in defence of Christine – this Plymouth Fury is his true love, and nothing will come between him and this vintage piece of machinery.

Another interesting element that embodies transition in this scene is the fact that Dennis is presented in a vulnerable position – shirtless and bandaged around his abdomen, his leg in a cast, his neck in a brace, bedridden and shot from a high angle with Arnie towering over him. This is the first time Arnie is presented in an angle that makes him seem more physically impressive then

Dennis and the coyness of his dialogue ("she lusts after my body") slowly evolves into something far more distressing and eerie. When he talks about his parents, it is deadly serious and as if he is killing them off with disdain, disinterest and disobedience.

Also, in Stephen King's novel and in deleted sequences that ended up on the cutting room floor for the film, Arnie would sign Dennis's cast and his penmanship would change over the course of various signage suggesting a deep change in his personality à la spiritual possession. Much like other movies dealing with teenage boy possession such as *Amityville II: The Possession* (1982), the detachment from family is fundamentally at the core of what turns them from sensitive young men to cold and demented sociopaths. In the case of Sonny Montelli (Jack Magner) in *Amityville II: The Possession* (a character loosely based on real life psychotic Ronnie "Butch" DeFeo who murdered his family) who is inhabited by demonic forces that plague the infamous Long Island home, he guns down his parents in a late night massacre. However with Arnie, the "possession" takes shape in the ownership of the malevolent sentient car; he is not driven to kill because Christine does this for him – however his personality changes for the worse and, as depicted in the final scene, has the potential for destruction.

KEITH GORDON: I think that idea of parents inadvertently trying to kill their children is an extremely interesting idea. It's a great piece of writing mainly because it's a very classic idea, there is a lot of psychology behind it. You know fathers have such an immense amount of competitiveness with their sons, and mothers with their daughters, it seems to always be the parent of the same sex. I had that with my father when I was becoming an adult, he felt threatened or didn't understand me and certainly young people get that feeling from their elders and this era of movies was such a perfect time to tap into that as there was no real war going on, there was no civil rights issues really, it was a time when parents were the real enemy, or the main antagonist and there have been many movies that exploited that! Teen movies, dance movies and horror movies were becoming popular. The idea of teen years is really only a new thing when you think about it. In the old days, once you turned a certain age you were married and started to raise a family, but come to the turn of the century, especially from say the jazz age of the 1920s, there was this birthing of the teenage years, where young people had room to grow into the adults they were to become and parents were always opposing what they did and being the oppressor. The threatened oppressor who were one day going to be replaced by their offspring. *Christine* is all about this; Arnie's parents really don't know what's right for Arnie, so him running into the metaphorical "arms" of this car really resonates with a generation of angry disenfranchised teenagers.

JOHN CARPENTER: Stephen King writes fantastic characters – he really knows people very well, and the relationships he builds throughout his works shared by his characters is probably the most appealing element of his writing to me. The relationship between Arnie and Dennis in *Christine* is just great, and then Arnie's relationship with the car as well, I just love all that interplay. I mean *Christine* is a character study, it most definitely is a character study. It talks about this pathetic kid who finds some kind of salvation, and then self-destruction, through owning this car. So directing a film that was a character study with a haunted car running around killing people was fun to do.

BILL PHILLIPS: Having read the book I knew when he was going to snap. I do recall buying a book on a sale table in Hanover, NH in about 1975. I think it was entitled "5,000 Dirty Limericks." I remember writing that into the hospital visit. Arnie gives that book to Dennis. And since it wasn't a common title, I ended up giving the production my copy. Come to think of it, I should try to get it back! It's probably too late. I remember that in the book there was some discussion about Arnie's changing handwriting, as evidence by the way he signed Dennis' cast. The idea was that, in the book, he was slowly coming to resemble Roland LeBay, so his handwriting was changing to reflect that. I think my script had some vestiges of that left in – artefacts of the book. But I think they were (wisely) cut from the film. One never knows in a performance how much the actor brought to it versus how much the director pointed the actor in a certain direction. From what I've seen of Keith's acting, and also what I've heard of John's high regard for Keith as an actor, I wouldn't be surprised if Keith brought most of this performance with him. On the other hand, John is very good with nuance, so it also wouldn't surprise me if he said a thing or two to Keith. Keith did a great job of depicting Arnie. In fact, of all the excellent performances in this film, I think Keith's is the one that stands out the most. I wasn't a fan of the line about parents killing their kids. I didn't like it because as a child and as a parent (I already had two kids), I not only didn't share those sentiments, I couldn't imagine how anyone could have them. It's sort of like not being able to imagine why someone would become a mass murderer or a child molester. It just wasn't part of who I was. On the other hand, I recognized that it seemed to fit Arnie's particular pathology, and I certainly wasn't inclined to second-guess Stephen King on the subject of psychopathology!

RICHARD KOBRITZ: It really is a well-made picture and I say that objectively and keeping myself at arm's length from it, but it is a really well done film. It plays on television all the time, there is a massive fan base, and you look back at it and it not only brings back loads of memories, but it really shows us that John really did a bang up job on it. If you make horror films they need to exist for all time. Somewhere in the world *Christine* is playing.

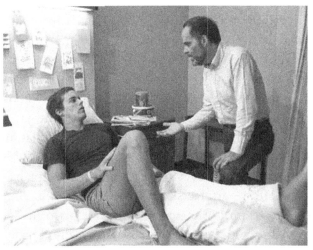

Producer Richard Kobritz has a talk with actor John Stockwell during one of the hospital visit scenes.

"YOU'RE MINE AND WE BELONG TOGETHER":
Christine tries to kill Leigh

In Roger Ebert's review of *Christine*, the famed critic makes mention of cars being more important to teenage boys than anything else in their developing world – even holding priority over girls and dating. In this pivotal sequence where Christine exhibits signs of pure jealousy, this is an essential overriding thematic ingredient. In John Carpenter's film stemming from Stephen King's novel, the notion of cars taking precedence over the emotional connection made between teenage boys and girls is at the core of what essentially is more than a possession story – it is a tale of obsessive objectophilia where an automobile (sentient and with her own "personal" agenda) takes control and drives the course of action. This Plymouth Fury is not to be reckoned with and her determination and zeal is an unstoppable force that wedges solid blockages in between her driver (the vulnerable Arnie Cunningham) and his established friendships (Dennis Guilder) and potentially even more fulfilling relationships (the budding romance with Leigh Cabot).

This perfectly realised scene opens in the heart of fifties nostalgia – the American drive-in. Here we find Christine parked alongside other cars and unaffected by the relentless rain, with her blood red paint job completely vivid and vibrant even amidst such grim and bleak surroundings. The rain gushes down, splashing upon her white rooftop and looks as though it is showering her in heavenly worship rather than drenching her in an undistinguished manner; in Carpenter's presentation of Christine, she is continually looked upon with deep respect and framed in sheer elegance and pristine beauty. Here in this rainy sequence, this is no exception. Whereas Arnie and Leigh step outside into the rain and look like washed up insignificant humans, the machinery that is Christine looks glamorous, like Esther Williams caught in a shower before diving into an MGM swimming pool in one of her otherworldly musicals that were popular during the fifties.

The film screening at the drive-in is the disco flavoured movie *Thank God It's Friday* (1978), which once again reflects a jarring comparison between the craze made popular by John Travolta hitting the dance floor in *Saturday Night Fever* and the old world of pure rock 'n' roll which was celebrated a year later in the nostalgia kick musical *Grease* (1978). Leigh Cabot's possible interest in disco is what brought them to see such a film – although the old adage of "who cares what picture we see" comes to mind with horny teens needing a place to neck, and that is exactly what *Christine* embraces: the hidden world of teens and what goes on in their cars. As the scene unfolds, we find Leigh and Arnie locked in a sexual embrace with his hand caressing her breast and her hand rubbing his crotch. Something breaks the mood, and in a flash Leigh suddenly jolts up and races out of Christine. Running into the downpour, Leigh makes her way to the concession stand taking shelter from the rain. Arnie follows her and is puzzled as to why she has pulled away from their romantic interlude. In a long history of teen cinema where young girls back out of sexual interplay because of fear, not being ready or the hidden anxiety of not being respected if they do follow through, it would make clear sense that a "good girl" like Leigh may not be keen on "rushing things" with Arnie, however, Leigh comes across as a worldly young lady, capable and confident and incredibly in tune with her sexuality, which makes what she tells Arnie all the more interesting and of course suited for this particular story – a story interested in teenage hang ups, but far more invested in the notion of a demonic car.

When she is asked what is wrong, Leigh replies "I can't. Here. In that car", she then angrily blurts out "I hate that car!" and then "You care more about that car than you care about me!" to which Arnie responds with "That's crazy, Leigh!" Here we come to understand that Leigh Cabot has an absolute distrust and fear of Christine – much like Dennis Guilder has – and she voices her opinion openly and honestly which both confuses Arnie and annoys him.

When Leigh is convinced to return to Christine, Arnie is baffled by her "jealousy" and responds to this by saying two inspired slices of dialogue: "It seems nobody likes my car these days" and "You know I thought girls were supposed to be jealous of other girls not cars".

Here in these two loaded lines massive character insight is happening. Arnie has now realised that outside of his parents, people just do not gel with Christine. They feel unsafe in her presence, disturbed and uncertain. He also wrestles with the idea of Christine being more than just a car, and that she is essentially a committed "lover" – something that will always be there for him, provide for him and defend him, outside of the realm of human desire. After this understanding, Leigh smacks the seat of Christine and Arnie quietly scolds her. Leigh bites back with "Don't like me slapping your girl?" This incredible duel between human girl and female-assigned machinery is intelligently composed and executed in the writing, performances and visual cues with Leigh's anger directed at this muscle car directly causing a violent attack from the vengeful Christine.

Cracking her own windshield, the car summons Arnie to get out of her and tend to the damaged glass while locking Leigh inside. Leigh has reached for her hamburger, taken a bite and then begins to choke. Christine flares up her inside lights, keeps the doors tightly shut and plays Ritchie Valens's "We Belong Together". Leigh struggles to breathe, clawing at her throat, her eyes wide and filled with mortal fear, her skin going deathly white, her body writhing in pain and gasping for air. Christine has her and is set on killing her while the desperate Arnie tries to free her. Leigh struggles to get out of the car and the imagery is just visually delicious: Leigh slamming the rain soaked windows lit up in extreme white lights, the multiple cuts that generate a sense of urgency, the thematic continuation of extreme close-ups that add to the frenzy and nightmarish intimacy of the horror and the tension that builds until a nearby drive-in patron notices what is going on and comes to the rescue, freeing Leigh from Christine's grip and performing the Heimlich manoeuvre which ends with Leigh breathing.

Christine's intelligence is also on show here. She is careful not to "out" her supernatural powers to the general public which is represented by the heroic man who helps save Leigh from choking. As soon as his gentleman approaches, Christine opens her doors and shuts down the lights and music – Leigh is safe, for now. But Leigh has been taught a lesson: "Don't get in the way of Arnie and I". The song choice mirrors this exact sentiment, that Arnie and Christine "belong together for eternity", and anyone who jeopardises that will be choked to death. This rivalry between Leigh and Christine will recede as the film progresses and make a transition into Leigh's genuine love for Arnie wanting him to break free from the clutches of this monstrous car (of which she summons the help of Dennis in order to attain such a goal). Also, it is interesting to note that Leigh would be the only female potential victim of Christine's, not only here in this sequence but in the climax where she will try and run her down on numerous occasions in Darnell's garage.

For the most part, Christine is a monstrous-feminine set on killing male bullies, and then tossing aside her lover in order to move forward and find the next unsuspecting loser, however, in this scene, Christine is a machine that will stop at nothing to travel from A to B. Also, Leigh is instantly linked to Roland LeBay's wife who suffocated to death in Christine – another woman who got in between a man and his car. In this regard, the gender of her victims vary, however in this particular incarnation of Christine and her relationship with Arnie Cunningham renders her a genie in the lamp who will punish those who persecute her teenage driver. Roland LeBay was an older man (married with a child), Arnie is a teenager (bullied and put upon), therefore it is an interesting factor that Christine will take on such personal narrative with distinction and uniqueness.

JOHN CARPENTER: The way I constructed the sequence where Alexandra Paul is choking in Christine was all borrowed from Hitchcock. I may have storyboarded the whole procession of her taking a bite of the burger, then choking, then trying to get out of the car, but I don't think I did. What I wanted to do with the scene was shoot it in a series of close-ups, I wanted it to be an entire action sequence but made by a collection of small shots.

ALEXANDRA PAUL: There was a close up of me touching his crotch. John wanted that. I don't think it was in the script. But remember, also in the eighties, there was much more sex in movies back then. Most movies had to have at least one breast shot. They had had least one lovemaking scene usually that showed the woman's breasts, and then something happened at the late eighties, early nineties when there was a lot more puritanical, more right-wing stuff, family values stuff came in. In the nineties you saw very little sex in films. Then in other films, whether it was a thriller, you always had somebody having at least one sex scene. So we were not teenagers, but there was no sex scene. I think if it was shot in the late '80s or early '90s there definitely wouldn't have been there except kissing. It was my first kissing/make-out scene. Keith was a little older. He lived with his girlfriend, so he was more... comfortable with it and relaxed. I liked Keith and he went out of his way to make me feel comfortable in that shot.

BILL PHILLIPS: As I recall, I just followed the chronology described in the book. My bias as an adapter is to always use the author's story as written, if it works. This involves asking if it's as cinematic as it can be (movies invite much more visual depiction and external action... books psychological and internal monologues). It also, of course, is determined by what can fit into the two-hour experience of a book versus a twenty-hour experience of a book.

ALEXANDRA PAUL: It was only my second time at a drive-in, so that was neat. I was nervous about making out with Keith, who is the nicest guy in the world but I was only 19 and shy about all that. Because there was fake rain outside the car, it was freezing when the good Samaritan pulls me out to give me the Heimlich manoeuvre! And I was vegetarian. I don't recall there being a veggie burger (it was 1983, after all – vegetarians were few and far between) so I only ate the bun. John kept asking me to be more and more panicked about not being able to breathe. Those are my memories. Back then it was unusual to be a vegetarian. I have been a vegetarian since I was fourteen, and I didn't ask for a veggie burger. Now I would ask for something that was not meat, or even a couple years later I would have asked for it, but then I didn't. I think I would very likely just not have told anybody. I think all I did was just push it back so that I didn't have to eat it and I just ate the bun because I didn't want anyone to have to go out of their way and get me a vegetarian burger.

KIM GOTTLIEB-WALKER: Keith was so open and enthusiastic. He wanted to learn everything about filmmaking and directing, so instead of retreating to the Winnebago between scenes, he would hand out near John and the cameras to see exactly how John would prepare each scene and work with the crew and actors. It is the way he learned how to become the terrific director he is today! Alexandra Paul was a very sweet girl… and a vegetarian, which required moving the meat to one side in the hamburger she chokes on, so she is actually choking on bread and lettuce!

ALEXANDRA PAUL: There were twenty one cars bought for the film, in various states of disrepair. The call sheet would list which Christines were to be used that shooting day – the cars that didn't have a motor were in the garage scenes, and the trashed ones were used in the beginning of the movie. There was "Muscle Christine #1", "Muscle Christine #2" and they did the chase sequences. The best was the special effects team, which devised the body parts that generate back to new. I remember a Time magazine article snarkily reviewed the movie and wrote, "and that cheesy way the car grows back by running the camera backwards". Well, it was not that way at all! The special effects team created rubbery car parts that they inflated during the scene. It was so clever and really hard to do to make it look just right. I thought it was awesome.

BILL KOBRITZ: The book takes place in Pittsburgh, and Stephen King did that as a homage to his friend George A. Romero and thinking about shooting that film in Pittsburgh and in the snow – because there are many scenes that occur in Winter and in the snow in the novel – was the first thing that didn't interest John, so he decided to transpose the locale to California and half shoot it in Pasadena where he filmed *Halloween*. We went from there. We talked over the scenes, and John would make changes. There is that great scene where the girl chokes at the drive-in, very similar to what happened to Roland LeBay's wife who doesn't end up so lucky, so that whole scene made more sense in California where there would be drive-in theatres still operating. We took from the book but we never felt that we were prisoners of the book.

DONALD M. MORGAN: I really didn't do too many horror films. I did *Starman* (1984) – I guess you could consider that as a genre film. That was pretty much the way I learned. I wasn't a film student. I started in the business as an aerial-cameraman for Nelson Tyler who is a very famous aerial photographer and built Tyler mount helicopters. I didn't know how to light anything. I never lit a set. I would just hang out of a helicopter and do whatever. So when I started getting people saying while you're out there could you grab this shot and grab that shot I would do stuff with whatever available light there was. It was mainly exteriors. When they started asking me to light stuff, I didn't know how. I didn't know any of the names of the lights or anything, so I bought a book of 100 famous paintings (which I still have), and I started looking at what artists did, and I thought I could do that with lights. I actually learned to light by looking at Rembrandt and different artists. I liked the mood. By the time I did *Christine*, I had been doing movies and movie of the week, so I really didn't reference anything then – I just went by my gut. I just did what I thought was right. John allowed that. John liked what I was doing, and of course, he made suggestions, but he left the lighting pretty much up to me. I don't remember him saying that he wanted it brighter, he just liked what I was doing. I've always "lit" from the gut. I just have a gut feeling about a situation and I "lit" like that. But it all started looking through paintings. I didn't even know who I was looking at. I would just look at paintings. I loved a lot of Rembrandt stuff. I loved the warm and dark and moody. So I didn't really reference any particular thing when I was working on *Christine*.

ALEXANDRA PAUL: I hadn't seen any of John's films prior because it fell into a sort of genre that was sci-fi/horror. My impression of John... I was so young... I was nineteen and I looked up to a director like he was a father, so I looked up at him like he was going to tell me what to do. And I was so terrified on that set! I don't think he realised how terrified I was. He was pretty quiet around me. There was one time when I was supposed to cry and I couldn't, and so he brings me into his bus and I start to cry! Too bad the cameras weren't on! I always had this thing where I thought they really meant to hire a pretty, curvaceous blonde like Kelly Preston… like why didn't they hire her for the lead? Why did they hire me? I said "I think you just hired me because you felt sorry for me!" and his face looked shocked and then angry, and then said, "Do you think I would hire somebody for the lead in my movie because I felt sorry for them?!" I just couldn't believe why… I just couldn't see myself… it took me a while to get secure enough as an actor to really go "I'm the best one for the job!" So he told me later that I really freaked him out because he wasn't used to such emotion with an actor and also probably because I was so young, but he was always so kind, I remember, very nice.

BILL GIBSON: Bill Gibson's Christine Movie Car is the most expansive, immersive *Christine* experience travelling today, now with eleven years of thrilling fans under her wheels. Gibson took his passion for the 1983 Stephen King novel and film, and poured it into a loving restoration that stands as a detail-for-detail screen accurate representation of the titular homicidal vehicle, made of actual parts from cars featured in the John Carpenter directed horror classic. Not only do fans get to meet Bill and his 2013 Mopar Hall of Fame inducted Plymouth, but they get to spend time pouring over the world's largest mobile *Christine* museum, featuring memorabilia, props, collectibles and original merchandise that can only be seen at one of Christine Movie Car's appearances. This lovely lady who just happens to have an actual assembly date of 31 October 31 1957 has appeared on *Graveyard Carz* (2012-)and starred in films *Jacob* (2011), John Schneider's *Smothered* (2016), SyFy's *Sharknado 4: The 4th Awakens* (2016) and most recently in John Carpenter's Anthology Music Video (2017). She also has been featured in Fangoria, Horrorhound and several Mopar magazines. Christine Movie Car offers more than your average show car experience, as she comes to life before your eyes, headlights glowing, smoke rolling and doo wop tunes flowing. Gibson has outfitted his "girl" with state of the art effects that recreate actions from the movie, putting convention patrons "inside" the motion picture. Just hope she doesn't get too close! Often imitated, never duplicated, Bill Gibson's Christine Movie Car offers a rare treat for fright fans and hot rod lovers alike.

ALEXANDRA PAUL: We shot that drive-in sequence in one night. There was certainly only one drive-in in the area; there weren't many. It was in Culver City if I remember correctly, and they had to do the rain conditions, of course, because it wasn't raining, it being California. I'm pretty sure we shot it in one night. There aren't a lot of long shots. I think there's just one wide shot to establish. Then it's in the car. Even when he leaves the car, we see him running. There is that one shot because he tries to open the car door and it doesn't open right away. Carpenter made me go further. He'd say, "Do it more! Do it more! More!" More grabbing at my neck and things which was not my inclination, but he wanted me to do it more. Given the job, it seems more appropriate.

Leigh and Arnie get romantic, only to be interrupted by the jealous Christine.

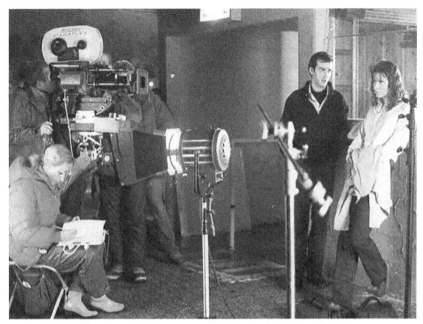

Shooting the argument by the concession stand at the drive-in.

Leigh Cabot (Alexandra Paul) becomes a potential victim of Christine.

Raining at the drive-in: the crew create the
rain effect while the film Thank God It's
Friday plays on the screen.

John Carpenter: director at work.

John Carpenter keeping the mood light on set.

Alexandra Paul and Keith Gordon pose for a publicity still whilst
shooting the drive-in sequence.

"I WONDER WHY I LOVE YOU LIKE I DO":
Leigh hates Christine

In the relentless rain, Christine pulls up out front of Leigh Cabot's house. This torrential downpour evokes imagery of classic Gothic horror but set in a suburban terrain, as if European sensibilities have penetrated the American landscape. With Rockbridge getting soaked, this relic of a bygone era – the titular Plymouth Fury – glides towards Leigh's house with Arnie at the wheel. This car is very happy to "drop off" Leigh and bid her farewell, as she is a threat to the unity shared between her and Arnie. The entire sequence leads up to Arnie promising that "everything is the same" when she stalls on him, as if upset with him – that he would have a human girlfriend, when she is much more than enough.

With suburbia drenched in November rain, Leigh bolts out of the car as if she is fleeing for her life. She races to her porch followed by Arnie who seems to undergo a major transition throughout the course of their confrontation. In the early moments of the to and fro, Arnie tries to understand Leigh's rage, then he gets defensive, then he turns threatening and then regresses back to desperate and pathetic. In the safety and comfort of Christine's "bosom" he returns to a place of happiness – or at least perceived happiness. Leigh's anger is warranted and it is the first time in the film a character senses something supernatural about Christine outside of hearsay and a "bad feeling". Leigh has experienced a violent attack from the car as a clear result of jealousy and she voices these feelings in this confrontation out on her parents' front porch. Protected by the compounds of family turf, the eloquent and smart Leigh insists that Arnie "Get rid of that car". Arnie asserts his protection of Christine, but Leigh goes on: "When I choked something happened…the radio came on, everything got bright!" She is aware of Christine's abilities and the danger that comes with owning such a car, and this is the first time Arnie is confronted with this fact: that this classic American muscle car may in fact be an agent of evil. The conversation gets even more heated when Leigh scolds Arnie about not even trying to help her when she was choking and she furthers her argument with the fact that Arnie even tried to stop the stranger from assisting. Completely consumed by the obsession he has for Christine, Arnie has turned a blind eye to everything outside of what happens and what is said about this automobile, and this includes his ability to help a choking girlfriend. When he becomes threatening and sinister, he brings sex into the picture: "You know what I think? I think you're just sexually frustrated…" – this is an insightful critique on what the film examines in regards to teenage sexuality; the hungry boys and the girls they pursue. However, here the scrutiny is reversed and a teenage girl's sexual appetite is up for "discussion", and the progressive and savvy, and also in charge and self-reliant Leigh, is forced to face her own sexual needs and the restrictions that come with it – also, the complexity of such carnal interest. With a sturdy blow, she pushes Arnie off of her and here we get a sense of her physical strength and athleticism – which will come into play during the final confrontation with Christine. Leigh is not only an intelligent and beautiful young woman, she is also physically capable and strong; making her a formidable adversary to Christine.

Alexandra Paul's performance in this sequence is dynamite and she powers Leigh Cabot with a vast array of character input. She comes into her own as a young woman not to be misunderstood nor bullied, however this does not ever deny her her sensitivity, nurturing nature and emotional connection to Arnie, after all, as seen in a follow up scene, she gives him another chance. Paul's dynamic chemistry with Keith Gordon is a highlight of the film as the two bounce off one another with effortless ease and bring the tension to the fore with great skill. Much like many teen dramas during the eighties, the combination of resourceful girls and needy boys is something that pops up in interesting and complicated films that for some reason get overshadowed by the overly discussed films of directors such as John Hughes. In films such as *Little Darlings* (1980), *The Last American Virgin* (1982) and *Smooth Talk* (1985), teenage girls and boys relate in varied manners with the girls being more aware than their male counterparts – Laura Dern's disinterest in teen boys and dangerous interest in the adult Treat Williams,

Kristy McNichols' heightened intelligence and Diane Franklin's vulnerability as an extension of her emotional power. Here in *Christine*, Leigh is seemingly more mature than the boys at Rockbridge (the ones who leered over her in the hall and at the library) and more together than the fragmented and damaged Arnie. Eventually, she will bond with Dennis Guilder – an emotionally available "good guy" – but thankfully the film does not tip over into them forming a romantic union. In early drafts this was the case, as the duo would fall in love outside of trying to free Arnie from the control of Christine, however, this would be dropped.

This scene is also the first time the songs from Christine's radio are mentioned. Leigh talks about the "old songs" that continually play, and how they scare her. Classic rock 'n' roll has morphed into something menacing and eerie, a ghostly memory of something that the youth of 1978 would never understand because "they weren't there". Leigh also says "Sometimes when we're making out, it just stalls…as if the car were jealous, Arnie…" and this jealousy concern is a vitally important ingredient to the very fibre of the film: Christine is a woman scorned, and hell hath no fury like her. Her main threat is Leigh Cabot and therefore her jealousy is warranted and may result in violence. With Leigh's parents' porch light coming on, there is a stunting of further discussion, as if the interference of adults breaks the argument and therefore puts a halt to understanding the true nature of Christine. The shaky grounds of Arnie and Leigh's relationship is at the fore of the scene (physically/literally) and yet in the background, John Carpenter plants Christine to the right of frame, stationed behind her man as if listening and eavesdropping, wanting Arnie to come back and apologise. Christine remains in frame for many scenes throughout the film, even when she is secondary to the purpose of the sequence – like an entity perpetually waiting and secretly listening.

When Arnie steps back into the driver's seat, Christine is annoyed with him. She refuses to rev up and with every turn of the key, her ignition remains quiet. Finally, Arnie gives in to the "romance" and promises her that "everything is the same", showcasing his undying love for Christine. Once reassured, Christine "cheers up" and her motor starts to purr. A big smile spreads across Arnie's face (he has forgotten Leigh for a moment) and Christine "speaks to him" playing Dion and the Belmonts' "I Wonder Why". The song's lyric ring out:

I wonder why I love you like I do
Is it because I think you love me too?
I wonder why I love you like I do, like I do…

JOHN CARPENTER: Hitchcock always has an influence on us directors – we owe a lot to his work and the way he develops characters and scenes. I tend to borrow as much as I can from him and of course you see that in films such as *Halloween*. However, generally speaking, the storytelling in *Christine* didn't really adhere to the way in which Hitchcock told his stories, for the most part. Hitchcock inspired some of the camera movement and composition of shots, but nothing really to do with the way the narrative unfolded.

DONALD M. MORGAN: John would say, "I'm gonna put Christine here. I want these two here. So frame that so we can see the car." That was pretty much the way it was handled. I got to admit, a lot of the stuff that we were doing that I didn't understand until I saw the movie. I wondered why a couple of times we were doing something, and rather than talk about it a whole lot, I knew that he knew what he wanted. My deal was the lighting though. I loved doing the lighting and of course the rest of it, but the thing that drew everyone crazy is that I always liked pretty much the wide open lens.

RICHARD KOBRITZ: The car was never referred to as a car, it was always called Christine by the cast and by the crew, and it was a girl. Certainly the Arnie character falls in love with her and is seduced by her. I don't think the word "car" was ever used on the set, it was always "Christine" and this Plymouth was always referred to as a "she" and as "her", and because of that, we all treated this car like a beautiful, deadly woman and it worked for the mood on the set. First of all, this car looked beautiful, she was red and if you look at the lines and the headlights, she is certainly a girl and the crew bought it!

KEITH GORDON: It is a love story with a car, quite literally. So that goes to that kind of sexual energy that particularly young males put into your connection to your car. You have an incredibly intimate relationship with this car that you are getting in and driving and touching. Driving a car is very sensual; you're feeling it with your hands, your body and if you work on a car, it's very physical and very connected. Also, cars are for a lot of young people where their first sexual experience has happened, and they make out in cars. So it's kind of your own little private world. That's the other thing about a car when you're a teenager; it is the one place you can escape your parents, and escape school, and escape, so it has a romanticism to that too, which is it is your hideaway, your secret cave that you run away to. Now, what's funny in terms of my own life is I grew up in New York City. Part of my culture in New York City is you didn't have a car; you got the subway. New York was never much of a car city. So I didn't grow up with that. I understood it because I loved cars. I was a kid who went to car shows and went to auto races and got Road & Track magazines for a long time when I was like 10 to 12/13-years-old. I was particularly into auto racing thing and formula one racing, and so I loved cars, too. I didn't grow up with the kind of California car culture, where the second you turn 15 and a half, you got your learners permit, and the second you could afford it, you owned a car, because, in New York City, you had to find a place to put a car. It was so impractical in Manhattan that a car just wasn't part of the reality of your experience. So for me, it was a lot of fun to play with it in the movie because I didn't get to have that. I was very aware of the car culture, but I didn't grow up with that certain thing where kids in California or in the Midwest, or a lot of places do, where a car is a part of your teenage years. I mean, a lot of people in New York I knew didn't get their first car well into their 20s because there was just no reason for it. If you ever needed a car for a trip, you would just rent a car, but it was just not practical for the city.

ALEXANDRA PAUL: They had the rain showering down from that machine and we do that scene on my porch. I think there was less rain; I think I was just wet. So it was cold, night shoots are not easy, they are very difficult… and then you add rain to it! But it ended up being fun! I personally prefer dialogue scenes. I am a very active person but when it comes to shooting – to filming – I am not crazy about the chase scenes. I've done so many of them. I like to act! So… it was fun… but the bulldozer and everything; I'm not an equipment person, so I couldn't care less about that. I learnt so much about cars and things, I never cared about cars. I did gain an appreciation of them while on that film, but I much prefer the dialogue scenes such as the one on the porch with Keith.

ADAM DEVLIN: Following a disastrous date at the drive-in with his girlfriend Leigh, where alone in Christine she almost chokes to death, Arnie drives Leigh home where she confesses she feels like Christine is jealous of her. When Arnie leaves, Christine won't start. After several attempts to get Christine going, Arnie tells Christine that nothing has changed, everything is the same – and Christine starts. As they drive away we hear "I Wonder Why" by Dion and the Belmonts. Originally released in 1958 its opening lines "Don't know why I love you like I do, don't know why I do / Don't know why I love you, don't know why I care…" This is clearly Christine "talking" to Arnie. It is essentially Christine making up with Arnie after a fight. It's as if Christine is jealous, as Leigh suggested. The use of this song at this point in the film skilfully shows the deepening "relationship" between Arnie and his car. Christine is now a full-blown "personality" and Arnie clearly has some sort of "feelings" for her. As Christine does for him. It's a masterful use of song to add context and layers to what is going on between Arnie and his car.

ALEXANDRA PAUL: I personally did not like my performance. When I saw it, I was completely freaked out, and it was probably because I was not used to seeing my acting on camera. My voice was very small, whispery. I was nineteen; I was not a powerful presence, and that came out of my little voice. I also feel like that, if things work for you as a person, like whether it is being funny or being helpful or being a certain way, then you keep doing it, and so I think I had really perfected the sort of innocent but not confrontational person because I wanted everyone to like me, that's me Alexandra in real life who was like that. So as a person, I was not powerful, and so I think that came out in terms of her, which is okay because a lot of girls aren't that way. I was not a woman yet, and so it took me another eight years to really get more powerful. And actually, when I cast in *Baywatch* (1992-1997), I asked if they allowed me to create my own character and I requested that she be someone who was powerful. I wanted to work on that as an actor because I had been cast for a long time in sweet, girl-next-door roles. That's basically what I was playing in Leigh; that's what they were looking for, the sweet girl-next-door. I think that was how the book was written, the nice girl. Probably why they didn't cast Kelly because she's got a sexiness to her. She has an innocence that's like a baby doll innocence which maybe was too provocative. Having gone into that psychology, I had taken acting classes and was very serious about the craft of acting and how to develop character. I had done a whole history, even though you never see her family, you never know who she is, Leigh outside of Arnie in high school.

STEVEN TASH: I got the Stephen King book right away. Actors go to the script and book first looking for their characters name to appear on various pages and scenes to see what's going to be demanded of them in the role. There was just enough material to work with in the book for me integrate and soak up as Rich. A good week or so before my call day I found out somehow where they'd be shooting. I took the work I'd been preparing as Rich and basically stalked the shoot from across the street of this beautiful house. I saw Christine parked in the driveway; I caught a glimpse of Arnie and his girlfriend, Leigh. And I started disliking this Arnie guy right away… the beautiful red car, the hot girlfriend… I, as Rich, had never seen a house this gorgeous… and as Rich I wanted to strike out at something, anything. And I watched that car like it was alive. I needed to make my mark. Rich had shown up to me that night. I was pacing up and down the sidewalk at this point in the misty night air, and I saw a couple of crew people notice me. I'm sure I was a sight pacing in the light from the street lamps, dressed all disheveled as Rich. Before it would turn into anything more I walked away. But I was ready for my call day to shoot.

Leigh Cabot in the storm; the human rival to the demonic Christine.

Producer Richard Kobritz talks with Keith Gordon on set.

Arnie Cunningham's devotion to Christine will eventually lead to his downfall.

THE RAPE: Christine is visited by Buddy Repperton and his pals

The masterfully composed original score for *Christine* came from John Carpenter himself (a Renaissance man in the purest sense) and fellow composer Alan Howarth. Howarth would work with Carpenter on a number of films such as *Big Trouble in Little China* (1986) and *They Live* (1988), and here, the score is minimal and minimalist. In a motion picture so soundtrack heavy, when the original score comes into play, the attention levels are at a peak, because something is either going to be revelatory or action packed – both ingredients propelling the story into another gear, alternate perspective and progressive development that usually involves the capabilities of its monster, this supernatural Plymouth Fury. The musical interlude that has Christine leaving Leigh Cabot's house and cruising back to Darnell's garage in the rain, only to be stalked by Buddy Repperton and his gang is deftly entitled "The Rape". While thunder and lightning hit the soundscape (more evocation of classic European horror), the Carpenter/Howarth score creeps in, meticulously handled with direct precision, leading to what would ultimately be a scene of gang rape. The synthetisers and electronic music counter the almost all-the-way-through rock 'n' roll score, and this very eighties almost technical sustained melancholic and haunting instrumentation presents a scene that is not only nasty, but will result in much more horrific events to follow.

Like goons ready to take instruction, Buddy's gang stand by Christine armed with personal weaponry (a chain, knives, mallets etc) and eagerly wait for their leader to begin the carnage. Buddy jumps onto Christine's hood and then climbs onto her rooftop and brings his sledgehammer down with all his force. The musical expression as heard in Carpenter/Howarth's piece comes to a halt as soon as Buddy Repperton thrusts his sledgehammer into Christine's windshield, shattering it and exposing her interiors. The entire sequence plays out like a vicious attack on a woman, as seen in many rape themed films prior to the release of *Christine*. At one point, Christine fights back with her "voice". She desperately uses Little Richard's "Keep A-Knockin'" to warn the boys to keep away, but she is "silenced" as Moochie smashes the radio and knocks it to pieces. Originally Moochie would defecate on the dashboard, but this would be removed from the final cut, and instead made mention of when Arnie has dinner with his parents.

The bullies revel in the destruction of Christine, from the time they watch Arnie park her inside Darnell's garage, sneak inside as he walks away closing the roller door, and right through the process of smashing her to smithereens. The violent attack on the car is primal, ugly and fuelled with hate. Christine is violated, molested, battered and bruised, and her eventual vengeance on these tormentors will ring true to form as many rape and revenge movies that had a popularity streak during the seventies and early eighties. Most importantly, Christine herself will become an agent of revenge as well as a protector of Arnie Cunningham, and she not only aligns herself with rape and revenge cinema figures such as Zoë Lund's mute heroine in Abel Ferrara's *Ms. .45* (1981) who takes on maleness after she is brutally raped twice, but also adopting the likes of Charles Bronson's Paul Kersey in Michael Winner's *Death Wish* (1974) who avenges the rape of his daughter. Connecting these two figures of vengeance to *Christine* is important in that she is a machine that will avenge her own undoing (Repperton and his friends "raping" her) and avenging the abuse "her man" Arnie has suffered at the hands of such oppressive victimisers.

Lit in a shadowy dismal hue, but completely realist in its design, the gang rape of Christine is a confronting sequence simply because we have come to see the car as a sentient being with feelings. Albeit she is a cold blooded killer, prone to jealous fits, easily agitated and simply deadly, the fact that she is referred to as a "she" and known as a "she" in our collective mind's eye (and heart) as well as the film's human characters, make it difficult to separate machinery and feminine energy. This beautiful and sleek woman is isolated and left alone in the dark, only to have her body violated and raped. She is prodded and slashed, stabbed and crushed, and being silenced seems to close the scene as Moochie has his way with her car radio.

It is the final blow and final insult: the distressing element all too well known in rape culture where women (and men) are forced to stay quiet in the ugly face of sexual abuse.

WILLIAM OSTRANDER: I based Buddy on a guy in high school, right down to how he looked – that's where the side-burns came from and clothing and things like that. They were things I borrowed from people I knew growing up. The character of Buddy Repperton is someone you don't really go into it thinking whether you like him or don't like him, you just find that person and you do what you are asked to do with that character. I inhabited him. You let parts of yourself that are like that character come through, and you tell your truth. One thing that I felt was important was that he had to have some a sense of "cool". After I did my first scene with Steve Tash, I got called into the office by the producer, Robert Kobritz and John Carpenter. It was after my first-night filming, and they had seen dailies and then they had called me in to talk to me, and I went, "Oh crap, I'm gonna get fired! I must have sucked!" But Richard and John said "Can you make Buddy more mean? We don't want him to be too cool." I said, "Sure... yeah, of course, I can do that." But I felt that he had to have something. Where I grew up, the guys that I based this character on weren't the sharpest tools in the shed. Everyone's afraid of him. He was also a good athlete though, he wasn't just a stupid bully – he's actually a really good athlete. Part of the reason you are afraid of these guys is because they are big or they're strong, or they are athletically inclined and ahead of you; so in the scene when I smash Christine, one of my little moments of pride – nobody ever noticed it of course – was when I come in, I stand in front of the car and take my coat off, and I toss it over to the side, and it lands perfectly on a stand. It was my Fonzie moment! Also jumping up on the car had to look very cool. I wanted him to be more than just a piece of shit, he was more ath-letically inclined than some of the other kids because of his age in high school. If you look at hockey players, one of the things is that seventy percent of all professional players are more developed than their peers. The reason for that is because when you are developing, six months makes a difference in someone's development. The kids that were born after January 1st, which is the cut-off date for the New Year, and between January 1st and March 1st had an advantage over the rest of their classmates in age and in development. When you have that advantage and development, then you are the first person picked for the Varsity football team and the basketball team, and then you get noticed because you are stronger and more developed and so forth and then you get picked for the special team or for the travel team and whole thing. And then you get extra curfew, and it accelerates the whole thing. So people that are born and are a little older in their class tend to do better in athletics by the more potential and more practice that they have. To me, that's kind of what Buddy Repperton needed to have. He needed to have just a little bit more than some of the other guys, just for the fact that he was older than the others.

BILL PHILLIPS: The actual script had much more specific incidents in it, but John found that they were falling way behind schedule getting all of it shot, so he had to cut a lot.

RICHARD KOBRITZ: Bill Phillips did no more than two drafts of the script and we would OK sections and he would go on, he would go further on. He was never off course at all, he would do his thing and if he came back with a change that John wasn't happy with, he would take direction well. He was an excellent collaborator.

MALCOLM DANARE: When I shot that movie, I was twenty-two-years-old. I laugh at it now. You know the expression "if I knew then what I know now" there would have been so many things that I would have done differently. I would have asked John Carpenter. I would have asked the producer. When you are younger, and you want to please everybody around you, you do what you are told to do. With the "rape" scene, John basically said, "Look, I'm gonna roll about three or four different cameras. And I'm gonna roll these things for about ten minutes, and what you guys are gonna do is just annihilate the car." There are different weapons here to annihilate the car. And obviously, I was on my side of the car. Bill was on top of the car. Stuart and Steve were in the back, and what John said is,

"I'm gonna roll" I think it was three or four cameras. And basically, I was the only idiot, really, and it was my fault. I did not put gloves on at the beginning of the shooting of that scene. If you watch that scene closely, you'll see that I pick up the concussion hammer and I go to hit the window of Christine once or twice – the left side of the window on the driver's side window –and it finally breaks, but when it breaks, a tonne of glass went in between my hand and the handle of the hammer. And I could not stop the scene. I just knew that I couldn't stop the scene because Carpenter said, "Whatever happens, you just keep going!" And I was just beating the shit out of the car. So once that glass went in between my hand it was the most excruciating pain ever! I see over on a workbench a chisel. So I get the chisel, and I just start pounding into the top of the roof of the car. But when we finally said "cut" I was bleeding everywhere. There was blood all over me, all over my hands, glass went into my face. I mean, it was crazy. It was a pretty brutal night. It was so painful; there was really nothing that I could have done other than just kept the scene going. If you watch it closely, now that scene, you'll see that when I hit the window, the glass goes in between my hand. You'll see me drop that hammer and go, "Awww, shit".' It was a bummer, but you know, you have to keep it going! I don't know if it was difficult, because once the scene was shot where we smash the car to pieces, then you start to shoot close-ups and insert scenes. You actually start doing the inserts where I go into the car and I take that huge long knife, and I start ripping up the seats, and then I grab that same hammer or chisel, or whatever you want to call it, and I smash out the radio. So those were all done in sequence.

ALAN HOWARTH: Musically some of the best stuff was done during that period. That was when movies went from Hitchcock and the orchestral scoring to the rock scoring and the synthesising scoring. In a lot of ways, because one guy with synthesisers suddenly became cheap music; there were a lot of people that did a lot of bad stuff, too. But out of that boil-down, there are things that are continued to be recognised now. Much like people are now discovering Led Zeppelin, after they have gone through all the boy bands and all that stuff. Pink Floyd, King Crimson, Genesis, The Who, Yes.

Now musicians are discovering this and going, "this stuff is incredible!" I'll use Led Zeppelin and Cream. They all went to the original blues guys; Muddy Waters, Howlin' Wolf, who were doing this on a single guitar and a black blues performance, and they heard something there that was prophetic, and they put it into their creativity, and they did the next generation of that stuff. Like those couple of kids that do *Stranger Things* (2016-). Clearly, they are huge fans of the John Carpenter and Alan Howarth score. I'll say it sounds close enough to what we were doing, and the whole thing takes place in the '80s. Almost every scene is a homage to another scene in earlier classic horror movies. The camera angle or the setup or how that scene worked in that movie, he's utilising that tool in his movie. So it is a combination. If you didn't know all this stuff, you'd just watch it and think it is cool. If you're a big fan you have a different referential experience. It's good; I'm enjoying it. Recently I did an independent movie called *Hoax*; it's a Bigfoot movie. A bunch of kids go into the woods; they get killed, the TV crew try to find out what is going on. The TV crew say, "I think there is a Bigfoot, I'm going to go and prove it" and all this goes down. It literally came to me and said, 'I want you to use the analogue synthesisers that you used in the '80s. I want you to replicate what you did back then on *Halloween*. Well, why am I going to say no? I know how to do it, and it's fun! So we're providing a service. I'm not going to push back and say, "No, I need to do this, this, and this." In fact, every now and then I pull out some of my current, unbelievable sampled orchestra or amazing orchestral textures. "No, no, no. I don't want you to use any of that! Take that off. I want that simple thing that you did back then." In some ways holding back was difficult. It's like a guy walking in with a whole machine shop of tools. "No, no. I just want you to use that one drill over there. Make it with all of that." It was very restricting. Of course, I know how to do it, but I kept running away with the circus and getting reeled back in because he was very good as a director. He knew what he wanted, and I got it for him. I have had to do things that are not horror movies, and I don't have anything established there. One of my clients was doing all these nature films for documentary films. I did all this beautiful music! Completely different. When you first hear it, you wouldn't go, "Oh, that's Alan Howarth". But it is. I'm also involved with video games. Now I'm working with a company called Magic Leap which is creating mixed realities, which is sort of the third generation of virtual reality. This is very loopy stuff because the technology restricts you. You don't have a tape recorder where you put a thirty-minute thing on it. It's made in all little bits and bobs that are weaved together interactively based on what happens during the user's experience, whether it is a game or something else. So it's another whole technology that I have just recently learned on interactive music software, learning how it works. So I'm still a kid; I just keep learning!

WILLIAM OSTRANDER: As far as being a movie fan, I don't even think I saw six films before I was a teen! I grew up on a farm, and I just didn't seek out a lot of movie experiences, honestly, certainly nothing as specific as a genre films. I saw *Jaws* (1975) and *American Graffiti* (1973). But I didn't really have a lot of film experience. But I know that *Christine* resonates with a lot of people. Especially for people that are into cars. Probably one of the top five questions that I always get is, "What did it feel like to destroy that car?" Collectors today see a 1958 Plymouth Fury in pristine condition, and someone takes a sledgehammer to it and they are shocked! This was in 1983 so fifties cars weren't still all the rage yet. I think people that respond to that movie are people that are car people, the people that in junior high school saw high schoolers that saw high school characters and archetypes and were concerned about that. I just was part of that. I didn't really recognise that at the time. During the smashing up of Christine, I didn't get injured or anything like that. I didn't get scared. But the car was freshly waxed so it was very slippery! So I nearly slipped and fell. You can see it in the film. It was really fun. John said go crazy. Beat the crap out of it, and then they wanted me to continue to beat the crap out of it from the inside of the car! The only mistake that I made there was by actually hitting the battery! The production guys were stressed but thankfully they didn't get splashed with the acid from hitting the battery, but other than that, I didn't have any concerns for safety. According to Stephen King, the company only made five thousand of these cars – this Plymouth Fury model – which is why he liked it originally. If you notice the push button transmission, this was a really unusual looking car. It wasn't the fanciest car but it could go a hundred and thirty miles an hour. It was a fast fucking car! And the push button transmission was a quite quirky, unusual thing. So Stephen King told me he chose that car because it reminded him of a kid he'd seen in high school who was an oddball character.

MALCOLM DANARE: There is a scene where you see my character actually take a dump on the dashboard. You don't see that, but you actually see the character of Moochie, really taking a dump on the dashboard. There were a few little sequences cut out of the death scene that would have made it a little longer. But obviously, the Moochie death scene is about six-minutes long anyway. The only thing I think that was cut out was when we smash the car to pieces and maybe a few things from the football field, but that might be it, that I can remember.

"GET AWAY FROM HER!": Arnie discovers Christine in shambles

The day after Christine's "rape", Leigh Cabot waits for Arnie outside Darnell's garage. She paces, looking worried – after all, her night previously wasn't the most pleasant. Coming into frame is Arnie wearing his red jacket, akin to James Dean's in Nicholas Ray's vitally important teen melodrama *Rebel Without a Cause*. He tells her that he needs to get his wallet out of Christine and asks her to come with him. She agrees and the two slowly stroll towards the garage. Inside, Arnie happily discusses their immediate futures together – he suggests that they both start applying for the same colleges. This is now definitely the last time we see an iota of decency in Arnie and his optimism is guided by the beams of light that shine through like bright shafts of hope through the windows of the dreary garage. Arnie is hopeful that he and Leigh will stay together after high school is over and Leigh is surprised by his enthusiastic interest in them being at the same college.

Arnie envisions a life after high school which is something that none of the characters have before mentioned, and something that the teens in the previous youth-centric Stephen King adaptation, *Carrie* never did – in that film, high school was everybody's "world". However, silencing Arnie's enthusiastic outlook for the future is what catches his eye in the distance: the destroyed Christine.

He squeezes on Leigh's hand hurting her – his emotional pain and anguish carrying over to her in a physical gesture – and he walks over to his smashed up car with confusion, sorrow and quiet rage. Keith Gordon plays the tragedy beautifully here, tending to Christine's crushed rear view mirror, nursing it with care and devotion. He reflects the external damage he sees before him with his mannerisms and mood, his body crouched over and looking as though he is going to be sick, whilst at the same time, trying to come to terms with what he bears witness to: his hard work gone to waste and his best friend/pseudo-lover destroyed.

Leigh tries to offer some compassionate solace, however when she gets close he turns aggressive and lashes out at her, thrashing her and pushing her away. She touches his shoulder, wanting to help, but she is turned away by the angry Arnie who screams out "Don't touch me, shitter!" The term "shitter" has been used before in the film, with George LeBay referring to "shitters getting in the way of his brother and Christine", and the term would be used more profoundly later in the film where Arnie declares "death to the shitters of the world" with Dennis Guilder in the passenger seat, terrified of his own best friend. Leigh has now stepped down in regard here, and she too has become a "shitter" – someone who has stepped between a man and his Christine. Arnie follows this attack with "This is just what you wanted!" suggesting that Leigh is yet another anti-Christine person who inadvertently has contributed to her destruction.

KEITH GORDON: Christine is so specifically female and there's a whole sexual thing with the car always. At least in my head and certainly when I talked with John. There is always an undercurrent of sexuality that happens with the car. So when they are jumping on her and smashing her and all that there is something of a violation, of a rape feeling to it, and that was as intentional as anything else. I don't know if John wanted an audience to be literally thinking that or just feel it. But we did talk about everything with that car – there was a sexuality to it. It was part of the fun of it and also part of what gave it an energy. I mean right down to the last moment when Arnie dies, and he touches the little V in the front grill, that was absolutely meant to be a sexual moment. I've always felt that there was something that would be on a bunch of guys smashing up an old car, something more personal and a violation, and even within the sense of a movie with a sense of humour, I think that scene is disturbing and creepy. I mean, the way it is lit, the way the actors pull it off. It feels like something dirtier is going on than breaking some glass. So in the scene where I find her trashed, I played it out as a total violation.

John Carpenter stands back and watches Keith Gordon explode with rage at the sight of the destroyed Christine.

Arnie is about to lunge at Leigh after finding his beloved Christine smashed up.

"TAKE YOUR MITTS OFF ME, MOTHERFUCKER":
Arnie takes on his parents

The first time we ever see Jim Backus's character of the henpecked ineffectual father to the troubled James Dean in *Rebel Without a Cause*, we find him on his knees dressed in a frilly apron, tending to cutlery that has spilled upon the middle class carpeted floor. Dean's response is one of disgust and agitation as this is the man who is supposed to be the patriarch of the household, however, instead he is beaten down to a mess of a man, dwarfed by the stoic power of his wife. James Dean would later have an altercation with both of his parental figures at the staircase of the house, something that would become physical and harrowing to watch. Here in this scene in *Christine*, a tribute is about to unfold to director Nicholas Ray's classic teen melodrama from 1955.

Sitting at the dinner table is the solemn Regina Cunningham, her husband Michael and Arnie who looks as though he hasn't touched one ounce of food. Here, the disgruntled and angst-ridden teenager that has since made his/her prominent appearance in American cinema since the fifties is about to duke it out with parents who are losing their young to societal decay or in this case, the lure of a sentient Plymouth Fury who has just been trashed by local thugs.

This scene's most important factor is that one of the film's characters (outside of Arnie) seems to have undergone a transition, a shift in personality and energy. That is Regina. She is no longer the assertive and domineering woman that we have all come to know and hate, instead she is defeated and even shows emotion, an arc that is just as vitally important as Arnie's development from dweeb to slimy cretin. Regina opens the scene's dialogue box with "Arnie, I'm sorry", holding back tears, while Arnie dismisses her apology and calls her selfish in a sequence that mirrors films about alienated teenage boys, cold mothers and fumbling fathers such as Robert Redford's extraordinary *Ordinary People* (1980). In that Academy Award winning introspective melodrama, Mary Tyler Moore (in a role so vastly different to her warm and loveable careerist feminist icon from her ground breaking sitcom *The Mary Tyler Moore Show* (1970-1977)) plays the distant and unfeeling mother grieving the loss of one son while resenting the surviving son in Timothy Hutton, while Donald Sutherland as Hutton's father, desperately tries to salvage his relationship with his boy by trying to rise up against such suffocating personal oppression.

Here in *Christine*, Michael Cunningham finally takes action, shedding the metaphoric "apron" that once acted as a shackle to Jim Backus in *Rebel Without a Cause* and taking a lead from Donald Sutherland in *Ordinary People* by moving against the current (against the restraint of dissociative wives/mothers) and stands up to his son, determined to shake some sense into him. However, Arnie will not have any of this. He rejects the idea of his parents buying him a new car, he spews out vile dialogue ("Well fuck you"), he explains that one of the bullies "took a shit on the dashboard" (a reference to Moochie defecating on Christine's interior which would be ultimately cut) and he leaves the table "without being excused" – an incredible insult to the trappings of middle class "politeness". Following him into the hallway and honouring the aforementioned homage that director John Carpenter will pay tribute to *Rebel Without a Cause*, Michael confronts Arnie beneath the staircase and with Arnie in the same red jacket worn by James Dean in Nicholas Ray's classic the scene plays out like a darker and more malicious take on Dean arguing with his parents.

Ultimately however, Michael is still serving under the rule of Regina in that he demands Arnie "go and apologise to your mother" and that he and Regina would like to help in Arnie buying a new car – which is essentially the core thing that angers Arnie more than anything else. When Michael pushes Arnie into a wall, Arnie reacts violently and grabs his father's throat with a stern grip and a cold, dead stare. This is the final time we see both Regina and Michael, and the power play has completely switched – Arnie is the dominant force here, his parents are ineffective nobodies, swamped by the dimly lit recesses of quaint but oppressive suburbia. The image of Arnie holding Michael's neck with great rage is looked upon from a low angle, and the colors and framing most certainly reflect the unique visual stylings of John Carpenter. In fact, it is one of the most Carpenter-esque looking images in the entire film, and in many ways this is reflective of the next point the film will make – that violence is about to blossom and that the realm of the supernatural will be far more pronounced and active.

RICHARD KOBRITZ: I had always seen Christine Belford as someone who could play a lot older than what she actually was. I had seen her do a couple of great movies of the week and I thought that I'd love to work with her. She certainly could do it and there was no problem.

KEITH GORDON: There was a play I had done not long before *Christine* called *Album*, that involved the character going through a lot of transformation. The play took four young people and followed them from age 14 through to age 18, so they all changed a lot over the course of the play, but it wasn't like a Jekyll and Hyde thing, it was both my characters did go from a really nerdy 14-year-old to this kind of pretty kind of cool, edge of crazy, Bob Dylan fanatic; and was this young kind of rebel... a young suburban rebel. He wasn't as much of a rebel as you would have liked to think he was. I had done something very recently before this that involved a character changing as it went along, and there was something like my voice over the course of the play dropped an octave and a half, and that was something I also did in *Christine*. There was definitely a very different vocal register in the sort of "uncool" Arnie and the later "cooler" and later "crazy" Arnie. I definitely played with voice stuff, and I had also done that for this play called *Album*. It just seemed logical. But in one case, because of age and in this case because the character was so different, among one of the things that would change would be his voice. So I didn't spend a lot of time thinking "What did I do for *Album*?" It was different in terms of the tone; it was sort of a comedy, and certainly a drama and it let me stretch those acting muscles. With Arnie, it was sort of finding a lot of that stuff; it was finding what is his voice, what is his body language like, how did it change? A big thing for me was finding confidence. Originally, the first costumes we were trying on were very standard 1980s clothes. Even for the later Arnie and there was something missing in them. I was probably driving the poor costume designer crazy because I was not being very articulate about what it was that I thought there was something more that we needed. When we stumbled into the slightly 1950s James Dean jacket and those sorts of things, I had that same kind of red colour. Suddenly with that, the character started to make more sense to me. As actors, sometimes it's weird what informs you. It's like if I put those clothes on, I was like, "Oh, this feels right to me, and it's sort of feeding, and the idea of a fifties thing." The car was from the fifties and, you know Roberts Blossom's character had been in his prime in the fifties. So suddenly if the Arnie that's reborn to me was more of a '50s character, that to me just gave me something to jump off of as an actor that was just a little bit more specific and not just random crazy guy. That became very important to me, and it was just funny because it was something I honestly hadn't thought that much about; I hadn't made that connection of maybe Arnie is going back in time as he's going through this transformation. It was only trying on those clothes as we went through the process of shopping for things that I kind of got that idea. And that's the thing, for an actor, for anyone creative you never know where one thing will set a bell off that will then inform everything else. What is fun about it is a lot of the most important stuff you ever do is stuff you stumble into, not the stuff you plan out ahead of time. A lot of my favourite moments as a director, as an actor, as anything... writing, are not the ones I thought about forever, but the ones that caught me by surprise, and I think that's the fun of it!

ELISSA ROSE: The climax of Arnie's transformation occurs after Christine's body is violated by the gang of his college enemies. Hell hath no fury like this scorned woman. She exacts revenge worthy of a deadly femme fatale of Greek Mythology (the likes of Elektra or the biblical Salome), morphing Arnie into a stone cold killer. Devoid of empathy, his style in turn elevates to level 12 bad boy. His key wardrobe piece – the Garbadine "Ricky" jacket, has now become a luxe blood red velvet, resolutely recalling the red Ricky jacket worn by the character of Jim Stark played by James Dean in

Rebel Without a Cause. His complete disregard for authority and anything that is not his main lady Christine is crystallized in the scene where he is confronted by Detective Rudolph Junkins (Harry Dean Stanton), which sees Arnie costumed in a rock 'n' roll style leather vest, black satin shirt and quiffed hair.

John Carpenter walks Keith Gordon through the stairwell confrontation scene.

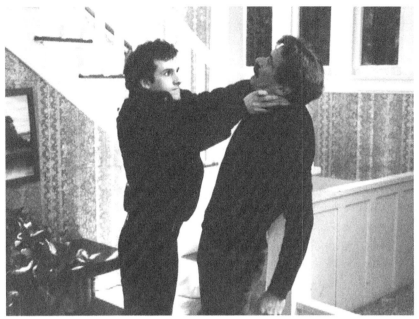

Arnie's (Keith Gordon) demonic turn as he strangles his father
Michael (Robert Darnell).

"SHOW ME": The resurrection

Opening on the damaged "heart" of Christine – her broken engine, smashed and dinted – the self-resurrection of this monster machine is a combination of "us against the world", demented romance, perverse sexuality and *objectophilia*. Also, from a technical perspective this is a major showcase of innovative camera trickery, where classic in-camera special effects will come into play and deliver a car reconstructing itself after being damaged. With cinematographer Donald M. Morgan's elegant take on painting a collage of fractions of Christine, carefully spliced together from the editing magic of Marion Rothman and overlooked and conceived by maverick director John Carpenter, we bear witness to this banged up victim of a good thrashing come back to "life" – her fenders folding back into place, her rear view mirror restoring itself, the towbar manoeuvring itself back into shape and her headlights beaming with glaring defiant fury. This entire scene would become the point of conversation for years to come from critics and fans alike who revelled in the intelligence in Carpenter's idea to show the resurrection of Christine. Essentially, early development of the film had the Plymouth Fury restore herself off-camera, but thankfully, Carpenter with producer Richard Kobritz agreeing, this event moment in the film – a testament to this car not only being malevolent but also resourceful and a genuine supernatural entity – would be a showstopper in the classic sense epitomising the notion of a magical car.

The sequence is a showcase of one of Christine's incredible powers, that she can rebuild herself and fix herself up, and although she is first introduced as a wreck – and one may question why didn't she just restore herself from the get-go – it makes absolute sense that she was sitting there at LeBay's junkyard, eagerly waiting for her next "suitor" who will be "good with his hands" and lovingly bring her to "life". In many regards, Arnie Cunningham's tender touch was a test conducted by Christine and as this scene opens with Arnie set to work on her, he is a genuinely dedicated devotee to this muscle car. It is interesting to note, that although Arnie has become creepy and unlikeable, here his sensitivity is still present in his conversation with Christine and elicits a sense of the old Arnie shining through. As he leans over his beloved totalled car he says "We'll make it better, huh? They can't hurt us anymore. Not if we work together. We'll show those shitters what we can do" and the sense of the lonely and desperate Arnie comes to the fore, but only for a tiny moment – when Christine shows him that she can rebuild herself, he becomes self-assured, determined and ready to take on the world.

The image of Arnie standing in front of Christine and turning around: "Okay... show me", is a theatrical win. The use of "Harlem Nocturne", a sexually charged musical piece originally orchestrated by Earle Hagen and Dick Rogers from 1939, is another inspired decision and it works beautifully as it seeps into the score forcing a wonderful transition from the John Carpenter/Alan Howarth interlude which makes way for what will ultimately be presented as a play on a striptease. The camera work – moving in on Arnie and holding him at polar opposites to his car – reads much like a shoot-out in a Western, but instead it is presented as a piece of sexual energy. Arnie's expression is that of a man watching a beautiful woman perform a slow striptease as the headlights beam towards him, highlighting the intense and provocative theatricality of it all.

Much like the seldom seen New Zealand film *Mr. Wrong* (1984) directed by Gaylene Preston where a young woman buys a car to claim independence from her parents and also earlier than that, the *Twilight Zone* episode "You Drive" (1964), *Christine* presents a car that is not only supernatural in nature, but also an extension to a young person's liberation and also an arm to violent destruction. Mr. Wrong has the heroine of the piece undergo a mental breakdown as she soon discovers the car she has purchased has a horrific past and has a malevolent presence lurking within, whereas in the *Twilight Zone* episode, the police officer who commits a hit and run, killing a paperboy, has his own car turn on him, as it develops a mind of its own. *Christine*, which sits in the middle of these two chronologically, utilizes both of these aspects – in a sense Arnie is liberated by owning the Plymouth Fury but it does lead to his downfall and he is eventually perplexed (but then consumed) by the violence she inflicts.

In the horror anthology film *Nightmares* (1983), one of the chapters primarily focuses on the mysteries of faith and uses a Satanic car as its antagonist that drives the story's principal back into the arms of the religion he has started to doubt. Lance Henriksen plays troubled priest MacLeod stationed at a remote parish in Mexico where he is haunted by the death of a young child who had been gunned down and left to bleed to death in the arms of his devastated parents. Upon finding the bloodied dead child, MacLeod insists they call an ambulance and that he perform a resuscitation, but instead the parents and his peers insists he give the last rites and pray over the limp body of this recently deceased youngster. When he delivers the sermon at the child's funeral, he treats it as a throwaway and is almost sickened by the role religion plays in the face of tragedy. Deciding that he has lost his faith, MacLeod leaves the church and sets out on a long drive back to the United States. He takes a tank of holy water with him, which he considers only to be regular tap water and essential for hot days on the road. Not long after setting upon the dusty track, MacLeod is stalked by a black Chevrolet C20 Fleetside that gets progressively aggressive in its attack on the disillusioned priest. In one inspired moment, there is a cut to the interior of this maniacal car and it is taken from the driver's seat where an inverted crucifix hangs over the rear view mirror.

This suggestion of the Chevrolet being driven by Satan himself is an indication that this short story entitled "The Benediction" will have a religiously fevered showdown as its fundamental core. With a brilliantly concocted cat-and-mouse set up that is thoroughly entertaining, this lonely road hijinks (heavily inspired by Steven Spielberg's *Duel* (1971) from a decade earlier) is a testament to director Joseph Sargent's smooth scrutiny and examination of the power of faith, which he manages to deliver with a sturdy devotion that is pure, simple and dedicated to full circle storytelling that heavily relies on a swift and reasonable resolution. As the Satanic Chevrolet torments MacLeod to the point of smashing into him, flipping his car over, speeding and darting around him in a frenzied and ter-

rifying fashion, the tension builds to the point of all arrows leading
to MacLeod's demise. However, because the short story (entitled
"chapters" in Sargent's film) takes you on an earlier journey of his
dismissal of Christian faith and a newfound disownment of religious doctrine, we are given an intelligent and plausible arc where
this fallen priest will literally throw his faith with great gusto at the
heart of evil itself and conquer malevolence and regain his love for
the cloth. Much like the haunted and faith-doubting Father Karras
(Jason Miller) in *The Exorcist* (1973) who regains his faith when
he is asked by Chris MacNeil (Ellen Burstyn) if her young daughter Regan (Linda Blair) will die during the lengthy exorcism in the
third act of that film, here MacLeod uses what is left of his belief
system and tosses it directly at the demonic vehicle. In what would
be a final moment of defence, the battered and bleeding MacLeod
throws the vat of "tap water" at the Satanic car and it is learned
that evidently, this is in fact holy water, because it vanquishes the
speeding and roaring Chevrolet. In some of the promotional material for *Christine*, the use of Satan and demonology was employed
– one has to look at the oft-used tagline "Body by Plymouth, soul by
Satan" – however, the Judeo-Christian element to Carpenter's film
(and Stephen King's novel) never make reference to the car being
an agent of the devil. Christine, by her very nature, is born evil – a
bad seed, "bad to the bone" as the opening song suggests – and this
has nothing to do with a bible dwelling entity or prince of darkness.
In this chapter "The Benediction" from Joseph Sargent's *Nightmares*,
the car is most definitely clearly defined as a Satanic force, and this is
all because of that one shot that depicts an inverted crucifix (which
is a fixture of demonic practice, black mass and witchcraft). Even
the score by Craig Safan evokes feelings of Satanic influence, something that would become almost clichéd and all derived from previous devil-themed chillers such as *The Omen* (1976); however, Safan's
more interesting moments in his score are found when the Chevrolet chases MacLeod down the freeway.

JOHN CARPENTER: We shot the scene where Christine puts
herself back together in reverse. So what we did was we sucked
in the car, so it was compressed and pushed into itself and then

when we got around to shooting it, we filmed the entire action in reverse, so it looked as though the car was pulling out, and pushing itself outward. The way I wanted to play it out was like a striptease, I wanted the car to be putting on some kind of performance for Arnie, and the way Keith Gordon plays it and with the look and style of the sequence, it all becomes a kind of erotic dance or a striptease from this car, if that makes sense. I wanted the music to also reflect this angle and I used "Harlem Nocturne" for it, so that added to that quality as well. I like that scene a lot, I'm pretty proud of that moment.

DONALD M. MORGAN: All that stuff in the car coming back and you'd see the fenders straighten out and the bumper, we did a lot of that after the movie. We did what we could. We built some fenders out of some sort of plastic, and it was supposed to pop back out and it just never looked right. So they had us come back, and we spent – I don't remember how many nights, but you know when the tractor runs over it and you see, I think you saw a shot of the radio busting out, and the front would crush in, and you'd see steam coming out from the radiator being popped. All that stuff was done after the movie. We went up to and shot it all with the camera outside Darnell's, so when they turn around it all comes back. What we went back for, we shot the sequence, and I think when they put it together they realised that they didn't really have enough of the set popping back. And that's when we went back and those were all insert shots. You know they weren't wide shots because they were just pieces of the car. Like we had a couple of fenders and a hood, and he would cut all the basing out, and we would just do inserts of stuff that they would cut in the movie. We were five weeks doing the masters when the tractor rolled over the car, and you saw that wide. He wanted to do more inserts of stuff popping. We had eighteen of the cars, in that we made an assembly line. At the end of a shot where it starts out, we did a crane shot from one of those old fans they used to have. I put smoke in there, and the studio had a special generator 'cause you know if you reboost clarity on a generator, sometimes you can blow it out and that's how they made those lightning strikes. I took that generator, and I had a lightning effect way in the background so that it would look like welding and so on. You could see this flashing of light. It actually was a lightning machine that they made special to make lightning. And I put that and smoke in the assembly line, and we shot the cars coming at us on that crane shot, and then in the wide shot, you'd see different guys welding and guys doing all this work and then in the background there's flashing. I found it made it look really deep. And all these cars coming out the back, and it was pretty exciting! And eighteen of those cars they bought and they used. When we were at Darnell's garage, they had a body shop in the back. As we'd tear cars up, they would take parts and just keep making other Christine's okay again. They had a full-time body shop the whole five weeks that we were in that building.

KEITH GORDON: I wasn't around much to see the model cars. Because of the tightness of time we shot all the special effects involving the full scale cars all at once and then in post production which I really wasn't around for is where John used the models. And just watching the models is just amazing, they come across as so flawless and perfect! We didn't want to rely too much on them, but they came off looking really great. All the wonderful camera tricks like reversing the film to show the fenders and what not bending back into shape when Christine resurrects herself. There are some wonderful moments in *Christine* that look like they're taken straight out of a Western — where the camera shoots from between the back of my legs with Christine in the distance, I mean that is right out of a face off in a Western. Just great stuff! What I do love about both of these great directors is that they were both open to input from their cast and crew. I teach a lot in film school and one of the main things that scares young filmmakers is not being able to control their film or their art; they are scared to just let go and let someone else make a decision or make even a suggestion that will benefit the final product. They feel threatened and there is no room to feel threatened when making art. And by the time of *Christine*, I think Carpenter knew this perfectly well, it was at that time in his career where he wanted an easy smooth ride and got it because he was amazing at his job, is ultimately amazingly talented and trusted his cast and his crew. He never had to prove that he was a great director. I love that scene! It was fun to shoot and really fun to watch! It was so sexy and completely sexualized. It was exactly like having your girlfriend do a striptease for you. And the music John used was "Harlem Nocturne" which was just perfect! I mean John has an amazing ear for music, he's a great composer but in the case of *Christine* he really gets to show off his love for other people's music and choose such perfect songs for the "voice" of the car. *Christine* was the most fun I've ever had as an actor! I got to play Jekyll and Hyde! *Christine* was a film that I just adored working on. I mean I would go to the set on days that I wasn't working and just look at the cars the crew were working on, the setting up of the dolly track, the lighting design, everything. It was a blast! And John Carpenter and the rest of the team just made the entire experience a hell of a lot of fun while delivering this amazingly smart and very sexy horror movie!

RICHARD KOBRITZ: In the original script, the rejuvenation of Christine was done off-screen and with sound effects and there would be a close up of Arnie's face and his face would begin to glow as you would hear the car reassemble – the cracking of chrome, the slashing of paint and so forth. But you weren't going to see any of that. In the rough cut – with all the music and everything – I said to John, "I think we got a problem". I thought it was too much of a cheat, I really thought we had to show the audience what's happening – we can't play on this kid's face no matter how good an actor he is. There was always this underlying thing where someone would say "How come you don't show the car fixing itself?" John agreed but he didn't know how it would work. But we gave the special effects guy, Roy Arbogast, three or four weeks. Roy had worked on *Jaws*, and that actual rejuvenation of the car wasn't shot until September, and the film had wrapped in July. It took him that long to do. When he showed us the dailies for it and John was impressed and said "Let's use it!" Roy reminded me years later that John said "Now we got a movie" after seeing that car resurrection. Everything was real – there were no miniatures, there was no plastic, everything was organically done. Today you would do it in a totally different way, and you would build the car from the grill up, but that wouldn't be real, here it was!

BILL PHILLIPS: The original special effects of the car putting itself together on-screen was not in the script. John and Richard felt the film was lacking something at this crucial moment, so they invented a way to do this (before Computer Generated Imagery was invented). It involved using a camera positioned upside-down with the film run backwards while special effects crew pulls molded car parts out of their natural shape into a crumpled state. Then with the film run forward and the sound effects of "uncrumpling metal" to help sell it. It works beautifully, and I think even if they remake the film with the aid of computers, there's something special about the way this was done.

KEITH GORDON: Well the "Show me" scene was a flat-out sexual seduction. That was what John and I had talked about with that. That was if you could have sex with a car that was what was going on in that scene. That was really fun! I mean, playing with that was just great... and it was funny. That's part of what I love about the movie; the movie just has this sense of humour about itself that I think is really crucial, and it has a sense of humour without being goofy. I think of *Misery* and *Christine* and they are kind of funny, but they're not like "haha" funny, and they're not like "nudge, nudge, wink, wink" funny, you can still get completely emotionally involved but the film acknowledges the absurdity in the situation, and I think it's a really tricky thing to do. For a filmmaker it probably sounds a lot easier than it is to pull off because the problem is if it feels like it is nudging you and winking you, it kind of kills your belief in the story. Then you can't get emotionally involved if it takes itself too seriously. There is something I remember John talking about during rehearsal was trying to find this tone and not wanting it to be too serious because he said, "At a certain point, it's a movie about a killer car, and I feel like if we be completely serious about ourselves then the audience will laugh at us!" Whereas if we can keep a sense of humour about it, the audience will laugh with us! I think he was very aware of that and conscious of that in the way he did things. It never becomes a joke, it has a sense of humour or acknowledges its own absurdities without ever becoming jokey. I think jokiness would kill what you're talking about. I do think the film is lovely though because it has real emotion and you do feel really sad. It is a tragedy, but it also has a sense of playfulness, and I think if it lacked either one it wouldn't work. If it lacked the tragedy, it would feel like a one-joke thing, and you'd go "Oh, killer car. Got it. Fine," but if it lacked the humour, you might get a little "Oh my God. It's like a killer car. Stop." I feel like by having that balance it really allows it to flourish.

ROY ARBOGAST: We had hydraulics and bendable cylinders attached to the car. I remember Bill Phillips, John and Richard came out one day and we did our very own "Show me" scene! We worked out the buttons and levers that would crumble the parts of the car and it worked out nicely. The studio heads would see this and they were happy with how this was achieved and it lead to the film being green lit. The final "Show me" scene was all shot in reverse. We had enough cars by that time through inserts – all shot in my work station.

ALAN HOWARTH: John came with themes; he's the theme guy. In fact, in a lot of ways being a musician. If you would look at the musicality of John's material, it's super simple. You'd almost think, "Hey, that's too simple to really work!" In *Christine*, you have low rumbling sounds, and it created tension; it works in the cue, and very interesting. There was an article in Rolling Stone recently, which was done not by our peer group but by the younger guys – the millennials. The thirty-five greatest film scores of all time. Number 1 was *Halloween*. Number 2 was *Halloween III*, and Number 14 was *Christine*. Three out of thirty-five of the greatest film scores of all time by this group was judged to be works that we had done together. It's John's movie; it's his edit. He's got the first pass on this stuff, so he elected that a particular cue would span several scenes, and it was painted and created. It was his creative choice to link them together, and I think it was for dramatic reasons to see Arnie's conflict and him realising that this car is more important to him than anything now that he is possessed by the car. This is where the car now starts to take him over, and he goes in, and he sees that it is destroyed, and then the whole amazing photography of Christine popping out her fenders and becoming Christine from the wreckage. It's a great moment. I considered that John was the pilot and I was the co-pilot. So we went where he wanted to go. It was his movie. It's different when you are a composer, and you're creating a score for a director and a director comes by every now and then and sees how the score is going and gives you input. It's like having the director in the chair. I was in artistic and technical support, but the choices of where things go are his. One of John's philosophies is just let the actors act. So he feels that the music only comes when the acting has come off of the dialogue into some transition or some underscoring or something to help tell the story of what they're thinking or what they are anticipating or what is going on.

Arnie Cunningham (Keith Gordon) mournfully looks over the totalled Christine, still unaware of her supernatural ability to restore herself.

John Carpenter oversees the famous "Show Me" sequence, while Keith Gordon listens and takes it all in.

"LITTLE BITTY PRETTY ONE":
Moochie is killed by Christine

Stephen King's sole directorial effort – loosely based on his short story "Trucks" from his anthology book "Night Shift" from 1978 – would be *Maximum Overdrive* (1986). A sci-fi film dealing with the supernatural after effects of the tail-end influence left behind by a comet, the film would feature inanimate machines against people. Trucks and other vehicles would be effected and cause chaos on the streets and this connective theme links this darkly humorous AC/DC scored King creation to the far more sexually charged and straight in tone *Christine*. In this sequence where Christine will make her first kill since the opening prologue, the opening shot somehow foreshadows events to unravel in *Maximum Overdrive*, where a large Mack Truck pulls over on a dimly lit street stretching out beneath a heavy overpass. Moochie, the heavy set bully, jumps out of the truck and it clearly suggests that this angst-ridden youngster doesn't drive or own a car and that he has a sturdy streak of recklessness that drives him to hitchhike. Moochie, much like the other teens in the film, live by their wits and on their own terms, and within that narrative construct, they are also susceptible to landing on the cold streets of isolation and dead-ends. This is indicative in this stalk 'n' smash sequence where Moochie is alienated, left alone and hunted down by the vengeful Christine.

The framing of the sequence is superbly handled by John Carpenter: he sets up each image early on to present a threatening Christine in full view from afar, quietly waiting and gracefully stalking the teen thug. Along with masterful editing from Marion Rothman, the way Christine cruises the streets that are dwarfed by the overpass and bend in varied directions is akin to the presentation of a classicist movie monster such as the Wolf Man creeping up on an unsuspected Evelyn Ankers. How Christine is introduced in this sequence is vitally important to the mystique of the horror – she is face front, headlights shining, gleaming in the moonlight; a monstrous entity glazing at its victim with a dead stare. We hear her singing out to Moochie and the song choice is a sarcastic mocking. Popularized by rock 'n' roll and R&B vocalist Thurston Harris, "Little Bitty Pretty One" is the number ringing out from the ominous Christine, and it is a play on the role of the taunt – this Plymouth Fury is somehow making fun of Moochie's appearance. Moochie's response is beset in deep fear and naturally he suspects Arnie Cunningham at the wheel, of course unaware that this sentient machine is driving on her own: possessed by rage and dedicated to honouring her current ward. She is also furious at the rape she has endured, and chooses Moochie as her first victim who seems the most disposable and also the easiest target. Moochie calls out "You ain't mad are ya?" in response to recalling the "gang rape" of Christine, and this sets off her headlights to beam kicking off the Carpenter/Alan Howarth score. It pulsates and drives the kinetic energy of the sequence as we follow Moochie running through the abandoned streets and into the loading docks.

Christine smashes through cyclone fences and chases Moochie who runs for his life. She is presented as a relentless leviathan and vengeful witch, and the sequence ends with Moochie being cornered and crushed to death. There was some petty criticism in the staging of the death of Moochie in that there was talk of why he wasn't able to jump on top of Christine's bonnet and leap over – however, this essentially can be countered by the fact that Christine could easily have backed up, stalked him and killed him in another area of space and in a variant of crushing him or running him down. A far more interesting criticism made about the film (as an overall assessment rather than just about this scene in question) was that there was a decidedly profound lack of gore in the death sequences. The novel itself is rather heavy with lengthy descriptions of legs being shredded by Christine, bodies being run down and crushed and busted up, however here in Carpenter's film, the subtlety in the on-screen violence is the choice of how to go about things during an era of visceral extreme bloodshed on screen.

JOHN CARPENTER: I don't know why I didn't want to make the film bloody or excessively gory, because the book as I recall has moments of really detailed gore. I think we had an R rating, as I recall, but it may have been something to do with *The Thing*.

BILL PHILLIPS: As much as I admire King's psychological descriptions of writing gory scenes, I feel that the screen demands these events to be visually interesting. When you're reading a book, your mind gets to supply images suggested by the text, but when you're watching a film, an incident is only as interesting as it is made on the screen. One of my few original contributions to the script was the notion of Moochie running into a forklift-loading bay... one that was too narrow to permit Christine to come in after him. Moochie (and the viewer) had no reason to believe the car wanted to crush him so badly that it was willing (and able) to gun its engine and strip its fenders to allow it to move into that narrow space. I love that image. Of course, whenever I see Malcolm Denare (who played Moochie), he always complains that there isn't a day that goes by that some fan doesn't recognize him and ask why he didn't just jump up on the hood. I told him to say "because that wasn't in the script!" But seriously (if you can be serious in discussing a killer car movie), some people suggest that he would be in too much shock to be able to think straight enough to avoid getting killed. Oh, well... it's a movie. I'm glad we didn't have to watch his guts get spread all over the screen... one thing I like about John's direction is that he's not a gore-fanatic. That's a good thing!

RICHARD KOBRITZ: As far as the slasher and gore boom went during the film's release, I really did believe that we had better characters and a better director and that somehow we would survive going up against such a fashionable trend. How right I was or how wrong I was, history can tell. But I knew that we couldn't have the car kill constantly. The horror film's primary objective is to scare people and you can do that with great performances, you can do that with lousy performances, you can do that in a slasher film way, you could do it in a *Blair Witch Project* (1999) style, and I think that's the real goal. *Christine* tried and achieve it through acting and character and that great set piece where the car fixes herself and rejuvenates herself which – at the time – was an unheard of special effect. We didn't want to play the normal game in my opinion.

MALCOLM DANARE: John Carpenter said, "You wanna be in a t-shirt the whole time?" I said, "Nah." Because Bill is going to be wearing a t-shirt and a leather jacket. I don't think they were called 'Hoodies' yet. I think they were just called "sweatshirts with hoods". I thought to myself "I wanna wear a sweatshirt with a hood". But because it was the eighties, I thought it would be really cool to wear like a bright blue one or some type of really colourful one. I was wrong. Like in '83, that's when all the eighties silliness came out. Then they put me in the grey hoodie. I didn't care about that, but I always knew that I wanted the hoodie. It's totally urban, and I think when you really look back on it, I was one of the first people to wear a hoodie in a movie.

MALCOLM DANARE: One of the first public screenings I went to, there was this African-American girl sitting in front of me, and she goes, "Kill that motherfucking, fat motherfucker!" Because everyone wants chubby Moochie to die in it. The screening was really interesting. I remember sitting next to Michael Douglas at the screening. And afterwards, he looked at me and said, "That was a pretty great death scene! A lot of people don't get death scenes like that, that last that long." But it was a stunning death scene, and it was long. But it was really interesting going to the actual premiere of the movie. Because people loved it. I remember some critic saying that it was one of the best, young high school movies he had ever seen! The reason why *Christine* is still so popular is because of the car. It really is only one of the few films of that time that hasn't been remade yet! Horror people really want to see that film remade. I think it is about the car. I really do. When I go to these [*Christine* conventions, people are just passionate! The one question that I get all the time, and it's funny because I always yell at Bill Phillips now – the one question that I get all the time, people are always asking me this. "Well, I don't understand why Moochie just didn't jump on the hood of the car?" to get away while he is in the loading dock. The reason he didn't jump on the hood is because it isn't written that way! It's a movie! There was one convention I did a couple of years ago, and I remember this guy standing in line, and he was just staring me down. And I was just feeling very uneasy by this guy. He kept getting closer and closer and finally when he got to me – and you have the handler next to you – and I said, "Hey man, how are you doing?" and he just kind of looks at me and he goes, "Guys in my school picked on me and they were just like you." And I thought to myself, I am dead! This guy is going to pull out a gun and kill me. I really think the Buddy Repperton character and the Moochie character really go deep into some people. Because they're bullies and it bothers some people.

JOHN CARPENTER: Moochie's death was very fun to do. It was an elaborate sequence where we go through the streets and then the car entraps him and gets in that alleyway and rams towards him. When it squishes him, we made sure we had the car locked in and made sure that it wouldn't move so it wouldn't hurt him! I loved doing that scene, I was really happy with how it turned out. I think it looks great.

MALCOLM DANARE: There were a number of cars used for my death scene. There was the one that smashed through the fence. Then there was the one that was smashing up through the side. I was in the presence of three cars in those three days of shooting. I said to Terry Leonard the stunt coordinator – as the car is chasing me down from the alleyway – "I can probably run nine or however many miles an hour. What happens if I fall? You're going to go over me. You're going to run over me!" And he goes, "I promise you, Malcolm, I am driving the car as fast as you run. So it is going to look as though I am going fast but I promise that if you do fall, I won't go over you." I said, "Alright. I trust you, Terry. I trust you." If you were being chased by a car it is still pretty damn scary! I remember when we first started the scene. I said to Carpenter, "Hey, you know what would be a little cool moment, John?" And John was already so far ahead of me, I said, "What would happen if I went out in the middle of the street and I said, 'You're not mad, are you?' I don't remember if that was a Bill Phillips line or if it was my line. I go, "but what would be real cool is if the headlights came on!" He goes, "Malcolm, shut the fuck up! I already know how to shoot this film." I was trying to tell John Carpenter what to do! If you watch the death scene, Moochie will run out of the alleyway and the sequence right before he goes to jump over the fence, the sequence probably took thirty takes. I would say maybe more to actually hit the mark John Carpenter wanted; I absolutely could not hit the mark. And we did it over and over and over. We tried everything for me to hit this mark. The reason I think he wanted me to hit the mark so perfectly, is because when I am standing there, you see the car headlights above me. I said, "You know what, John? Let me fucking look down at the ground. Let me just look down at the ground instead of me trying to stop at the take." So you actually see me look down at the ground, and I stop. That's where I needed to stop. You'll have to have seen the sequence to understand what I am talking about. It's pretty interesting.

DONALD M. MORGAN: We would get permits that John would OK. And he found that great location; that was a real location. We were able to work in there with no cars that we didn't want in there, so I don't know if it was a new location, or they were still building it or what it was, but I still remember that there was nothing around that we didn't want around. We didn't have to wait for cars to come through and then do some more work. It was pretty much ours, so we worked all night on that stuff. You know John always insisted that we shoot anamorphic wide lens and the only thing that John absolutely would not allow is a zoom. He did not like a zoom lens; he just didn't like the look of. He thought that television had been done to death where they zoom in on someone's face. He wanted the camera to move in on people. And I remember trying to talk to him into letting me make just a little adjustment as we get over there that we'll bury it. "No. I don't want a zoom lens!" The only time we use zoom lenses was the zoom in those days; the Anamorphic zoom would allow you to get closer than the prime lenses. So a lot of times on close-ups I would use the zoom without making it move, and he'd let me do that if I didn't use it as a zoom lens, I'd just use it as a fixed lens. He did not like a zoom. So a lot of stuff that we did when we got to any kind of real close-up... tight, tight close-up, was letting me put a Diopter and getting closer I could use the zoom in that way which we did a few times. John liked the camera to do the moving – not the lens! That was a stickler, and we had to abide by it.

ALAN HOWARTH: All the songs were established prior to the story. So the songs were in place. We knew what was going to be 'Bad to the Bone' and 'Harlem Nocturne' and all the other things that were going to be put in there. In fact, when we did the soundtrack album, the first one, the underscore that John and I do pretty much absent from the album was all the songs. We only had two numbers on there; it was the two action cues for when she chases Moochie and when she chases the other bad guy at the gas station, which were pretty much the same music cue, but done in different versions. At the same time I strung together what is now the John Carpenter/Alan Howarth score to *Christine*, as an after-thought and kind of put it away, and a couple years later Varèse Sarabande came back to us and said, "Do you still have the music that you and John did? We'd like to do that as its own separate thing" and I said, "Actually, I do, and I'll even do a nice mix" and I did my introduction on the tape and that was it. So I sensed that there was something there: the marketing, the momentum and all the '50s and '60s songs were what spoke for the car.

ADAM DEVLIN: Following Christine being vandalised and her showing Arnie that she can magically repair herself we see one of the thugs that vandalised her getting dropped off in the night. As he walks home we hear Thurston Harris's 1957 hit "Little Biddy Pretty One". The youth is in the boondocks, under a motorway. He looks around to see where the music is coming from and he spots Chris-tine. Christine starts up and intrigued – it was only last night that he and his friends almost destroyed her after all – he slowly starts walk-ing toward her. Christine slowly starts driving through the pillars holding up the motorway overhead. We can't see who, if anyone, is driving her. Christine is using this track to tell her attacker that she is indestructible and despite him almost destroying her the previous night, she is indeed still a "little biddy pretty one". It's a boppy, toe-tapping number, all innocence and virtue and perfectly lulls one into a sense of ease about her somehow, miraculously, being "as new" again. It's repeated opening line hum "Mmm-mmm-mmm-mmm-mmm-mmm-mmm-mm" is infectious and so light and bubbly; it perfectly foil for what is about to happen.

MALCOLM DANARE: The death scene of Moochie was a pretty intense part of the film because it was such a long death scene. That scene took about three days to shoot. It was a long scene. There are so many memorable moments in it, but obviously, the most memorable moment was that scene because John Carpenter, Bill Ostrander, me and Steven Tash did a convention a couple of years ago and it was the first time that we had all been together, and it was funny because I had mentioned this moment. And the moment that had scared me and terrified me the most wasn't being chased down in the alley by the car because I really trusted Terry Leonard – it was when the car gets Moochie in the loading dock and the character can't go anywhere, the way they shot that was on the other side of the wall – the wall that was behind me that I was up against was a bulldozer. And it had a very heavy duty wire going through a little hole in between my legs that was connected to the the actual chassis of the car. So when that car is being pulled though, it's being pulled through by a bulldozer on the other side with this thick wire going through my legs going into the chassis of the car. So the craziest thing about that was if that wire had of snapped from the car it would have killed me instantly. Instantaneously it would have cut me in half – there's no doubt about it! Basically, there was another machine pulling the car towards me. So it was absolutely terrifying. I can't stand the way on Wikipedia where they say, oh the fenders were plastic or rubber or whatever. Trust me, and it is coming from me, and you can ask John, that car that was being pulled through that loading dock was real and the fenders were real and they weren't rubber and they weren't plastic. The noise that car was making as it was being crunched through was horrifying! It was really one of the most terrifying moments of my life! I will always remember it. And that is why I said some of the things that I did in that film. What I know now, what I didn't know then, I wouldn't have done that type of stunt. The only thing that actually prevented that car from cutting me – not cutting me in half – actually smashing me up against the wall was that they had this sort of metal, those things you see on police cars that come out the front. about five feet. They're like metal fenders – that kind of was on the bottom. It never would have gotten to me, the car. It never would have smashed me against the wall. It would have stopped. What was terrifying was the wire that was between my legs. You know, literally, it was terrifying! I even thought, "Man, I am twenty-years-old, if this thing breaks or rips or pulled – I am a dead man!"

ROY ARBOGAST: We had a big water truck that had a main cable run through it through to the set with an actual big building construction attached and we put on some flexible fenders and wedged that car into him! We had to be very careful not to get him crushed, so we had this cable that we would reel in a little bit at a time so it would gradually move in on the boy.

The long process of rigging Christine to a truck.

Christine sets out to kill Moochie.

Moochie (Malcolm Danare) is chased by the vengeful Christine.

Christine rams towards Moochie.

"DID YOU HEAR ABOUT WHAT HAPPENED TO MOOCHIE?": Arnie visits Dennis in hospital again

Using the title cards once again to give a place of time and comment on the progressive decline in Arnie Cunningham's mental and emotional state, as well as his descent into madness, we learn that it is Thanksgiving, and as the camera pans across the broken leg of Dennis Guilder, who remains in hospital, we see the Thanksgiving football game clearly in view on the television set. Dennis is asleep, unaware of the horrors that have claimed Moochie, and he is woken by the eerie presence of Arnie, who has become linked to Christine in more ways than one. Here it is the way he appears out of nowhere just like his car appeared on the dead streets watching Moochie.

During the scene, Dennis still refers to Arnie as "asshole" and there is a sense of playfulness that is stunted, because Arnie is completely serious and, much like his car with her blacked out windshield, appears kind of dead inside. His transition is apparent in his mood, a creepy sense of authority over Dennis and his commanding presence with self-assurance firmly in place. In the novel and in a deleted scene, the role of Arnie's signature on Dennis's cast is an indication of his gradual change, his hand writing would change over the course of time and over the course of various signing of the plaster. This scene establishes the thorough change in Arnie when he is in contact with Dennis – the power dynamic reversed – however, follow up scenes where the film introduces a police intervention, Arnie resorts back to a boy "fumbling in the dark". Here, however, by the bedside of his injured friend, Arnie holds the court and remains threatening and this is highlighted and even promised by stating that Buddy Repperton won't be trashing Christine again, before leaving the hospital room with a cool "Stay loose" – a sinister take on fifties slang.

KEITH GORDON: It was really just the most fun acting job I ever had on film. I loved going to work every day. The part was great; the people were great; I loved the actors I was working with; I love John. It was just fun! I went out and hung out all day on the set on the days that I wasn't working and part of that was my film geek side that wanted to see how they did things, but it was a really fun set. It was just a great job! It was one of those jobs that I was really sad when it was over because I was having such a good time. And certainly, maybe one or two experiences working in the theatre were as good. And that's the biggest thing I remember. On a personal level, I just remember laughing. I remember, there's a still photograph that I wish I had of John – I was doing off-camera and John was making faces at me and being like we were twelve-years-old. And for me to be with John Carpenter, this hero of mine, and being that goofy and fun was like can I just do this for the rest of my life! There's a still photograph where he's pretending to scream at me, and I'm trying not to laugh, and to me it captures the movie! And it was really the experience. I love the film. I am proud of the film but the thing I think of is just how great it was to go to work every day! And I still remember it much more than most jobs that I had, what it was like on the set each day. I remember shooting the make-out scene and then shooting the scene in the rain and the scenes with John Stockwell where I was visiting him in the hospital. I remember what it all felt like more than most jobs because it was so much fun! And so it stuck with me. Most things kind of blur together over these many, many years, but that one never did.

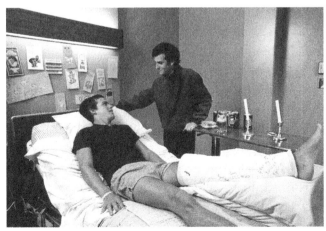

Arnie pays a visit to Dennis in hospital. His change in personality worries the injured football jock.

"I JUST WANNA ASK YOU ABOUT YOUR CAR":
Enter Detective Junkins

The entrance of Detective Rudolph Junkins (Harry Dean Stanton) is a much scrutinized additive in horror films of the seventies and eighties where police intervention is a necessary subplot inserted into what usually consists of supernatural activity. Much like Lieutenant Kinderman (Lee J. Cobb) coming into play in *The Exorcist*, the entrance of Junkins is a late ingredient that serves a core purpose: that reality is still most definitely steady in place, and that even though this story is about a possessed car that has a mind of its own, the world of logic is still secure. But for fans and critics alike, a lot of these police procedural inserts area slight nuisance as an audience is given a serving of the characters catching up with plot and catching up on what the audience itself already knows. However, screenwriter Bill Phillips takes Stephen King's source material involving Detective Junkins and delivers it with style, swiftness and calculated dramatic allure. Phillips gives King's hard boiled flatfoot a classic design, as if he has emerged from a forties sensibility, which makes the character an interesting and captivating late addition. Junkins sees Arnie Cunningham as a suspect in the death of Moochie, and as this scene unfolds, he has already started his detective work – he has already spoken to the local police, Arnie's parents Regina and Michael as well as Leigh Cabot, and when he approaches Arnie, his analytical mind is already clearly focused and informed. However, by the end of the film (he shares the final scene along with Dennis Guilder and Leigh) he is left speechless, finally forced to comprehend the element of the supernatural that has now surfaced in what would normally be a standard police procedural involving a troubled young man hell-bent on getting vengeance on the thugs that "hurt his girl". But here, in the first introduction to the character he is much like Kinderman, in that his investigation is clear and direct – a disturbed youngster (be they the demonically possessed Regan MacNeil or the newfound creepy Arnie) is attached to a murder (the death of movie director Burke Dennings (Jack MacGowran) and the death of local slacker Moochie).

Producer Richard Kobritz and John Carpenter toyed around with the notion of creating a spin off series for the character of Rudolph Junkins, who, much like his television counterparts Columbo (Peter Falk) or even more so directly related Kolchak the Night Stalker (Darrin McGavin) would solve various crimes, some with a supernatural element and others without.

Harry Dean Stanton walks through the role with great ease and smooth coolness. His career during this period would lend itself to giving in to incredibly moving and mannered performances in films such as *Repo Man* and *Paris, Texas* (both from 1984). Here he handles the questioning, investigation and treating Arnie as a suspect with a stoic higher learning – he is a detective who has "seen it all" and someone who has no interest in wasting his time. With Christine as the point of conversation, the film firmly stays invested in her as the focal point and central figure, and instead of this sequence playing out like a standard question and answer back and forth, it is a nice reminder that Arnie is still running up against an adult authority – and here, the most formidable: the police officials.

The dialogue also comments on the course of action and the deflective nature of Junkins's questions, he remarks "I really like this shade of red", and here the conversation shifts from a genuine admiration of Christine's beauty to her driver being a suspect in the death of Moochie. On top of this transition is the musical interlude that creeps in; John Carpenter and Alan Howarth's electronic hum rings in, establishing newly developed enemies being a detective and a complicated teenager with an unhealthy obsession. Junkins continues: "Usually when someone trashes a car, we get photographs" and the reality of a police procedural fusing with the supernatural elements bring the violence home and even unsettles Arnie who is slowly understanding the true power in his Plymouth.

The scene ends with talk of Moochie's body being cut in half and the grotesque description is a reminder that Stephen King's source novel was in fact very brutal in nature and graphic in the description of the carnage Christine would inflict. Junkins explains that "They had to scrape his legs up with a shovel" to which Arnie coldly replies "Isn't that what you're supposed to do with shit? Scrape it up with a shovel?" – the film's slight preoccupation with faecal matter and its celebratory nature of the profane is turned into something sinister and dark here, where human life is actually in conversation and compared to "shit". *Christine* is a film that truly has a deep rooted misanthropy inbuilt into its very fabric, and this is something that John Carpenter handles with distinguished care; the film paints an image of the outsider as distressed victim of his own world, and someone who cannot break out of permanent ruts. These ruts are also self-made, and self-governed, and in true misanthropic form, Arnie dismisses human emotive connection by turning off his heart.

RICHARD KOBRITZ: Harry Dean Stanton had that wonderful strange face, and he was so good at playing Detective Junkins that John Carpenter and I entertained the idea of doing a spin-off show. We said to each other "What if we did a TV series called "Junkins" and have this shaggy cop going around solving supernatural-themed crimes and sometimes just straight criminal activity!" This was the era of *Columbo* and so it would have been pretty interesting to see what could have resulted. But it is so hard to translate from one genre to another and to jump from features to television – I mean, I remember after we did *Salem's Lot*, NBC or one of the other networks wanted a five script commitment for a *Salem's Lot* TV series and it would be supernatural activities happening in various small towns. But the scripts were terrible, and we of course never made them. I mean these scripts were forced and awful – there was one where someone had written an evil car radio story. Originally, it was conceived that the *Salem's Lot* spin-off would deal with vampires, that was the original intention, but I don't even remember Barlow ever being a part of it. I know that I read the scripts and made some changes but I knew from day one that the writers were having problems with it and it was just not very good.

KEITH GORDON: Bill Phillips did a great job! To take what was a four-hundred-page novel and condense it into a two-hour movie and stay true to the essence of it, and yet not just be a slave to it. You can get into trouble with adaptations, when people feel like oh, it's Stephen King, we can't change anything! Bill did a really admirable job of making the movie its own thing and still keep the spirit of the book. It was well written.

BILL PHILLIPS: I remember being so impressed and pleased that Harry Dean Stanton was going to play him. At the pre-production party, I think he was putting me on when he asked me if the script was based on a book or something. It was the number one best-seller in the world at that moment. I never got to know him well enough to know if he was kidding or not. I choose to believe he was kidding. I always hate it when stories try to invent ways to keep the police out of the tale… probably because their presence could complicate the story considerably. But King handled that well here, and I just did my part.

KEITH GORDON: With Harry Dean Stanton, first of all, it was great because we did a lot which I enjoyed as an actor. Harry Dean always wanted to keep trying more and more and different things, and I love that because coming out of stage work, I love doing a billion takes because it makes you feel like, "oh, let's just keep trying different stuff!" So there were versions of those scenes with Harry which were cooler and tougher and there were versions that were probably even more nervous than what John used. Probably in the editing room, John created a bit of a mix too of different tonalities that we did in different takes, and Harry did that. In some takes, he would come at me much more hard, and some takes he would much more lean back, like let this kid trip on his own two feet. Other times he would be more intimidating, and so we had a lot of fun, as actors doing this dance together, and then John in the editing room took different colourations and also help create those performances in a way from the different raw material that we gave him. We also talked. The one thing that John did say was he wanted the first scene at the car from Arnie to keep his cool pretty well, and then the second scene when Christine has been destroyed, that the kid inside of him almost wants to confess. There's suddenly different tonalities from each other because one it is still about standing up to him and trying to figure out how to get him to back off, and the other, there is a real part of him that wants to stop the whole thing and wants to get free of Christine. So that is something that John had put in my ear and each of those scenes has a different feel to it because of that.

MALCOLM DANARE: Harry Dean Stanton's character says, "They had to shovel him up". John Carpenter really made you think about what Moochie looked like, especially when he was shovelled up when he was cut in two. If there were blood, it would have been fine, if there was no blood I'm with it. And there was no blood; there was really never any blood, other than at the end.

ALAN HOWARTH: I had the studio – it was all my gear. John brought his movie over on a videotape. He would sit at the black and white keys and push them down, and do the first pass on the score because it is his movie; he knows what he wants. But then the engineering: if we needed this or that or how about that, and certainly all the sequencing, and the drum machine. I don't remem-ber using a drum machine at all – in sequencing, that was all my side of the equation to keep everything going and make sure the red light was on and recording and run those machines which were all my gear. So he had virtually no interest in it other than to make it cool. A couple of times I tried and other times when I got a little more dense with the sequence against computer that I tried to explain what I wanted. He said, "I don't even want to know. That is your job." When I was in high school, I remember writing a paper that was a themed paper on music. This was the Stockhausen stuff that for a lot of people was noise, and for me, it was still music. So sound design is music still to me. I don't think of it separately. It's the same instruments; it's the application whether you're going to paint sound effects or sound sculpting or making musical rhythms and phrases. It's all the same. I'm visually driven. .

As Detective Rudolph Junkins, Harry Dean Stanton would love the fact that he got to play a "good guy" for once as he questions Arnie (Keith Gordon) after the death of Moochie.

"ARNIE, I CARE ABOUT YOU": Arnie calls Leigh

This would mark the final moment of seeing a glimmer of decency in Arnie which is completely thrown out the window as soon as Leigh gives him the answer he doesn't want to hear. Waking her from sleep, Arnie calls Leigh (the first time we see her in her own home) and asks for one more chance. She tells him that she cares about him, but he wants a straight response. In many ways, Arnie's regressive transition from sensitive nerd to disturbed fifties throwback has also made its mark in the way he responds to modern relationships. Here is a boy who just wants a direct answer, and not willing to talk things through or even capable of understanding the complexities of a teenage romance. Leigh's comment of "caring for him" is an open-ended statement that could eschew many possibilities of directional flow of conversation, but Arnie's cutting "Will you give me a fucking yes or no?" is a testament to older more "traditional" standards of teenage American dating of a bygone era. He ends the conversation with a nasty "Well fuck you bitch!", hanging up and then desperately picking the handle, clocking for a response "Hello? Hello…?"

Arnie's breakdown is a response to him being completely out of touch with humanity and it is countered by a cut to Leigh sobbing in bed. Her consideration is juxtaposed with his turmoil and the death of his pathos and understanding. Leigh's deep care for Arnie is not only an indication of the character's security and sensitivity, but from a narrative perspective it is also something that will send her into the arms of Dennis Guilder.

KEITH GORDON: John was very kind and patient with my wanting to look into the lens and ask "why are you doing this?" and "why this shot?" He would tease me about it. Once he knew I wanted to direct, he gave me a hard time about it but in a wonderful big brother sort of way, but he was also very patient; he'd be like "come here, look at this… okay. Now, you see, we're doing this and it's going to get darker over there"… but in terms of directing the challenge was tone: finding that fine line with Arnie, to be serious but not too serious; and to be real but not too real. We were experimenting as we were even shooting it. People always assume that directors have this locked in idea in their head, but most of the really best directors I have worked with as an actor were also open to the fact that it wasn't just going to be what they had in their head; that they were going to be finding some stuff out during the scenes with the actors – they'd get us there and things would happen. John had a real openness to it, but at the same time wanted to keep on a large level the more global themes and ideas that he wanted in the story. He was just really good at communicating what he liked and what he didn't like and what was working for him within that, but allowing it to sort of happen in the moment. Without him, I would never have found any tone for the character. I probably would have gone for something completely naturalistic and real and it probably would have been boring and not good.

"BEAST OF BURDEN": Christine stalks
Buddy Repperton and co.

From what would mark the complete end of Arnie and Leigh's budding but much troubled romance, the film shifts its gears to taking out the rest of the gang that Moochie belonged to. Thus, the revenge angle of the film continues, as we are sent to a local suburban liquor store, where we find Buddy Repperton and Rich Cholony shopping for booze and headed to their violent deaths at the bloodied "hands" of Christine. The liquor store is a perfect starting point place of action for such carnage that is to follow, as it represents a descendent of the dimly lit saloons that pepper many classic American Westerns from the Golden Age of Hollywood that director John Carpenter treasures so dearly. In *Black Moon Rising* (1986), another car-centric film which was co-written by Carpenter, the very opening is set in a convenience store with Tommy Lee Jones as a rogue left-over cowboy surveying the scene which is interrupted by an attempted robbery. In many regards, what happens here is an updating on the Western saloon as a place of eruptive violence, and here in *Christine*, the launching place of where Buddy and Rich (as well as fellow thug Don Vandenberg) will meet their demise is yet another extension of Western tropes – a place where drinking/purchasing alcohol will move into a place of explosive violence. Another social factor that benefits in having this opening for this lengthy sequence set at a liquor store is the fact that the problem of teens and drink driving is an element that penetrates the realist mind frame the film dances with – thinking back to the entrance of Detective Junkins (a character completely new to the fold and unaware of any supernatural going-ons – unlike the suspicious Leigh and Dennis) who is there to serve such purpose. The idea of teens dead as a result of combining drinking and driving makes literal sense in a film like this one, and could possibly be used as an alibi outside of supernatural intervention.

Another interesting and complex interloping element that comes into play here is the scrutiny of male sexual prowess. Buddy trivialises and mocks Rich's sexual advances to a passerby who has also purchased something from the store. She walks towards her car, Rich calls out some obnoxious catcall and Buddy undermines him, which makes a sidelined commentary on both his cynicism when it comes to his friends "picking up" and on his own lack of female companionship. *Christine*, unlike most very female-centric horror movies of the time, seems to be incredibly invested in teenage boys and the relationships shared between such characters – there is a brotherhood uninterrupted by girls, and when it is interrupted, it proves to be disastrous. Therefore, as much as *Christine* is a male-focused horror film (once again, something rare in the genre), the obvious monstrousness is presented as female and as woman as feminine-destructive and later even *vagina dentata* when the crazed killer car develops shark-like teeth hell-bent on killing Leigh and Dennis (the heteronormative couple that can succeed outside of the trappings of such a bleak plot).

While The Rolling Stones's "Beast of Burden" plays on the car radio, Buddy and Rich are stalked by Christine. Once again, the musical choice is poignant and telling; and even when the track belongs to another car (Dennis's being the other) and therefore from a contemporary period and not from 1957, the purpose is warranted and fitting. As a Greek Chorus, the song summons a mechanical "beast of burden", a machine that will run these dead-end kids down into the ground. Along with the inspired musical choice, the use of light plays vital importance where high beams blind the young men and become overbearing in oppression – if cars usually represent a place of independence and freedom from parental figures and society as a whole in cinema history, in *Christine*, they are a place of terror and entrapment.

Of course Buddy and Rich believe it to be a fellow reckless thug chasing them down (not yet clear that it is Arnie's red Plymouth Fury) and Rich flips the bird calling out "Asshole!" (more references to the anal/faecal) while the framing and composition leads into a frenzied car chase that builds into a literal explosive climax. The way the sequence is mounted and plotted reads like fellow car chase

sequences in film history – there are dramatic cuts of the speeding
cars that add to the hyperactivity of the sequence, there is an almost
Noir-esque aesthetic in the way they are presented zooming across
the wet grounds and the cross cut precision of the editing and the
aggressive nature of the energy builds into what would be a dynamic conclusion with three dead teenagers as the sequence's casualties.

The third teen and final member of Buddy's gang is Don Van-
denburg who works at a garage that seems isolated, far from the
suburban terrain. Christine powers towards there, following Buddy
and Rich. Here is where each teen realises it is Arnie Cunningham's car ("Is that Cunningham?"), and at this place of car culture
(a garage) there is a wonderful play on the polar counterpart to the
earlier scene at the high school garage, where now we are inside a
working station and Arnie (although not present at all) will come
up trumps. It seems like such a long time ago since he slipped upon
his yogurt and smashed his glasses at the bullying hand of Buddy
Repperton. Now, Christine, his angel of mercy, has stalked his per-
secutors and is ready to spill their blood, and she kills them with
grand fury and rage. However, before she takes them on, she rams
into Buddy's car and it is left completely totalled. Distraught by
this, Buddy's break in his voice ("Look at my car!") verifies a sense
of insecurity within the tough bravado, and soon after he bears witness to his friends violently killed. Once again, there is a conscience
lack of gore here, and instead, director Carpenter opts for a masterfully executed staging of an explosion with beautiful use of color
and light with fragments of the garage in an explosive state raining towards the fore of the frame. Christine destroys the garage
and with that kills Don and Rich, finally remerging from the fiery
busted up station as a vehicle enflamed, headed straight for Buddy.

The final image, set to the throbbing score of Carpenter and Alan
Howarth, has Buddy running for his life – his body sprinting into
action stalked by the hateful Christine who is completely covered
with raging flames like a demon car zooming through the night.
This is the most obvious in terms of Christine being compared to
something hell-born or Satanic, and her driving down the blackened street is a pure image of hell on earth. However, a car-centric
horror movie from some years earlier had more in common with

the influence of the demonic and Satanic culture. The politics and belief systems dictated by the controversial but incredibly fashionable Church of Satan – and the teachings of its leader Anton LaVey – would become one of the most talked about topics of "in-vogue" conversation during the late sixties and seventies. It is therefore not surprising that Elliot Silverstein's *The Car* from Universal Pictures opens with a quote from LaVey, which quickly establishes the film as a car-centric curio deeply indebted to the devil and occultism. Having the film's monstrous machine (a customised 1971 black Lincoln Continental Mark III) associated with the powers of darkness, allows the film to tap into the current trend of Satanic-themed horror, made vastly popular with the success of *The Exorcist* and its imitators. However, even though this film would have Satanic High Priest Anton LaVey as its technical advisor, the film owes more to Native American Indian spiritualism than the world of the dark underlord and is plotted and constructed in a manner that responds to tipping its well-designed hat to Universal's previously released spectacular hit *Jaws*, rather than resembling the aforementioned Warner Bros. venture about a possessed little girl. Outside of LaVey's quote (which comes from the "Invocation of Destruction" in his Satanic Bible) and minor involvement in the production, *The Car* utilizes one more ingredient that is born from religious horror-themed cinema, and that is the grandiose and inspired music. Set alight by Leonard Rosenman's thunderous and forceful score which boasts deep bass notes pounding an impenetrable sense of impending doom, *The Car's* inventive and elegant reconstruction of the Latin hymn "Dies irae" is a terrifying re-working of a musical arrangement that symbolically reflects the purpose of the Last Judgment – something that Elliot Silverstein's film thematically embraces. But as previously mentioned, *The Car* seems to ignore its religious promise, instead it opts for a non-demonic leviathan, much more akin to the shark in Steven Spielberg's massive blockbuster and also as relentlessly ferocious as the same director's maniacal truck in his made for TV master work *Duel*. Universal Pictures would be responsible for a thoroughly Satanic car in an anthology horror film from 1983 entitled *Nightmares*, which would pit Lance Henriksen against a car from hell, complete with an inverted crucifix hanging from the rear view mirror. Thankfully, the lack of religiously driven horror in *The Car* works to its benefit – because the movie is a wonderful riff on a small town terrorized by an uncompromising and unfeeling evil.

The opening sequence set to glorious Californian light is a marvel in celebration to the golden desert land of an America that film audiences know all too well; it is as if it is the world of the movie Western but now embraced by a modern sensibility. The film doesn't walk into revisionist Western territory, but it does embrace the glorious openness of the wilderness and is peppered with rogue cowboys searching for meaning and assurance. The film's first victims are also just as archetypal as the Western tropes that dance in and out of the narrative construct; they are a young couple racing on their bicycles and are representative of good health, vibrancy, energy and youthful zeal. Much like Chrissie in *Jaws*, they are the monster's first victims and this long legacy of early victims being young people – sacrificial lambs – is perpetuated and used intelligently.

As opposed to these young people who are killed, the film's protagonist Captain Wade Parent (James Brolin) is someone who looks as though he'd refuse to die, or refuse to even be put in such dire situations. The cyclists come across as risk takers, racing down winding roads and in flirtatious competition, while Wade instantly comes across as someone who revels in comfort and order and design. He has a relatively new girlfriend Lauren (Kathleen Lloyd) and two young daughters Lynn and Debbie (Kim and Kyle Richards) and his life seems to be back on track after separating with the mother of his two girls. As stoic and as masculine as Wade is (Brolin cannot be anything else, and this works in his favour as an actor), he is also sensitive enough to want his offspring to feel comfortable with the new situation at hand and Lauren is much the same ("I just want the girls to like me"). Lauren is presented as an outsider to the Parent household, while the eldest daughter at least has a slight understanding of divorce, with the film lending itself to sitting underneath the flag post of divorce culture in narrative based art forms. Wade is also similar to many policemen in American seventies cinema, that haunted hunted type – living in the shadow of his all-too-good sheriff father who has recently died. It is as if the entire town of Santa Ynez rests upon his shoulders, and he carries the burden of every citizen's concern like Atlas carrying the earth, however, Wade is someone who only responds to possibilities if it enforces his station of comfort and sense of order.

Adding to the mix of this stylish and taut thriller is legendary character actor R.G. Armstrong in possibly his most repugnant role as a dynamite and explosives dealer who beats his wife (Doris Dowling) – in many regards he is a caricature of poor white trash, and is essentially loathsome for the sake of being loathsome. He is also hurriedly established as an "enemy of the progressive people" when he is first introduced berating his wife as well as a young hitchhiker who annoys him with his French horn. The hitchhiker comes face to face with the murderous car moments after his altercation with Armstrong's roughie, and extending his thumb hoping this supernatural automobile is in fact a normal civilian with a hankering for picking up wayward youths, he dreams of the driver being a beautiful thirty four year old nymphomaniac. Sadly of course it doesn't work out for the young musician, and the car speeds towards him, aiming to kill him. He calls out "Up yours with a splintered fiddle, ya son of a bitch!" and moments later the car spins around and strikes him dead. Here, the film employs its third victim as a more cynical representation of late seventies youth as opposed to the almost too-wholesome thrill seekers from earlier. Interwoven within the film – and outside of social commentary made on the strained relationships between the old guard and the youth of America – are some small town secrecy subplots, however these are delivered without any fanfare, instead they are presented just as is, but also cleverly as an extension of plot development. For instance, the police investigation sheds some light on character interaction; a clear example is the fact that the Sheriff (John Marley) harbours a romantic and more importantly nurturing interest in Armstrong's downtrodden wife, while the film's vested interest in Native American Indian culture also acts as meaty marrow to the narrative bone when an elderly indigenous woman is interviewed by a fellow tribesman officer – giving the film a culturally sensitive edge that unifies the indigenous and the European settlers. "Bad things are coming with the wind" says the elder Native woman in her native tongue and later it is discovered that she mentions that the car she saw drive down the sheriff had no driver – a wonderful play on the invasion and rape of her land by the faceless "pioneers" who drove her and her people out of their communities and villages.

Adding to this mix of nicely crafted additives that make up a thoroughly engaging ride, are cult movie star Ronny Cox as a policeman who used to drink and has now been driven back to the bottle, suspicions about various characters building as deaths are investigated and the police station itself – a usually quiet place – now disrupted by this new enemy of the people that is embodied by the rampaging car. The major set piece to this film presents Lauren taking on the maniac machine. She is a teacher and in many ways, one of the kids. In an early scene, it is found out that she is also ogled by one of the boys who sketches her nude, and is scolded by her older more conservative peers. The core scene that is the most exciting has Lauren leading a marching band rehearsal for an annual parade, only to have it interrupted by the terrifying car that wishes to run down her students and everyone in its path. The trapping of a small town event that marks a celebration is akin to the 4th of July celebrations in *Jaws*, and this pops up in various films facing disasters. The wind storm – harking back to what the Indian woman said – pushing the terrified children around while the car zooms through, hell-bent on killing the entire congregation of students and adults, is a dramatic ingredient and as Lauren (the born leader) calls out and directs the petrified people, instructing that they "go up to the cliffs!" it is learned that the car won't enter the gravesite Lauren leads everyone into – it doesn't touch hallowed ground. Lauren's braveness is on show here, and her screaming at the car and antagonising the supposed "driver" with furious taunts is somewhat an empowering moment, not only for her, but for her peers (including the stuffy older woman who took issue with a boy's healthy interest in the female form) and students, building a sturdy solidarity. It also wins the hearts of Wade's daughters who see her as a heroic figure, taking on the car. Sadly later in the film, Lauren, left alone at her place, is stalked by the car and killed in her own home. Crashing into her living room at full high speed, this incredibly composed sequence has the car's headlights seen through the window while she talks to Wade on the telephone. The framing is a classic Hitchcockian visual cue and it works remarkably well, with building terror that leaves no time to breathe – the sheer force and ferocity of this speeding car permits no moment for Lauren to react or respond. In the last act of the film, Brolin's Wade is left to confront the car and it comes to be a lengthy battle initially involving the other police officers but then ending with him facing off with the monstrous car, a la classic Hollywood Westerns. When Wade is left inside the wreckage of Lauren's home, here we see a damaged man, who was so used to comfort and order – now engulfed by mess. Assisted by a stern Indian cop and a fragile alcoholic cop, there is a beautiful moment where no word of dialogue is uttered and time is seen passing. When the moment comes to "speak" in the wreckage at Lauren's house, Wade desperately refuses to hear and believe that the car is a supernatural force, even when he is confronted with facts that point to this reasoning. Like the fierceness of the wind that ushers in the demonic car, this denial and stubborn refusal to acknowledge an otherworldly entity that drives this vehicle to homicide will pass and Wade (as well as Brolin) will become a man determined to act against a monstrosity that has left its mark on his now shambolic world.

WILLIAM OSTRANDER: During filming Richard Kobritz spoke to other actors, but he never said a word to me about my character or what we were doing, other than that he liked what he was seeing after my very first night of filming at the liquor store. That was part of the reason they wanted us to be sure what we were going to do because, in that scene, I come out of the liquor store, and even though it was seemingly a nonchalant scene where there was nothing to it, they just wanted to make sure that I was going to go in the direction that they wanted to. Other than that scene, I never really had much to do with Richard. When he came to the set, John was playing jokes on him, which always made it very entertaining.

STEVEN TASH: I got close, as one could, to Buddy Repperton. I asked Bill Ostrander if he wanted to drive out together to a site we would be at just outside of L.A. County. He said, "Yeah. Okay." I think those were pretty much the only words he spoke after that – we rode out in near silence. I saw our characters taking shape right there, Buddy, brooding, stoic, with Rich, anxious, feeling wiry next to this rock that was Buddy.

BILL PHILLIPS: Stephen King has great dialogue. He also has an ability to get you into the head of his characters. One thing I noticed immediately, though, is that because he is so adept at writing verbally, sometimes the translation of that image onto the screen doesn't work. This is because he convinces you with words that something has a certain impact. An example I use is this (not based on anything he's ever written, as far as I know.) If he described someone's head starting to melt like a Hershey bar, the teeth represented by the almonds and keeping their form, we'd all understand the horror of this image in our mind's eye. But if you were to put that on the screen, it would look silly. While I love his words, sometimes his images can stand translating. This is handy for a screenwriter. It gives us something to do. For example, in the book, Buddy is killed on a snowy road in a Pennsylvania winter. When the car runs over him, all that is left is a "grease spot" on the road. But there are a couple problems with that: 1) we weren't filming in snow; 2) the image of a grease spot on a snowy road is rather unspectacular. It reads well… but on the screen, it would be difficult to detect and probably boring to see.

JOHN CARPENTER: I get very stressed on stunts because there is always that chance that somebody will get hurt. We had amazing stunt drivers and fantastic stunt people, and the cars were all cherried out, so thankfully everything worked out very well. Terry Leonard was the stunt coordinator and he was a legendary character. I don't remember how long the scene where the car drives down the road on fire, but I do recall that we had a lot of trouble from the car itself because the thing was on fire and the engine kept going out, so the car would just stop mid-run. We had to keep babying the car, and finally it worked. We would set it on fire, and then Terry Leonard would start it out from the garage and then it would stall, and we would have to stop start and shoot all over again. I remember it took about two nights to film that sequence.

DONALD M. MORGAN: It was something to see that car totally on fire and this guy driving! I don't know how he did it, but he did a good job of it! It was a gruelling night and the exposure when the explosion happened. They say that all is tricky. When an explosion is used in film, I would have the guy stop/stomped down the flame. We'd be lit for night which could be wide open. The lenses would be pretty much wide open. And then as the explosion happened, I would have the guys hand down the explosion as it went up, so it kept the red and the colour of the explosion real good. I saw a lot of the time, obviously explosions where they kind of whiteout and not be very colourful. And so that was a little trick that we did to make it look real.

WILLIAM OSTRANDER: A lot of people love John Carpenter's sense of humor. Especially, what you really like about him is that he is a bit of an auteur. He does music, he can shoot things, he can write, he can direct. John knows a lot of different aspects of filmmaking and is capable of lots of different filmmaking, but he doesn't take it seriously. By that, I don't mean to be flippant or dismissive of him. He does by getting his job done; he's not caught up in the vanity of filmmaking. I think that is the nicest thing I can say about him. He's really not caught up in the vanity of filmmaking and really is about making a movie. In the scene when the car is on fire and chasing me down the road to run me over, I asked "So why am I running down the middle of the road?" and he just looked at me and said, "Because it's a movie." I had a great relationship with John and I treasure that relationship even more now as the years have gone by after working with many directors. The relationship that I had with John was a very positive one. He was very unfeathered with ego and vanity. I would usually go to John, and I would say to him, "Okay, in this scene, I could do A, B or C. What do you like?" and he'd say, "I like A" and we'd do that. Then he'd come back and say, "I like that. But let's do B." I really appreciated that because he gave you the confidence and the chance to be creative. He wasn't looking to you to necessarily give a line reading that he heard in his mind. If he did mean that, he'd find a way of getting it to the right point instead of just mimicking what he wanted. Either way, in whatever way we got there, I appreciated the freedom and being able to play with my creativity. I love that as an actor it made you feel invested, like you were bringing something to the film personally – your contribution mattered and it wasn't a case of simply fitting a role because you fit the costume or that the writer or director wanted you to say it this way. On occasion, there is value in that approach too, but on a daily basis, the way John worked was much better.

KIM GOTTLIEB-WALKER: The construction crew had created a gas station out in the middle of nowhere for us to blow up. Cars going by on the road didn't realize it was fake and would have to be waved away from trying to get gas there. I was, by then, about six months pregnant, and shooting from the top of a huge ladder (with people spotting me from below in case I got blown off it). But my belly fit neatly between the rings, which gave me more support! Also, Don would have crew members build little protective barricades to protect me during scenes where flying debris or cars might be creating potential hazards. John's practical joke on Kobritz was probably the best John ever managed to pull off. Richard had a fancy Porsche that he adored and would cover every day to protect it. Without his knowledge, John substituted an old junky Volkswagon under the cover, and had the bulldozer run over it. Richard thought his autobaby was being flattened!

DONALD M. MORGAN: The crew was really protective of Kim Gottlieb because she was pregnant and she always wanted to crawl up ladders and do this and do that. In one of the scenes when the car crashes at the office in the garage, and the man slides out on the hood and dies, I said, "She's pregnant and she wants to stand near there." So I had my grips build a big wall for her so it would protect her. The whole crew was really protective of her.

ROY ARBOGAST: Every member of my team was important. Bill Lee was my foreman for many years and one of the best in Hollywood. When the car fell onto the kid we had a hydraulic system that fell down and was pretty dicey, and it should have fell down far more dramatically, but we got scared and kept it well sustained. Bobby Dawson was another great SFX guy, he blew up the gas station – he was a top explosives guy at the time. Dick Wood was one of my main guys also. We have done so many movies together! Bobby Dawson was a legend in pyro work. Terry Leonard the stunt coordinator would sit through the entire sequence on fire. We lit everything up on fire – the gas station, the car and so forth – and all of a sudden Terry wouldn't come out of the fire, because the car had died, because the fire was so big that there was no room for carbonating, so Terry came out dizzy from the heat and intensity of the flames. This happened a fair few times, the fire was so big that there was no air to breathe. When we worked on *The Thing* on the ice, the same thing happened. When we had fire work, there was still no oxygen for it to go out. But on *Christine*, Terry hit his marks and he was fine. The first time he did it and didn't come out of the car, it seemed like hours. We were all so terrified that something bad had happened. But by the second time, it didn't matter – he came out of it fine.

WILLIAM OSTRANDER: When we are stalked by Christine that was shot on a sound stage with a camera rigged at the front half of the Camaro I drove. They would use bars to leverage the car and move it when we turned to give it force and that would impact the moments where we would be stopping and starting. They simulated that by hand when we did it. John Carpenter told me that he was a helicopter pilot and that they used helicopter lights to light up behind us. That is why the light was so piercingly bright. I remember him telling me to get it at that level of luminosity they used helicopter lights. So that is my understanding anyway. The only take on it that I would have is from the same point of view as the audience had. Seeing it in the movie itself. Nobody told us that when we were doing it. So it didn't have any influence on me. As far as having a Camaro in the movie, that was a case of: I showed up, and that's the car that I was given! I don't know who had Buddy drive that kind of car, maybe Bill Phillips. I don't remember. I don't even know if it was in the book. I never read the novel. There was a choice in that for me; I don't know if it is the right choice or the wrong choice. When John and Bill Phillips were creating this film, I thought, it's the film, it's not the book. And therefore, they may have a take on it that Stephen King wouldn't have thought of or didn't like or wouldn't have been cinematic or visual. So to me, it was more important to stay true to the script, so I didn't feel compelled to go back and read the book. I felt I was trying to honour the new version that's the way they filmed.

DONALD M. MORGAN: There was one shot where there's the headlight coming up behind, and the guys are in the car; they see the headlights coming up on the car, and they're speeding away. That was all done on the stage, and we had lights mounted on a dolly and dollied in, and you could just see the bright lights. So a little bit of that was shot on, you know, we'd do wider shots outside. We did quite a bit of interior shots done on stage. It looked like streetlights going by and to make it look moving we took one of the sound booms, and we put a light on it, and we would swing it where they could move the mic where they wanted it, and it could be up high out of the way. And we'd put a light on that, and we'd swing it by the windshield, and you'd see the light go by like it was streetlights! I gave it a feeling of movement.

RICHARD KOBRITZ: We did tests with the lighting on the second unit and we tested Christine at night and how her head lights would be brighter and stronger than other car lights. The problem was when we got her out on some country road and put on these lights, and it would turn on all of the halogen lights on the highway, so it defeated the purpose. In pre-production we learned what to do, the whole film was a learning experience.

DONALD M. MORGAN: The challenges were always, "Here's the time you got, do it!" The pressure of how much time we always had and the foot-in to the film business that I got. Of course, on a bigger film, you had a little more time to light, but it was always a challenge to get done. If you were doing car stuff and it was getting late, and it was supposed to be day, you'd have the challenge of rushing to try to make the day before it got too dark. Not on *Christine*, but I remember on a film where it just turned dark, and we had two people sitting next to a car. I took a piece of 12 x 12 frame of silk and put it behind trees and lit it so that it had that kind of white look between the trees and then I lit the trees and lit the people and tried to match the daylight. Those were the challenges of trying to make the day and the amount of time. In one case, they had the car all cut up in pieces, and they put it on a flatbed. So that we had the hood and fenders, and the bottom of the car was all cut out, and the back of it was cut out, so I was over the actors, and they would drive in the truck, and they wanted the lights to blow out everything. I mounted two Xenon lights in the front, and I had every kind of light you could imagine you could blow out and it was lit on the inside of the car which was blown out, too. They wanted when we were driving anything it would over-expose, so I rigged lights on this truck and they took me out on the road, and it didn't do anything! I had all these lights there, and they had all these street lights that were on would turn off because they were on sensors and they would think it was daylight and they would go off as we were driving along. But it never really wiped out anything, and it knew because they put us on a road if they'd have driven downtown, it would have worked. But we blew a whole night doing that. I got a lot of flack for that! At that time we lit the car on the flatbed – the inside of the car was kind of like that, too. Anyway, it was a whole blow out. It didn't work!

WILLIAM OSTRANDER: "Beast of Burden" has to be one of my favourite songs and I'm glad it's there, but it wasn't something that I knew was on the radio when we were driving. While we were filming it, I might have responded to that song itself. If I had heard that while I was cruising along in my car that might have influenced my behaviour. It wasn't, so I didn't even think about it at all. I would have liked to have known that it would be playing. It's cool.

STEVEN TASH: I'm pretty sure this was Day 1 shoot for me, possibly Buddy. The Camaro – next to the Mustang Mach One this was my favorite car when I was young. And note: better than an Oscar, Hot Wheels/Mattel made the Christine 1967 Camaro car and released it. I was a collector as a kid, so that was a treat for me. The liquor store, with the girly mags right there on the counter. And the Stones – my all-time favorite rock band, blasting "Beast of Burden" from out of the Camaro! I've lived plenty of nights likes this growing up in L.A. with friends – so much youthful energy flowing through veins if felt like you'd burst. I wish we had had a little more room to improv on set... we had a second or two here and there but nothing that deepened, enriched our characters any more. But this little scene in pure enriched filmmaking style of what Mr. Carpenter does here, visually, sonically, I think was such a beautiful key homage to what only perspective can provide, along with the eyes and heart of what an artist can render, which was to me a pinnacle kind of night, maybe one of many nights young guy friends have... feeling alive and possibly looking for some easy troublemaking, if it were to show up. And it does – right as I'm rocking out to the Stones – the bright lights of Christine come up behind us. In regards to the shot of me flipping off Christine, Carpenter said at that time to me, this shot will be one of the most close-up shots ever filmed! We did that scene, take –after take, like nearly fifteen or so versions of me saying my line and flipping Christine off. The camera was maybe eight inches from my face.

RICHARD KOBRITZ: I do remember we used the song "Beast of Burden" in the scene where Christine is stalking Buddy Repperton and his friend, and our musical director Michael Ochs wanted to get permission but the guys from The Rolling Stones were incredibly hesitant. So we called a friend of Michael's in New York and we explained where the song would be used and how it would be used and finally Mick Jagger got in touch and asked questions about it. His first question was of course "What is this movie about?" and I said " a killer car, it's based on a best seller" and he asked "Who wrote the book?" and I told him "Stephen King" and with that, Mick Jagger told his lawyer "Let 'em have the song." So they gave us the song for free!

ALAN HOWARTH: John had just come off *The Thing*. There's a couple of cues that we did in the very end of *The Thing* which I will just call supplemental cues. Like burning the one guy outside the camp... I forget all the characters names. They were literally just like *Christine* but they just lay there. The John Carpenter signature thing of the drone sustained tones that the suspense of the sustained underpins horror of what is happening, and so it was done very organically. It wasn't calculated, it was more like a jam than it was ever something that was written out and expressed in the floor plan of what it was going to be.

STEVEN TASH: Coming out of Stella Adler, the master teacher of acting in the world at the time, and onto this set was a huge transition. With Carpenter, he's pretty hands off, just show up prepared. I liked the experience okay, but was hungry for more, deeper character work. I haven't seen the film in total... I saw plenty of scenes by others during the shoot and it was satisfaction enough to have done the work. The most I had seen of the finished film was this one particular day years later, it was at one of those actor convention events... I looked up at a monitor nearby that was playing scenes from *Christine* – and almost didn't recognize me in the monitor. I saw how deeply I had transported myself into Rich, the way he held himself, his eyes, a depth of character, an absence of me, Steven, and I was blown away by that; and proud to have delivered, and been a part of it all.

WILLIAM OSTRANDER: Stephen King was never on the set of *Christine* to my knowledge. But when I was working on a picture in New Mexico, I got a call from my agent asking me to make a quick trip to Los Angeles to meet him at the Beverly Hills Hotel because he had a deal at that time with Dino De Laurentiis who delivered two scripts. He got offered to direct one of the two that he delivered. He wrote a script called *Maximum Overdrive*. Stephen King had an interest in me in playing the character that eventually Emilio Estevez played. With respect to Stephen King, I hated that *Maximum Overdrive* script anyway. I thought it was terrible, nothing exciting about it.

STEVEN TASH: I was blown away by the set, a gas station with every detail and nuance. I explored everywhere, the oil cans in the back shelves inside the mechanics area, the gas pumps outside. It was unreal how real it was. And it was a set about to be demolished; blown up. At one point this convertible sports car pulls off the road into the gas station, and the driver hops out to get some gas. What a laugh! Strange that he didn't see the fifty- plus people milling around… but that's how real this set looked – that this guy pulled off the freeway to fill up on gas. By the end of the night, past midnight, with the cast and crew and a few locals pushed back a good city block they charged the rig that blew the set into a large flaming ball of fire way high into the sky – and we all felt it as though it was 25 feet in front of us and not a block away. It was a sight to behold. This is all quintessential guy's stuff. As I speak these words – it's the same thing I hear from fans all the time all over the country – it's a film that celebrates youth and being a guy, and all the guy archetypes are there… but especially, the tinkerer, the car geeks, cool cars and good FM radio music, the smell of gas and oil, and a ball of fire in the night sky – and of course, no hell on earth like a woman's wrath. Christine; what a bitch! Production had a stunt guy there to shoot my death scene. I approached John Carpenter and asked if I could do the stunt myself. He quickly agreed. Now, I didn't know what I was in for but the energy on that set for what was going down, Christine killing Rich and Buddy, and the gas station going up in flames and smoke, well I was feeling it. The stunt guy is standing against the green barrel, ready to go, dressed in duplicate of my black pants and Frye boots. Essentially what happens is there are several guys that will push the entire rig with camera straight at me *full speed*. I'm to fall back at a calculated point on to the blue mat as the camera rig with the side of the Camaro comes right over me full speed. After filming the stunt I can tell you that I have never felt that kind of adrenaline pulsating through my being. I could not come down for a day. A good 24 hours. No sleep. A highpoint of the shoot for me.

ADAM DEVLIN: As the thugs that nearly destroyed Christine are leaving a convenience store, after buying some booze at night, they head off in their car and we hear another "contemporary" track. This time it is the Rolling Stones's "Beast of Burden". As they speed through the streets, we see some headlights come up behind them. As the song plays the headlights get closer and the driver realises he is being followed. He decides enough is enough. The song cuts out as he decided to take on whoever it is that's following him. This is an inspired choice of song for this point in the movie. Firstly, being a contemporary track (the film is set in 1978, the year this track by the Rolling Stones was released as a single) that is being listened to in the thug's car, it clearly shows us that it is not Christine "speaking". It shows us that these young men are your typical rock 'n' roll type bad boys – all testosterone and bravado. Secondly, this track is a nice juxtaposition as Christine is about to very much become a "beast of burden" as she seeks revenge for what these thugs did to her. The song hints, mockingly, at what is about to happen. Christine is in fact a "beast" and she's about to become a very big "burden" indeed. And the machismo of Mick Jagger's staccato delivery of the lyrics perfectly sets up the following scenes.

Shooting the carnage that will unfold at the garage/gas station, where Christine kills the bullies.

John Carpenter and crew prepare the stalking sequence that will result in Buddy Repperton being run down.

Preparing the explosion at the gas station.

Prepping the Rich Cholony (Steven Tash) kill, where the young thug is pulled under the heavy machinery of Christine.

A Spanish lobby card.

Production still featuring Steven Tash as Rich flipping Christine the bird.

William Ostrander talks to John Carpenter about his impending death scene.

Christine smashes through Buddy's car.

"SHE'S AS SKINNY AS A STICK OF MACARONI":
Darnell is crushed to death by Christine

Throughout the film, the adult antagonists of Arnie Cunningham seem to get out scot-free (ie they are not killed by the murderous motorcar), however the loutish Will Darnell is crushed to death in the driver's seat of Christine in what seems to be an ambiguous but effective scene that seems to come from a realm of otherworldly seduction. Much like the brutal gang rape earlier involving the now deceased gang (and even to a lesser extent, Dennis Guilder's attempt to "open Christine's door" prompting Little Richard's angry response with "You Keep A-Knockin'"), this sequence unravels at Darnell's garage and involves a "sexual act" which turns deadly. Starting with Darnell sitting at his desk in his cruddy office (a sign referring to God plastered at the base), the scene unfolds quietly and without any fanfare or aggression as the previous sequence which saw the deaths of Arnie's teenage tormentors who were stalked, run down and burned alive. Here, Darnell is startled by the image of a burnt out Christine cruising into the garage, spattering and smoking, stalling and – as if completely exhausted – coming into her parking space ready to recoup and regenerate.

Darnell, still as loathsome as ever, even on his own with nobody evidently present to offend or upset, is dumbfounded by the entrance of Christine. He sees before him an absolute wreck, blackened with burnt fenders, singed to the very chrome and metal she is made of – a monstrous charred machine ready for the scrap heap. Her singed and burnt body with metallic "scar tissue" exposed is all the more terrifying an image because there seems to be no driver in the car and this is where Darnell reacts in both a terrified state and a childlike state of bewilderment. After making a feeble phone call – checking on Arnie and Arnie's whereabouts – Darnell arms himself with a rifle, indicative of the film still expressing the notion in its characters that Christine is not a haunted car but that she has a homicidal driver, most probably Arnie Cunningham. However, of course the rifle is obsolete as Darnell pries the door open – a musical cue to reveal no driver – and he is slowly somehow seduced by the crispy and charred Christine. Singing his hand on the door, but stepping inside comfortably as if beckoned, Darnell's physical response to the burned car is that of a man being welcomed into the arms of a seemingly affectionate woman. It is as if singing his hand was a mistake, and that Christine herself has made up her "mind" to instead not push Darnell away, but to envelop him and bring him close – to kill.

The song of choice here is "Bony Moronie" by Larry Williams (once again from the year of Christine's birth, 1957) and while the heavyset Darnell is crushed to death, the song makes mockery of his weight, singing the praises of an ultra-thin lover:

> *"I got a girl named Bony Moronie*
> *She's as skinny as a stick of macaroni*
> *Oughta see her rock and roll with her blue jeans on*
> *She's not very fat just skin and bo-o-one"*

MARION ROTHMAN: I've felt that editing is closest to directing. You feel it is "your baby". I think footage (angles, lighting) create the visual style. You take your rhythm from that and the performances. I can't recall specifics from editing *Christine*, but I loved the insert radio with music popping on for the first time, the odometer references, Christine's transformation and presentation at football, Moochie's death and I loved his line "I didn't mean anything bad". I also loved the drive-in and Robert Prosky (Darnell) getting crushed was my favorite scene. I like to think I always collaborate on the story flow. Before meeting with a prospective director, I would study the screenplay and present notes. That is a start in seeing if you and director have rapport.

VIRGINIA KATZ: I loved working with Marion. We worked together for years until I moved on as an editor. She was a great role model. I had only worked with men up to that point. I learned so much about being a woman in the cutting room. We worked well together. These were the days of film so assistant duties were different then they are today.

KIM GOTTLIEB-WALKER: Except for my belly being community property and everyone being very protective, me being pregnant did not interfere at all with my imperative to get the shots. I was just as energetic and having just as much fun as I always did working with John. The production took me from my third month to my seventh month... most fun pregnancy ever!

BILL PHILLIPS: I didn't particularly like the way Darnell was killed in the book… it seemed hard to believe to have a car climb stairs to kill someone. I know it's a bit silly to talk about credibility in a movie about a killer car, but I think one reason the film has endured this long is that we tried really hard to make it as believable as we could.

RICHARD KOBRITZ: We tried many things like having the camera in the driver's seat. And there were times where we had to replace the grill, especially near the end during the final confrontation and it was cut down to make it look more like a shark's mouth, but it was still on the car and the car was moving at its own volition. They would have to yell out "Quiet!" to the functioning shop which was positioned behind what was used as Darnell's garage, when they were about to roll, and then during that final confrontation they were rolling out Christines and wheeling them out at the blink of an eye.

KEITH GORDON: I was there when they shot Darnell's death scene. A lot of that is what a wonderful actor he was. He was just so good. Again, it was still playful. He nailed that tone! He made that character a real human being, and yet also a little comic and bigger than life at the same time. I thought he did that so well. He did it in a few other films, too. It was something he came by very naturally, this fine line of bigger than life but again not at all a joke. I just remember watching it, and I don't think there was a lot of John having to coach him to get him there. I think the whole transition from suspicion to kind of the turn-on of being in the car and the sensual delight of sitting behind the wheel of what it felt like, and then him being crushed, as I remember he did it amazingly. They did a few takes, but I felt like he just had this take on it where he did a rehearsal and John was very happy and very excited. I don't think it took a lot of hard work to get the performance. Technically, they had to get all the bits and pieces of him getting crushed, then they did it with the actor and made it look fluid, manually moving the seat. That scene to me more than anything is really performance based. It's all what Prosky brings. John shoots it great; he shoots everything great, but there's no big fancy shots in it that I remember. It's just that performance and the arc – the S curve of him going from negative to positive to dying. It's his face that sells it. I thought he was great. I loved him. I loved working with him; he was just the sweetest, nicest guy.

ROY ARBOGAST: My favorite sequence is when Christine comes into Darnell's garage, going 'Chug chug' and reversing into the parking spot. Just terrific stuff – still gives me chills. The car had a flexible steering wheel and the seat was rigged by hydraulics and bent into shape to crush him. We also had light bulbs inside to burn bright and they started to smoke because they had gotten so hot; the car started to catch fire because of this. This was also a tough shoot – it was all night long. None of John Carpenter's movies are easy.

ADAM DEVLIN: After Christine has sought revenge on the thugs that tried to destroy her, she returns to the garage, Mr Darnell is still on the garage office. Christine is all burnt and smouldering still following her 'revenge'. Darnell goes over to Christine and sits in the drivers seat. As he does this, the car door slams shut and the radio starts playing "Bony Moronie" by Larry Williams. Bony Moronie, released in 1957, was Larry Williams' third single release and went on to be recorded by a range of successful recording artists over several decades. We know in this scene that this is Christine communicating again – as her radio starts up just to play this track. The lyric is about the singer's girlfriend, who is as skinny as a stick of macaroni. As we hear these lyrics, Christine has locked Darnell in the driver's seats and she slowly starts moving the seat forward. Darnell is definitely not "as skinny as a stick of macaroni" and as the seat moves forward he is crushed to death. It's a clever play on words, showing that the fat Darnell is not meant to be in Christine (Arnie by the way is Christine's thin young suitor) – and since he's seen too much (a smouldering Christine returning after seeking revenge on her attackers), he too must die. Once the deed is done, the radio shut off again. The lyric "She's not very fat just skin and bone" is almost prophetically comical – if Darnell had of been thin, like Arnie, he may not have been squashed to death by Christine. This is very much a case of Christine saying that only Arnie shall drive her.

A burnt out Christine rolls into Darnell's garage.

"I GUESS NOBODY BE TRASHIN' YOUR CAR ANYMORE": Junkins confronts Arnie

The opening shot of Darnell's garage sign in broad daylight is the counter to seeing it in an establishing shot earlier in the film in the dead of night. With this stark and unforgiving light now revealing hidden truths, the film is ready to "out" the true nature of the evil that possesses Christine and has influenced Arnie Cunningham. This sequence also showcases the incredibly true inconsistency of Arnie's personality transition – as much as he has become self-possessed and ultimately creepy and disturbed, here his vulnerability is still maintained as he is asked endless probing questions from Detective Rudolph Junkins, who makes his second appearance still in the mindset that Arnie is most certainly the "monster" of the piece.

Arnie racing inside of Darnell's garage and confused by the situation is a brief moment where he has been "detached" from Christine; he has not seen her for the entire evening – her night of tracking down Buddy Repperton and his pals, as well as killing Darnell. Arnie's story that he tells Junkins is obviously true and the back and forth nature from defiant, to angry, to incredibly nervous Arnie is a wonderful display of acting talent from young Keith Gordon who steals the scene with his jitters and blank-faced confusion. What is the reveal for us the audience however, is the way in which John Carpenter chooses to reveal a newly restored Christine with Arnie racing towards her, and her coming into frame. It is ultimately the same shot that had Arnie discover her smashed to smithereens earlier in the film, where he snapped at Leigh ordering her to "Get away from her!" Here the car has rejuvenated and is no longer a burnt shell, she is back to her old self, looking gorgeous, gleaming and shiny, with the dead Will Darnell pressed up against her dashboard – shotgun by his side.

Smartly written exposition is then delivered (Junkins providing it) where it is noted that "someone" spotted Christine following Buddy Repperton the previous night, and this is followed up with

Junkins slightly accusatory line of "I guess no one will be trashin' your car anymore". While the interchange between Junkins and Arnie continues, a team of forensics circle Christine taking photos in a perverse take of a Hollywood glamour-puss being photographed for a brand new shoot to highlight her beauty and fame.

RICHARD KOBRITZ: Daniel A. Lomino's work we had seen and what intrigued me about his work was that he had just worked on Billy Wilder's last ever movie *Buddy Buddy* (1981), and it was a lousy movie. I remember asking Daniel about it and he was umming and ahhing and the main reason I asked is because I saw the working relationship and the chemistry between Walter Matthau and Jack Lemmon and looking at that it had been totally exhausted, and just not good – especially that Matthau was so old by that point. Daniel agreed and told stories about the making of that movie, but I thought his credentials based on that movie and his past work were exceptional and it's good to give somebody who may not be on the tip of everybody's tongue a shot – and so we did. Donald M. Morgan worked with John on *Elvis* and I had worked with him on some early movie in the second unit – this goes beyond working on *Someone's Watching Me!*. John was happy with him, and so be it.

KEITH GORDON: In terms of *Christine*, I felt that given the tone of the movie, which to me has this odd sort of dark sense of humour, it doesn't play as pretend naturalism or I don't think when you watch the film you are thinking I am watching real life and John Carpenter creating a documentary film about teenagers or the police. There's a playfulness in the cinematic artificiality to it that I love. Within that, I don't find myself ever thinking about, "Well, does it make sense that the cops would act this way?" The film is a fairytale, it's a myth and those scenes are written really well. I think Bill Phillips did a great job with those scenes and the way John directed them and Harry Dean as a presence. Harry Dean is so kind of odd himself and interesting and complicated, and he makes that character, he does so much with those quiet moments with that character. That for me works great in *Christine*. I hate things that feel forced into a story. There are certainly films where you feel that. I mean horror films, also mysteries. It's even worse sometimes in thrillers and mysteries that even if they don't have a horror aspect, where you just feel the whole police element feels manipulated to make the story work. I never felt it with this film, but I also felt like in this film that almost anything went because you weren't asking an audience to believe. "This is a new crime in New York City in the year 2003." You are saying this is a killer car that this boy is in love with. Within that those scenes with Harry Dean just have a lovely, almost mythic quality. I don't think of it as accidental. John was very much a part of it. In the first scene with Harry Dean –there's something almost very Western about them. I mean, with the whole black vest on, and there's something about the gunslinger and meeting the law guy that was in there. There's something in there that is a little bit archetypal going on.

Harry Dean Stanton and John Carpenter run through a scene.

John Carpenter ensured there was a "family vibe" on the set of the film, and his sense of humour shone through during the shoot.

"HAPPY NEW YEAR": Leigh calls Dennis

Here is the first time we see Dennis Guilder in his own domain – his family home. In the novel there is talk of his mother (a writer – as Stephen King would commonly have the profession shared by many of the characters that populate his stories), an ill-fated cat named Captain Beefheart and a younger sister who we get in the film adaptation.

Finally with his leg free from the plaster cast, and sporting crutches, Dennis sits with his sister playing a board game as we learn that it is New Year's Eve. Leigh interrupts the game with a phone call requesting to see him – to discuss Christine. Mocking the phone call with "It's a girl", Dennis's sister flips the brotherhood element of the film on its head with a female taunting back at boys and their inabilities, and this tiny insight into Dennis's home life reflects a gender alteration in the progression of the film.

ALEXANDRA PAUL: It's a little tricky because you want to portray them as honourable, yet they are basically turning towards each other and defeating Arnie. But it's portrayed more of us trying to deal with our confusion of what is happening to somebody that we both love and care about. So that's why we turned to each other, but it's fitting that we don't end up [together]... it's more about us coming together because of our hurt over how Arnie has been acting rather than directed at each other only. Like I've mentioned, I was a little intimidated by John Stockwell because he was a couple of years older. So we got to know each other better afterwards because he dated another co-star of mine Rae Dawn Chong for a long time when I shot *American Flyers* (1985). There was only Kelly and she was only in a few days. There weren't any other women really on the set. So I didn't bond like Malcolm and Steve Tash, they became friends or closer. Of course, I dated Bill Ostrander, so that was an important relationship in my life.

French lobby card.

"I THOUGHT YOU WANTED TO TALK ABOUT CHRISTINE": Dennis and Leigh discuss the Plymouth Fury

Essentially, two things occur during this sequence – and one point is muted. First and foremost, exposition is presented in simplistic and docile terms: Leigh learns about the death of Christine's previous owners as Dennis explains it to her, and Dennis in turn learns that Leigh nearly choked to death in the car. There is also talk of Arnie's change in behaviour and personality and it is well established that both characters – the best friend Dennis and the girlfriend Leigh – are worried about his wellbeing. Secondly, what is happening here is the film establishing Dennis and Leigh as the central heroes who will eventually confront Christine and bring her to a scrapheap. In a movie that heavily relies on an anti-hero (Arnie Cunningham) and a monster that is not human nor animal (Christine), the story lends itself into territory that is relatively different to contemporary horror films of the time which had a cleanly and clearly designed hero (most notably heroine) who will face the monster and defeat it (or not). It is not until very late in the piece that Dennis and Leigh come into gear and form a union in order to "rescue" their beloved Arnie from the malevolent clutches of this sentient sadistic car.

What is muted in this sequence – and what was essentially developed in drafts of the screenplay as well as shot in deleted scenes – is the budding romance of Dennis and Leigh. In one sequence, Arnie would find them kissing and he would scream out in a bloodcurdling holler "Shitters!" – this would ultimately be dropped, as would the obvious tell-tale signs of Dennis and Leigh forming a romantic bond. They get close, hold one another, but a kiss is never shared; this is the beginning of what might be a healthy, positive relationship.

Leigh's fear of the car realized and Dennis makes the decision to help her to help Arnie and confront Christine. As Dennis and Leigh get close, John Carpenter is careful not to allow them to get too close by not cementing any kind of full blown romantic union essentially because it would create a narrative concern: the issue there, having the heroes "turn on Arnie" by betraying him and partaking in a relationship that is based on sex would diminish their power as heroic characters willing to risk their lives to save him.

BILL PHILLIPS: This was my first produced feature script. I never intended it to be more than two hours long. I find that most films that are three hours long usually contain a two-hour good film and a one-hour bad film. They are usually made by directors showing off because their last films made a particular studio a lot of money, freeing them (in their own minds) to do whatever they want to do. That kind of hubris leads to doing a mixed job at best. The discipline of a two-hour story is good. I told John and Richard that the reason the script was 136 pages long instead of 120 is that I used a lot of Stephen King's descriptions of things to add more atmosphere to the story. I was wrong that this wouldn't add length to the story. The rough cut of the film was thirty minutes too long. I've never written a script that long again. My idea was that Dennis and Leigh were concerned about Arnie and that their getting closer was inspired by their concern for Arnie. Once they realized that Arnie was no longer really Arnie, it was more acceptable that they would give in to feeling closer to each other. But it was never intended that they would be a bona fide couple. When the rough cut was too long, John and Richard had to decide how to shorten it. I feel that they made the right choices. Ironically, they had to cut the more 'soft', interpersonal scenes. These are the kinds of scenes that tend to make the writer look better, but let's face it: this is a film about a killer car. You can't cut the action scenes in a film like this. I felt bad for Alexandra, who had to see that many of her best scenes had been cut in order to keep the film short enough. Fortunately, most of these scenes have been preserved in DVD outtakes. I've seen them recently, and I think they work fine. But the decision to cut them out of the film, in order to keep the pacing fast, was the right decision.

RICHARD KOBRITZ: The studio had suggested Brooke Shields and Scott Baio for Leigh and Dennis, however, we never considered them and they were never in a casting call, they were just what Columbia used as a whole "Boy, we'd like this type of person for this role". Obviously they saw the tests and they signed off a deal where John Carpenter and I had final say and final cut of the cast and finished film.

KEITH GORDON: I think part of the concern was also not making them unsympathetic because the film does an interesting thing, because you go along with Arnie so much so on the journey, and ultimately though, they take over the central role in the movie. They become the heroes, and Arnie dies, not as the villain but sort of an anti-hero, so I think there is a trickiness and balance where if it seems too much like Leigh has just turned on Arnie, and now they are getting it on. When they were like making out, were more physical, you hate them a little bit. It made you feel like they're betraying a friend: Dennis betraying his best friend, she's betraying her boyfriend. It was one thing to feel them grow attracted to each other or to imagine after the story is over and that Arnie is dead, that they would become a couple. It didn't feel that way. When you saw that happen when Arnie was still around it kind of made you not feel for them, and I believe that was what was behind the decision to take that stuff out which makes sense to me. This may be my own theory, but I believe that was something John said at some point. It's a tricky thing because it is a bit of a triangle or a quadrangle with Christine. I think for the film to work you have to like everybody. Again, John had to be careful with the balance.

Finding comfort in one another's arms, Leigh and Dennis plan on what to do about Arnie.

From a deleted scene, Alexandra Paul and John Stockwell as Leigh and Dennis, form a more overt romantic union much to the outrage of Keith Gordon's Arnie.

Shooting what would become a deleted scene that would involve Arnie seeing Leigh and Dennis kiss, sending him into a hysterical rage.

John Stockwell and Alexandra Paul.

William Ostrander, Richard Kobritz, Alexandra Paul, John Stockwell and Keith Gordon on location with Christine.

"DEATH TO THE SHITTERS OF THE WORLD IN 1979!": Arnie and Dennis go cruising in Christine

It has to be said that John Carpenter has an uncanny ability to turn halcyon normalcy represented by the American suburb into something foreboding and menacing. The way Haddonfield is presented in *Halloween* is mythic in its depiction – the rich green lawns, the tract housing, the long stretches of pavement and so forth add to the mystique of other worldliness in an otherwise ordinary locale. Here in *Christine* – which in many ways mirrors a lot of the aesthetic from *Halloween* – the opening of this entire sequence has Leigh Cabot leave Dennis Guilder's house and cross the gleaming street. Much like a classic Film Noir where the sidewalks shimmer with an intensity that adds so much to not only visual trappings but to story and character, the rain soaked Californian suburban streets at night carry the nervous Leigh into the safety of darkness as she watches Christine approach, ready to collect the injured Dennis.

Much like anti-hero Walter Neff in the much lauded Billy Wilder Noir classic *Double Indemnity*, Dennis rings similar to the opening image during the credit sequence to the classic forties picture where Fred MacMurray is seen in silhouette hobbling along on crutches. Adding insult to injury, Arnie Cunningham pulls up and mocks him; laughing at his old friend who hops over towards the murderous Plymouth which dominates the quiet, dead street. Here is an age old New Years Eve tradition losing its charm and innocence – if Dennis and Arnie have always celebrated the wake of the new year together as teens, this will clearly be the last of it: the end of the road of their friendship, two boys who have grown apart.

Arnie's love and loyalty lies in the companionship he has found with his car and this is developed throughout the film, however in this sequence it is funnelled down absolute obsession and consumption. He even opens the dialogue with sturdy defensiveness, protecting his Christine ("You gotta watch what you call my car") and even speaks for her, giving her a "life" and "feelings" ("She's real sensitive"). All of this even pushes the reasonable and mentally stable Dennis to give in, apologising to Christine – and even though the line is delivered by actor John Stockwell with a tongue in cheek sensibility, it is still a dedicated honouring of Christine as a "real person". When Dennis mutters "Sorry, Christine", he is buying into her being a machine with feelings and in response to this comes the condescending "Good boy" from Arnie who sits in the "driver's seat" taking control over the situation and bringing the monstrousness home. One of the many hearts of darkness in *Christine* lies in the death of traditions that are comfortable for those who wish to remain in control. Dennis is a character who reasons with change, but is ultimately scared of it, and when he sees the transformation in Arnie's personality it doesn't just mean that he is terrified of his old friend's new personality, he is disturbed by the course of transition – that the trajectory he assumed would uphold is now in decline and soon to be lost forever. For Leigh, who hides in the bushes watching the boys enjoy their "secret outing", her concern is far more general; sincere and devoted but outside the realm of longevity and the past. She is still essentially the "new girl in town" and her connection to Arnie exists on another plateau, which is why she lets Dennis have the final word with the troubled owner of that deadly Plymouth Fury.

With Arnie at the wheel of Christine there is something completely demonic about his appearance. He is so gleefully sinister that he almost looks cartoonish, like a possessed character from one of those wonderful EC horror comics from the fifties and sixties. With this film being so dutifully dedicated to fifties sensibilities, aesthetic and culture, it makes absolute sense that the visual styling here would be painted up within a broad stylized pop canvas. Classic fifties teen centric horror takes over at this moment in the film, however the language and the very nature of what is discussed is incredibly modern in its fundamental message – or at least overt. Essentially what this sequence screams is the utter alienation of our "rebel" of the piece, who is a tragic figure, lost in time and space and lost in his own mental decay. Arnie Cunningham had potential (his intellect and how he was "good with his hands") but has been consumed by not only the influence of a malevolent sentient car, but by his loneliness and deep rooted sadness. Arnie has lost control and it is now Christine in the proverbial "driver's seat". This is physically realised when Arnie throws his hands off the steering wheel and the car zooms down the freeway much to the distress of the terrified Dennis.

Arnie, with his can of beer at hand, also delivers a toast that heralds "death to the shitters of the world" which is a testament to his misanthropy now morphing into something far more toxic and unhealthy. Dennis is repulsed by such a toast and suggests they celebrate/honour friendship which is more of Dennis clambering for the past and trying to salvage the comfort zone he knows so well – Arnie has the fumbling vulnerable mess. Dennis's fear is highlighted by the production design – shot on a sound stage, the use of light to give off the impression of passing cars zooming down a freeway strike Dennis's frightened expression illuminating such palpable fear. The same use of light paints a disturbing image of Arnie who basks in a cool blue surrounded by an enveloping black giving the impression of transformation, sickly desire and living death.

Countering the steady extreme speed of the car is the jolts in the dialogue and the way Arnie and Dennis bounce off one another in conversation. From off putting discussion of "car talk" ("This is great alignment, you just don't see this anymore") which pays into the nostalgia kick, to the degrees of jealousy and finally to the disturbing moment where Arnie actively trivialises and shuns the love of Leigh and champions the love of Christine over such potential human affections. Dennis pleads with him: "Leigh's on your side", but Arnie dismisses this but not without any acute insight into matters of the heart. Arnie alerts Dennis to his mental and emotional demise when he talks of love and mentions that "it (love) has a veracious appetite"; this is a masterfully handled entry into what will eventuate into a mesmerising soliloquy from Keith Gordon as the demented Arnie. In a speech that comes late in the film (a risk in many regards – one may think back to the stunning monologue delivered by Piper Laurie's religious zeal Margaret White in a former Stephen King adaptation in *Carrie*), Gordon throws himself into the fun and freedom of being a character actor exorcising everything that has shaped, manipulated and damaged the character of Arnie Cunningham. The speech is essentially a condensation of what the poor kid has gone through and where he is heading. He cries out about the importance (and unimportance) of someone believing in you and then cackles over the idea of Leigh being that person. He then brings his monologue around full circle with talk of the merits of owning Christine, celebrating the cold fact that "no shitter ever got between him and Christine". In a scene that is the complete polar opposite of an early sequence with Dennis in the driver's seat (the jock in control, the nerd his passenger), the final line in this game changing moment reflects Roland LeBay's pussy reference causing us the audience (as well as Dennis) to believe that Arnie is yet another prisoner of Christine, and possible potential victim to the bloodthirsty machine.

JOHN CARPENTER: I really love moving camera action, I think I fell in love with all that during film school – it's something I've always loved. I started watching a whole bunch of movies, and the films that resonated a lot as far as technical skill went, were the movies that had a lot of moving camera work. It was the dolly shots that I just fell in love with. It was just incredible. So I started using those in my movies, and by the time I got around to working on *Christine*, I had already made a number of films, and this was my first movie after my giant failure on *The Thing*, so I was just starting anew and I just threw in these dolly shots to give the film a feeling of perpetual movement. There was also a lot of steadycam work in certain places of the film, because I just love the look and feel of the steadycam. I just feel it gives a certain sense of fluidity to the movie, and in many cases it gets you more involved with the characters.

DONALD M. MORGAN: I have to give John credit for the moving camera work in the suburbs. John never wanted anything that stayed stagnant. Even if we were doing an establishing shot at the house, he wanted it moving, and I questioned that several times where I said, "If it's just a shot of the house, why would it be moving? That indicates something is doing it." And he said, "This is what I like!" So we just did it. And the end result I saw what it was about. He wants that camera moving all the time. So that was

John's way of doing stuff, and I learned a lot on *Elvis*. Then I did *Christine* and then *Starman*.

KEITH GORDON: Every director is very different. I worked with a lot of directors when I was acting, and I think people would be surprised how different each director is, in terms of their actual process and their energy and there are always more differences than similarities between any directors. John was a lot of fun. He brought a real playfulness to the process which I adored. There was something of a kid about him. He was always making movies with this sense of enthusiasm, and he kept things very light on the set. He spent a lot of energy on practical jokes, and sometimes it was silly, little things like stealing the microphone cover from the sound person when they weren't looking and watching them go crazy and sometimes it was very elaborate practical jokes. Maybe more than any director I have worked with I felt like he put effort into making the set a fun place to be! And creating an atmosphere that was very collegial. On a lot of movie sets the actors hang out as a group and the crew hangs out as a group. One of the things that I really remember about *Christine* was that everyone ate lunch together and there was just this sense of a normal job, and class barriers on movies were broken down and that all stems from John. In terms of his way of working, he wasn't someone who spent a lot of time talking about the subtext or sort of the motivation in tremendous detail, but he still would communicate a lot of what he wanted very well. What happened with us over time, and it's actually something that I then stole and used as a director with other actors later on. Often he would talk to me in very simple terms about if that was a five, give me a seven. Numbers were one way that he would do it; he would kind of bring me up or down. He definitely would direct me, but it wouldn't tend to be a 10-minute monologue about the meaning. It would tend to be a very simple phrase or two, or "Try one where you let the anger get away from you" or "Try one..." but it tended to be very simple, very clear and very actionable. It was [direction] that you could actually do things with. John generally did fewer takes than for example than Brian De Palma tended to. Brian would tend to almost always do multiple takes on everything and kind of intentionally get a tonne of variations. With John, it was really about when he got something that he was really happy with, and sometimes that would be take six, but sometimes it would be take two. He didn't tend to just do takes to experiment, although he was great if I ever said, "Can I do one more? I have an idea!" He was always very open to that, but he wouldn't just do more. Brian was more of a style of "Well we're here, we've lit everything. We've taken the time, let's experiment". John was more like, "We're here, but we've got it!" We never really did one take, it was always at least two or three, and sometimes you do a bunch if he wasn't sure about what he wanted. Or if he was finding things as we were doing it or he felt it was getting better and better. But Brian was more of an experimenter and John was more of trying for the thing that felt right to him, and when he did he felt like he had it. I've been surprised in a number of ways, directors sort of branch into two classes: the ones that very much want to take credit for being auteurs and the ones that tend to downplay. I mean John has never suffered pretension gladly. He is very much an artist, but I think he doesn't like to talk about film as art so much. He clearly is an artist but he does undersell how much art he brings to it. I think he talks in these very regular guy terms, but he's somebody who is truly an auteur. He's writing the music, he's a visionary and his movies aren't like anybody else's, but he's not someone who craves to be seen that way. I think a lot of John's favourite directors probably come from that if I remember correctly a big John Ford fan. Directors that were from the studio era and made a tonne of movies and some of them were great, some of them were good, but they always brought their best to it, and I think John grew up admiring those people. John Ford now we all think [of highly] but at the time he was just this working director and only later did everyone say John Ford was this auteur, this great filmmaker. But I don't know if the system did see people that way. Of course, on the other hand, John also puts his name right in the title. Technically the title is *John Carpenter's Christine*. So it is an interesting thing because there is part of him that wants to get the credit and deservedly so. But I think he also admires the pretentiousness of just filmmakers as craft people as opposed to self-conscious and self-inflating artists. I never felt with

John that he needed people to kiss his ring. There are a lot of directors who need that kind of ego reinforcement, and I just felt like John really didn't need that. He was confident enough in himself that he could be very at ease and relaxed and appreciative of the people around him. I think there's a reason a lot of the same crew work with him over and over again. There was a family atmosphere on that set, and it was like we were all having this adventure together, and I felt like that was very important to him. It was clear that he was the guy in charge. Some people have authority without needing to demand authority; they have respect without needing to demand respect. John was like that. Everyone would defer to him, but it wasn't because we were scared of him, it's because we knew he was really great at what he did, and he was really smart, and he was a good leader. I never work with a director without taking something away. With John, the biggest thing was, to me, the atmosphere that he created on set. I remember very distinctly thinking while we were making the movie, "If I ever get to make a movie" – because ever since I was a kid, I wanted to be a filmmaker – "I want my set to feel like this!" I remember when I watched John being playful or laughing or making [the set] a good place to be, thinking "Don't forget this! If you ever get to make a film, try to be like this", and I think I really have. I do it my own way, but I always want my sets to be a fun place for people to be, and I'm really frustrated if I don't achieve that as well as I want. So that was one of the single biggest things that I took with me as a filmmaker. It wasn't so much as a technique or you know a way to do a specific thing, it was more the whole feel of that movie. I felt like he did a good job at bringing out the best in everyone, and in setting up an atmosphere where actors and also crew – everyone felt appreciated and felt a part of the process and felt like their opinion was important and the camera operator, the still photographer, whoever you were, if you had something to say, John would listen. That seemed like a really good way to make a movie! So that was probably the big takeaway for me in terms of trying to bring that into my own work. My film *Waking the Dead* (2000) was probably my happiest experience as a filmmaker; as a director. We did achieve what John achieved on *Christine*, but it got very emotional. It was one of those things like on the last day of shooting everybody cried. It was like summer camp ending, and so that was maybe my most successful of all in terms of what John created where I think people were actually happy to be at work. Even though the film was very sad, there was a passion that everybody brought to it. That was partly because of the personalities of Billy Crudup and Jennifer Connelly who also brought the sweetness to set. Between the three of us, I think we established a tone that everybody else could fall into. That's the other thing, a director can do so much, but if your actors are angry, difficult people it's hard to set a good tone on set. If they're good people, it's a lot easier. I'm sure John has to do that, too. When you deal with an actor who's got a huge chip on their shoulder, there's only just so much you can do. *Christine* was like that, nobody on *Christine* was difficult. Everybody was really cool and interesting and fun, so that also fed into that atmosphere.

BILL PHILLIPS: I didn't have time to think about the significance of horror scenes set in the suburbs. I was too busy just writing the film and finishing the drafts on time. In retrospect, I think there is validity to setting some horror stories in the suburbs… but I don't see that as a requirement of any film. I remember hating *Poltergeist* because I could never buy that Jo Beth Williams would take a bath in a house in which her daughter had been kidnapped through her TV set, a house that was haunted and built on a burial ground. When the characters in a story are so compliant that they are willing to do stupid things, I feel separated from the story.

JOHN CARPENTER: Orson Welles used the moving camera a lot, and that was an obvious choice for me as a point of reference, another favorite filmmaker of mine is of course, John Ford, but he seldom used these kind of tracking shots or dolly shots. Alfred Hitchcock did and I think I derived a lot of *Christine*'s visuals come from both Orson Welles and Hitchcock. Welles used the crane a lot more than I ever did, but I tried to give the film a few shots here and there that would use a moving crane to give the feeling and sense of continual flow and movement.

DONALD M. MORGAN: I remember John being way different than any director I had worked with up to that point. He was very free with stuff. I remember one night when we were doing some Steadicam work, Alexandra came out of the house and walked across the street and she was hiding and Christine drove up, and that's when Keith Gordon walked down and got in the car, and they drove off. And he had me doing the Steadicam shot, I wasn't the operator, but I had a Steadicam operator. In my early days, it was not long after I started that I did *Christine* because I was pretty new, but when we'd do dolly shots, and we'd get to a certain point, we'd stop. And most directors say, "the dolly's still moving when it's supposed to be stopped! I want the pan and the zoom and everything to stop at the same time" – you know, to make a point. John didn't worry about that. I remember when we did the shot of him, Christine in the background and her in the foreground that we wrapped around. And when I got to a certain place, I said I'd like to do it again, and John said, "What was wrong with that?" and I said, "The operator didn't stop right here." He said, "I don't want it to stop. Just keep going. We"ll cut where we want it to cut." So he was freer, and for me, he was a lot of fun to work with!

RICHARD KOBRITZ: The car is the star of the film and I don't think anything would be remiss to say otherwise. But we did populate the film with great actors who could hold their own and John Carpenter dealt with them. He made sure that they were in character and I know that he and Keith Gordon had little signals that they would work with which would be a "more or less" kind of thing, and we were always more conscious of doing much more than a special effects movie or a slasher movie, and that this had to be character driven and that is the thing that we watched out for.

KEITH GORDON: [When I was driving Christine] was great fun to shoot! That was a scene where we very much did get the tone and kept the sense of humour alive, even though it was dark and real. We did a lot of playing with that scene. John had me do it much more broadly than was in the final movie; he had me do it much less subtly, more real than what is in the final film. He gave himself in that scene a good amount of choices. I think because that was a place where tonally it was hard to guess what would work. Also, the version that's in the film is a reshoot because the first version we did looking back was probably dangerous as hell! But basically, he wanted the reality of being in a car going very fast and for it to look very real outside. So basically, they bolted the front half of a Christine, but just the front half onto the front of this gigantic Mac truck and we were going down the highway at 90 miles an hour with cameras bolted on the outside. I don't think the Christine half had wheels on it. We were basically just stuck on the front of the truck! I'm sure it was very reinforced, but I remember at the time going, "Oh, I could die tonight!" But what happened was it was so loud that you really couldn't hear anything and it was basically just not very usable, and I think what happened, John said, "First of all, you couldn't really get the sense of how fast you were going." When they saw the dailies, it just didn't look like it was anywhere near as fast and as cool as they were hoping. They took these huge aeroplane landing lights and put them just above us on the truck, and so it was like Christine was lighting up the night, and John just said, "We couldn't hear you guys, and it didn't look that amazing." So we ended up shooting an entirely different way, and that's an amazing thing and another good lesson in directing from John. Rather than getting freaked out or frustrated or trying to do it again once you saw it didn't work, he utterly turned it on its head, and then we did it all in studio, in what's called "poor man's process", and it was all created with just lights, and if anything, I think that was much more interesting. It's not very realistic which I think is really good for that scene. It doesn't look like it's a real car and it's a real freeway. It looks kind of magical and like a '50s movie. That came out of it the second time around. The first time they went for a little reality, and it didn't work, but it was great for me because I had a practice run on that thing, I didn't expect to get. I got to go back and do it a second time which is always great because you got past the nerves of it. I'm really glad he didn't keep the original because it would have been an awful scene to have to loop the whole scene and replace all the dialogue, which would have been the case with the truck. He said not a word of that was going to be usable because it was just way too loud. I'm really bothered by scenes where I feel like the sounds are replaced later. It just has a certain lack of humanity that I don't love. So it worked out very well in the end, and of course, doing it on the stage, we could do it over and over again. It was easy. Everything with the truck we could do in one take and turn the truck around. It was much easier for John to say, "Go bigger with this. What happens if you just laugh here? Just crack up." I think it's a lot of the best stuff.

JOHN CARPENTER: The use of the houses and the streets in *Christine* and *Halloween* was incredibly important to me and to the films themselves. What I set out to do for both those pictures was create a mythical Midwest in the United States, something that really doesn't exist. There are neighbourhoods in Los Angeles that have a lot of these old East Coast type houses, and these are beautiful old houses and they are all set to these gorgeous tree-lined streets, so we hunted around for that. That is what visually connects *Christine* to something like *Halloween*; in essence, this sense of a fabricated and almost dreamlike suburbia.

KEITH GORDON: It's almost like a noir look: very dark. One of the things he plays with are the shadowy areas are very, very dark, and that adds a lot to it. When a lot of people do suburban streets, they tend to light the whole street up, and he really picks his places, like he did in *Halloween*, too. It's like it's just the light and shadow differences are very extreme, and I think he does that beautifully well. It makes suburbia very creepy; it makes those streets feel like what's hidden in this idyllic world? David Lynch does that very well, too. I think that is because they are not afraid to use the shadows and darkness.

RICHARD KOBRITZ: We never realised how hard it would be to assemble seventeen or eighteen functioning cars. But we had our transportation captain who was able to get junkers of the Plymouth Fury and he had about twenty four of them and he was able to cannibalise them into seventeen or eighteen. Several of which would do various things – one of them would be the fire Christine, the other would be the pristine Christine, and we were polishing all of them except for two by the end of the picture.

ADAM DEVLIN: As Dennis (Arnie's best friend) and Leigh (Arnie's girlfriend) start having concerns about Arnie and "Christine", they meet up to talk about what they can do and their concerns about Arnie and his growing obsession with Christine. They hatch a plot that if Arnie won't listen to them, Dennis will destroy Christine. As Arnie approaches Dennis's home in Christine we hear Ritchie Valens classic "Come on, Let's Go". The song is about a young love affair, with the singer pleading with his lover to "… never leave me". Leigh leaves, without Arnie seeing her, and the two men drive off in Christine. By this stage in the film, Arnie is a very different character – all swagger and bravado – and the use of this song by Ritchie Valens from 1958 is a clear indication that Christine is basically saying to Arnie that he isn't to leave her for anyone else. Dennis tells Arnie of their (his and Leigh) concerns for him. Arnie admits he is in love with Christine and goes on to show Dennis just how "close" they are, by driving without steering at high speed.

Keith Gordon
as Arnie
Cunningham.

Shooting on a sound stage: John Stockwell and Keith Gordon go for the last drive together.

John Carpenter, Keith Gordon and John Stockwell enjoy time on
set before the "Death to shitters" sequence.

"ROCK AND ROLL IS HERE TO STAY":
Dennis and Leigh take on Christine

In the pre-code film *Female* (1933), Ruth Chatterton is the head of a car manufacturer which is referred to as General Motors. It is learned that she has inherited the company from her father, and makes a mention of being the only person who can do the job. This incredibly gender-political film is an early example of the "Woman's Picture" that would make a mark on cinema history during the forties, and here Chatterton's gender amidst the world of cars (a male dominated arena) is scrutinised, championed, analysed and brought to the fore. Years later, and released in 1983 (the same year as *Christine*), *Heart Like A Wheel* features Bonnie Bedelia (who had already made her mark in a Stephen King adaptation playing small town school teacher Susan Norton in *Salem's Lot*) as a top fuel-drag racer, who has to fight against the inherit sexism that exists in the motorcar industry.

Christine is a film completely dedicated to gender politics, and it sits in between these two very different films about women and cars on its own socially aware plateau. It also remains incredibly different to both films in that it does not feature any women behind a steering wheel or culturally invested in cars, it presents a world of teenage boys (and damaged older men – Darnell, LeBay et al) and their inseparable "romance" with automobiles, and has the car gendered "herself" – bringing this Plymouth Fury to the fore as a contemporary to both Ruth Chatterton's savvy car-centric business woman and Bonnie Bedelia's dedicated sportswoman. During this sequence of the film – which is the final confrontation and show-down between our newfound "heroes" Dennis Guilder and Leigh Cabot and the monstrous bloodthirsty car – gender division and the relationship between boys, girls and gendered objects hit the axillary point and are themes that are driven into hyper drive. Ultimately, Christine desperately tries to kill Dennis and Leigh and in turn, is the monstrous-mechanical-feminine hell-bent on crippling normalcy and potentially healthy and well-mannered romance. Christine has now become the full fledged monster she always was, and during this sequence, she even develops large sharp teeth that are bared and hungry, ready to "feed". The relentless driving into corners, smashing into dark corridors, trapping Leigh in varied points at Darnell's garage and the endless speeding around with an unflinching desire to destroy are both magnificent choreographed moments in dynamic storytelling and staging of an action sequence, but also a brilliant acute take on the monster trying to destroy the heteronormative union of characters who "have a future".

Of course, a character who sadly "has no future" and must succumb to the deadly wrath of Christine is Arnie Cunningham who is summoned to confront Dennis and Leigh from a precursor to this final battle sequence set at Darnell's garage. In broad daylight – a sunny December day in Rockbridge – Dennis carves an instruction for Arnie into the pristine paint job of Christine. Here the young jock is marking her, branding her and calling upon his friend to meet him and end this insanity. From this tiny precursory moment, we see Dennis enter Darnell's garage: the place where Christine was restored and brought back to life becomes the place of her destruction. Cars are essential in many of Stephen King's works and sometimes respond to birthplaces of evil and then closing points (or points of death) for such malevolence. In *Carrie*, bully Chris Hargensen convinces her boyfriend Billy Nolan to help her with the prank that ends with the fiery destruction at the prom inside his car, later the duo are killed in the same car at the hands of the telekinetic enraged Carrie. In *Misery*, this concept of birthing/dying in a car is made one and the same as author Paul Sheldon is "rescued" from death by his "number one fan" Annie Wilkes, but then brought to her home to be tormented and have his artistic integrity jeopardised and metaphorically die at the same time.

Leigh waits outside in the dark and is let into the garage by Dennis – here, the world of boys makes allowances for concerned girlfriends to "experience" the "trouble". In many regards, this gesture from Dennis is the flipside to him not being allowed to "enter" Christine ("Keep A-Knockin'") earlier in the film. Leigh has earned her "entry fee" and it is she who will literally come face to face with the raging Christine. One of them remarks "It's kind of spooky in here huh?" and as they look around the dark space of the now dead Darnell's garage, they find that the place is cleaned out, emptied and no longer a place of restoration.

This is one of the only times in the film that a character refers to Christine as an "it", in a piece that has seen her referred to as a "she" throughout. Leigh calls Christine as an "it" – completely snubbing the dig she made earlier to Arnie, referring to the car as a girl ("Don't like me hitting your girl?"). Angered and equally distressed at the character transformation in her boyfriend, Leigh is ready to put an end to the nightmarish nonsense and guide Dennis into finally destroying the supernatural car (a car she refuses to gender and hence humanise).

The sole machine in the garage is a large bulldozer that Dennis hops into and jumpstarts. He improvises and finally masters the controls. In Stephen King's novel, a pink tanker truck called Petunia would eventually crush Christine, ending her reign of terror, but here, John Carpenter along with his writer Bill Phillips had the inspired concept to bring forth a great American bulldozer as the regal opponent to the equally all-American Christine. By the end of the frenzied sequence, this bulldozer would ultimately sodomise Christine and render her a scrapheap. The bulldozer would come to represent an icon of Americana and the "old world" of farming communities. Here is a machine of rural America, or hard work, labour, the American dream coming to fruition and only because of hard work and endless sacrifice. Christine is a leisure vehicle – a muscle car made for joyrides, for reckless teenagers and for juvenile delinquency. So it makes perfect sense that the earnest and honest bulldozer (a machine solely made for building a "better world") destroys her.

Christine zooms around the dark gloomy garage chasing Leigh, smashing through pillars and terrorizing the athletic young woman who makes more than one narrow escape. The fury in Christine is impenetrable and very real, so when it is discovered that Arnie is in fact in the driver's seat – letting "his girl" take on his "former girl" – it is even more harrowing and frightening. By the end of the sequence, Christine sings out that "Rock and Roll Is Here To Stay"

which is of course the iconic song from Philadelphia musical group
Danny and the Juniors which was released in 1958, an indication
that Christine's rage and fury will never die, and that there is always
a future for such energy, zeal and destruction. While the Plymouth
is rolled over by the heavy bulldozer, she cries this sentiment out
– until her radio goes bust. She promises that rock 'n' roll is most
certainly here to stay – and this is countered and commented upon
by Leigh in the final line of the film.

Arnie Cunningham's death is also a testament to the longevity of the great classic horror trope of the creepy ghoul sprouting
from nothing and scaring the traumatised heroine. This is another
example of monstrousness and fifties nostalgia coming together
and being a perfect marriage that will never cease to exist. Arnie
is thrust out of Christine (as if rejected by her) and falls into the
arms of Leigh. His chest bleeds heavily as he removes a large shard
of windshield glass (Christine has used him, and now he is to be
discarded in hope for a new "worthy owner") and dies at the grill of
his beloved Plymouth. His bloodied hand strokes the V of the grill
in an overtly sexual image of vaginal iconography – the blood, the
V-shaped logo, the tenderness, the "release". As Arnie dies, Christine's headlights dim, as if she is grieving the loss of someone who
truly was "good with his hands". But this mourning is fleeting, as
her true nature pricks up into gear – a dedication to killing, with
her focus on Leigh and Dennis.

The destruction of Christine and eventual death of Arnie run
simultaneously during this climactic moment in the film, however,
they unfold in opposing tones: Christine's demise is welcomed and
understandable, whereas Arnie's bloody death is tragic and depress-
ing. Dying from impalement, John Carpenter paints a beautifully poignant image of a young boy who has had his heart symbolically and
literally crushed and damaged by life – a teenager who has no place in
a world that is cruel and filled with sharp edges. Much like Christine
(who as aforementioned dims her lights in some warped mockery
of respect and mourning), Dennis and Leigh have a tiny moment to
mourn the loss of Arnie, both in despair but with no time to reflect.
This place of sorrow is interrupted by the advent of a crazed Christine,
and once again, this monster of the piece drives a knife straight into

the heart of sentiment and the desire to love, honour, care and respect. Throughout the movie, Christine herself demands all of these things; however, she will not allow others to have such "privileges" – her main objective, outside of destruction, is to deny her human counterparts these aforementioned glimmers of happiness.

JOHN CARPENTER: The big action scene at the end of the film took forever! It was the longest shoot I've had to deal with, I mean it just went on and on. The whole sequence was made up of a lot of shots, a whole heap of endless shots that we had to cut together to make that thing sail. It was all shot live, everything happened right in front of us – so none of the car pieces were separate pieces there, that was a full-fledged Plymouth, and the bulldozer itself was also an entire machine that "performed" for the camera. It took days and nights of endless waiting and sitting around and reconstructing ideas of how to shoot it, I mean this was the longest period of filmmaking ever. We were there for a long time.

DONALD M. MORGAN: It was five weeks in Darnell's garage. All that garage stuff at the end with the bulldozer crushing the car. I would always add stuff outside the windows, to get it moody. I think one of the interesting things about that film when they got it all done on schedule, and he'd shot the movie, he went back and did a reshoot. We went up to his ranch and we cut out all the voices out in the car, and he hydraulically pulled in, compression and it would break gears and all that kind of stuff as it crushed in. He had that with the camera upside down. John always loved doing everything in-camera.

ALEXANDRA PAUL: I actually am not a fan of chase scenes. I like the dialogue scenes and exploring the relationships between the characters. But it was fun working with John Stockwell in those climactic chase sequences where Christine is trying to run us down. Although we shot nights, which can be very hard. At 3am you start feeling nauseous because you are so tired. In those final scenes in the garage, I was doing a lot of pretending. I would say to myself, "OK Alexandra, now the car is coming at you really fast. Back up and look scared", which I like less as an actress than relating to a real person. But I was thrilled to be there every minute I was on set! It was my first feature film, so I was very grateful to be there no matter what time it was or what we were filming.

BILL PHILLIPS: I thought that a pink painted septic tanker named Petunia would elicit laughs, and that a bulldozer was a more credible opponent to Christine. John improved on that by finding a particularly tough-looking old-fashioned bulldozer.

JOHN CARPENTER: Alexandra has an identical twin sister and it was very bizarre because one day on the set, the wardrobe people dressed up the twin sister as Alexandra's character of Leigh, and they both came out to the set. I thought I was looking at Alexandra, but something was wrong – I couldn't put my finger on it, but I was like "Something is wrong…"

CAROLINE PAUL (Alexandra Paul's sister/prank on John Carpenter): This was Alexandra's first movie, and John Carpenter was just really awesome to her, just really nice. I had never met him before. He didn't even know that Alexandra had a twin. It was at the end of the movie, it was at the end of the shoot, and she did make sure it was a scene that was not important. It was just what they call "an insert". I snuck up into the makeup trailer and the only people that knew that this was happening was the make-up people and her co-star, John Stockwell. I step out of the trailer, looking just like my sister. I was sitting in the trailer, and my sister was sitting next to me, and they had those Bevelled mirrors, and I honestly couldn't tell who was who. It was very eerie, but the most striking thing about this whole thing was that when I stepped out of the trailer, and John Stockwell had to lead me to the set because I didn't know where I was going, but I was walking towards the bulldozer and all these people started saying, "Hey, Alexandra. What's going on, Alexandra?" Everybody from the grip, to the PA! I really under-stood in that moment that my sister was a super awesome person because I don't think that happens that much! They all loved her so much. I am not an actress. I was kind of thrown back on my heels. I thought I was going to have to walk over there and do nothing, say nothing except to John Carpenter and my whole plan was thrown off. But it was pretty neat to see how many people really loved her! You see, Alexandra and I started to look more and more alike as we got older. And so we had played a "twins" trick once before that was pretty big in front of my high school. We went to separate high schools. Makeup can do everything! So for this prank on *Christine*, I walked up to John Carpenter with John Stockwell because we were going to do the scene together. It was the bulldozer scene, and all they needed to shoot was the leg of Alexandra pushing the clutch. That was it. Only an insert. So John Stockwell and I walk up to John Carpenter, and Carpenter looked at me weird, and I thought I was pulling the wool over his eyes, and he said, "Do you have a cold?" I think he knew something was different but of course, he didn't know she had a twin so why would he think this is not her. I guess I present as "under the weather" or something! Otherwise, it was fine. John Stockwell then led me to the bulldozer and he sort of whispered what I had to do because I really don't know, and I'm expecting Alexandra to come at any time. But I have to say she totally missed her mark! They shot the scene and that was not supposed to happen! Alexandra was supposed to intervene well before that because you don't want to ruin a movie! I mean, it was just my leg, but nevertheless! So I pushed the clutch like they told me and they're like "It's a wrap!" Like I was a one-take actor, I'm happy to say. Then my sister came from the wings and said to him, "Did you fire me already?" or something like that and he was floored! None of the crew knew except for the makeup people. They were all floored too. As I remember they were laughing and they broke out in applause, and it was hilarious! There is some photos somewhere, but I don't have them. There are photos of either me talking to John Carpenter or Alexandra and me talking to John. I will say many shots hit the cutting room floor, and in fact, my leg is in that movie. Three seconds! If you blink, you miss it! It was literally the shortest scene ever, but it is my leg. I don't remember much about John Stockwell. I don't think he found it as funny as everybody else thought it was. He might have just thought that it was a pain to be leading this joke. I honestly didn't get a sense of him at all. He was a very good leader; he led me through the crew, right up to John Carpenter, and he didn't give anything away. Also, I think no other movie would have let that gag happen. This was John with the collaboration of the makeup people, and there must have been an AD that was maybe involved. I don't think normal movie sets would allow it because every second counts – money, and I broke all the union rules, accidentally, by being filmed. So I thought it was great! The only thing that struck me was just how much Alexandra had made an impression on people because it wasn't like they were saying that to John. They were definitely saying it to me/Alexandra. They were delighted to see my sister, who was not her – me. I don't think that I could have gotten the gist of that without being her. We're pretty much the same build. Again, it was like the makeup people made it amazing. When you can't tell yourself apart from your twin, you know that the makeup people are good!

MALCOLM DANARE: John Carpenter is a huge practical joker. Richard Kobritz, the producer of the film, drove a Porsche. Whenever he would get to the set, he would get out of his beautiful Porsche and put a car cover over it so nothing would happen. Carpenter and his gang took the Porche, took the car cover off the Porsche, got a Volkswagen or funny little car and put the same car cover over it and ran it over with a bulldozer. So everybody knew that the joke was going to happen, except Richard Korbritz! And he went absolutely bananas when they took that bulldozer and ran it over. It was the best practical joke I had seen in my life. It was a pretty amazing practical joke, but he loved it.

ROY ARBOGAST: There really are no similarities between films. We would read scripts and figure out what to do. So in *The Thing* we are on ice and building a fire at one point, and then in *Christine* we're out on the road. With John Carpenter, we never had studio department heads on top of us telling us what to do. We had total control on the SFX unit and how it went about. I always hired a team and I always got the best electricians, welders, rubber guys and so forth and away we'd go. I was always in charge of who my team was. The crew would rent my facility and they would pay my crew. I was never a businessman; all I ever wanted to do was work with my hands and deliver the goods in the SFX detailing of the film. We had to serve the script and at times storyboards – for *Christine*, there was only storyboards for the final sequence where the car is chasing down the kids and then crushed by the bulldozer. As SFX got more advanced I started to back off a bit, and take the backseat while more technically inclined guys would step forward, working with computers. I came from mechanics and my team were always practioners of mechanical work. I cannot stand what is happening now in SFX with CGI, I think it looks awful. But then again, I am not a massive fan of SFX driven movies – nor did I really watch them in the past – my favorite movies are classic musicals and dramas from the thirties and forties. To me, all the films I worked on were wonderful challenges. I am a very visual guy – a lot of the SFX guys from my era were amazing technical guys. I was never the best welder or electrician, I mean I knew it all, but I would hire the best. By the time of *Christine*, I knew so much in the art of SFX and once I got that script and sit down with John and we would go through it, I would get excited and start working! This was the same with Steven Spielberg. I remember working on *Close Encounters of the Third Kind* (1977) with Spielberg and was just amazed at how much of a visionary he was.

KEITH GORDON: I don't remember if touching the V was my idea or John's idea. There was stuff where he might have said, "Touch the car" and I was like, "Well what if I touch the V and it was sort of sexual". In terms of really staging the death and how he was going to shoot it, that is where I think as an actor you kind of shut up and go, "Oh you're John Carpenter. You're going to have really good ideas about this!" and then I might respond to it. We were always bantering and I might say, "Oh, if we're doing that, why don't I do this?" and then we would work out the physicality together, and that was fun in terms of what looked good to a camera in terms of my pulling the glass out. That was just really interesting for me because I was interested in filmmaking and we were trying to find an angle where I could basically cheat it, and it would look good. But he did it, I just said, "Well what if I did it like this? And what if I do it like that? So that was very interesting to do. There was also some of that that was reshot. Originally there wasn't as much of a death scene. Arnie went flying through the window and with the glass pull out, he might have added more of it, or even the whole idea of it was not the thing we shot when we first shot it, and then they made it more of a moment. We reshot that later. I remember in an embarrassing moment I actually made myself pass out on the set without meaning to. I was trying to make myself really red-faced, and so I would hold my breath like crazy before we did the shot where I was pulling the glass out and on one of the takes, I literally held my breath so intensely that I kind of passed out. They were like, "Are you kidding? Are you alright?" I don't think I ever acknowledged what happened because I felt so damned embarrassed. But you know that is part of being young and stupid. As a year-old actor you're trying to be all method and real, and if you make yourself pass out, you're not going to do this thing really well. That's the stuff you learn when you get older, and you look back. I remember at one point we were doing one of the scenes in the garage – the scene where I find Christine after she's been smashed up, and I remember taking some dirt from the ground in this garage and kind of rubbing it in my eye so my eye would be red. I look back and go, "Okay, I could have lost my eye-sight. That was really, really stupid!" That's why they have makeup people. Again, when you are a young actor, you want to be really real, and then you have a couple of bad lessons where you go, "Yeah. Really real is fine to a point, and then there's a reason why it is a movie!"

ALEXANDRA PAUL: There is a running shot where I have to hoist myself up out of Christine's way. Anyway, that was not me, that was a stunt person. If I'm running like a truck driver and bow-legged, then it was me and not a stunt person! My stand-in may have been my stunt double too, and I think it was Kurt Russell's sister. I think she was my stand-in. Because John had worked with Kurt a lot. Kurt came to the set I remember, and his sister was married to the first AD who became a very successful producer, Larry Franco. I didn't know a lot of actors because we lived in the country and the nearest movie theatre was eleven miles away, and we didn't have television a lot when I was growing up. But I did know Kurt Russell!

DONALD M. MORGAN: The only time that John ever used storyboards was the sequence with the bulldozer inside Darnell's garage. That was the only time that I ever saw storyboards, but there are so many little things that we had to shoot after the fact. Like when we'd do work with stunts, whether it be a fender or an actor, we would cut to something else but we always tried to do it so it had the same atmosphere, so I didn't have to go back and shoot additional inserts. I like to do some while we're doing the stunt, but you can't always do that while you're doing the scene because it's lit and it doesn't match. And sometimes you don't want to do it out of frame because you want to make a big point of a cutaway, so you do a little rewriting on that. That stuff was all storyboarded so we could keep track of it because we did it over a long period of time. I don't remember how long that sequence took, but it certainly wasn't done in one night –with the tractor driving in and all of the talk. It was a sequence that was storyboarded, and later on, if we didn't have stuff, we'd have to go grab this, this and this as the storyboard. That's the only time that John used the storyboard; he wanted to see it rehearsed and he was more fluent with it – more liquid.

ROY ARBOGAST: Spielberg and Carpenter are totally different. Spielberg is a visionary and a genius in that regard, but as far as doing practical things such as write his own music or fly his own helicopter, that was Carpenter's bag. I mean Spielberg's movies are some of the best I've worked on and he puts all of his trust in you as an SFX designer and executioner, but Carpenter is simply hands on. I remember working on *Jaws* and Spielberg being completely open to ideas from not only myself but his amazing editor Verna Fields who came up to us one day and said "Guys, you don't have to build the entire shark! I can show you why." So we went up to her moviola and went through some scenes and we saw that all we needed to do at some points was build portions of the shark, because of the way she edited it and cut it, which added to the film being as terrifying as it was. Spielberg had a vision but he was always open to concepts and ideas, and to not show the entire shark for most of *Jaws* was a perfect realisation for all of us. Verna was just beautiful – I knew her son well – and she was like everybody's mom. She would walk through the shops and down to the stages, this beautiful little heavyset lady just beaming with brains and brilliance, whereas Marion Rothman on *Christine* worked completely in post-production and with John only.

LISA RAE BARTOLOMEI: *Christine's* finale begins with the outdoor sounds of crickets at Darnell's car yard as Dennis breaks in through a creaky window. The racket of the roller-door then overwhelms the large reverberant space made predominately of metal and concrete. Even the smallest of sounds of footsteps and voice echo throughout the mechanics. As the outdoor sounds fade out we are left with a vast and spooky atmosphere in the emptiness of sound. A tense, anticipatory silence. When Dennis hotwires the Caterpillar, the overwhelming sound of the engine overpowers everything, its steady rhythmic roar countering the more emotive and aggressive expressions of Christine as she angrily attacks Leigh and Dennis in the finale. While Leigh and Dennis sit in the truck the sound shifts to the tighter deader sound of the small Caterpillars Cabin. When the Caterpillar comes to a stop underneath the seeming silence if you listen very carefully you can hear the quiet ticking of an idle motor. Christine laying in wait for her prey. This is then masked by the false alarm car pulling into the car yard. When Leigh steps into the caryard Christine reveals herself and the synthesiser and cars roar fill the space creating a sudden creative tension as Christine skids towards Leigh and destroys the other cars in the car yard demolition derby style. Christine's aggressive motor revs is a strong indicator of her enraged and psychotic state of mind. The music drops as Christine backs up for her final showdown and as a rising synth tone along with her engine build to the final confrontation in which Arnie is killed, thrown from Christine's window as glass smashes everywhere. The silence hints at an end to the horror, but then Christine's final stand begins with the use of a 1950s song to express Christine's mood. Before her damaged motor jumps into flight and confrontation with the Caterpillar a steady mechanical and metallic musical score plays under the rhythmic movement of the Caterpillar as it crushes Christine. The sound of metal and glass torn asunder accompany "Rock and

Roll is Here to Stay" as Christine is finally destroyed and then the sound cuts to a subtle thud as Christine is a square of crushed metal dumped in a car yard.

ADAM DEVLIN: As Dennis and Leigh attempt to destroy Christine in Darnell's garage, we see that Arnie is driving Christine and as Christine rams into the office, trying to kill Leigh, Arnie is catapulted out of Christine and dies due to a shard of glass through his chest. As he lay there dying, Christine's radio plays "Pledging My Love" by Johnny Ace. Originally released posthumously in 1954 after Johnny Ace had died of a self-inflicted gunshot wound, the use of this song – with its chorus "I'll forever love you / For the rest of my days / I'll never part from you / Or your loving ways…" perfectly captured what Christine is feeling about Arnie's death. The use of this song also tells us that Arnie's death is premature (like the death of Johnny Ace himself). It's a wonderful piece of cinema that tells us a lot about what is going on without dialogue. After Arnie's death, Dennis and Leigh set about to destroy Christine. It takes some time however they eventually destroy Christine and as she's "dying" she plays "Rock and Roll is Here to Stay". The song plays until Christine is completely destroyed and the next scene is a red block of compacted metal drops from a crane in a scrap metal yard – this is Christine, finally dead! It's an ironic choice as it is clear that Christine is done – she isn't here to stay this time. Or is she?

ALEXANDRA PAUL: We shot a lot of nights, and I remember the AD Larry Franco being very upbeat and positive. I think he got pissed off once, but I don't remember exactly. I have a vision of him yelling. But most of the time in the early morning, he'd been working all night, but he always had a very upbeat attitude and a lot of good energy. You know he was probably exhausted!

ROY ARBOGAST: That entire ending was so hard. It was such a big set and everything we did was a big deal. We had to get the tractor in there, we had to stage the cars and where they would go. I did not have anything to do with the car developing teeth. That was all John's idea! He actually called for "More! More" as far as the image of the teeth went! I wanted to do something different. John Carpenter is a night owl, he worked so hard and stayed up all night working on that sequence. It's funny, thinking about working with Carpenter. I feel like *The Thing* was the most fun to work on, but I did not like the post-production work on that; however, yes, working on it in the moment and camping out in the snow and that was just wonderful. When I watch movies like *The Thing* and *Christine* I don't look at them as movies anymore, I see them as memories – I remember how much fun I had, how hard it was to get certain things working, the parties, the friends; just everything. I am very lucky to have worked on these great movies and very happy to be part of movie history.

John Carpenter directs Alexandra Paul during the lengthy climax.

John Stockwell, Alexandra Paul and John Carpenter prepare the bulldozer sequence. Unknown to Carpenter, Stockwell and Paul would be part of an onset prank involving Paul's sister Caroline during this shoot.

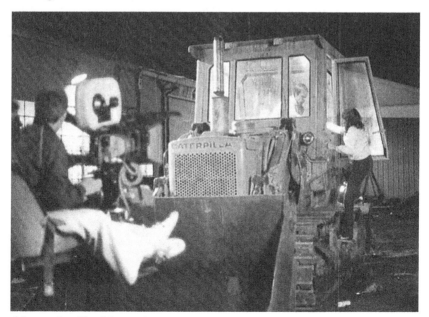

Alexandra Paul leaps into action.

Alexandra Paul and John Stockwell ready to take on Christine.

The bulldozer that eventually crushes Christine.

Christine is crushed by the bulldozer as the crew re-group to continue work on the gruelling endless sequence.

A cannibalised Christine is governed by the SFX crew.

Christine develops teeth.

The bulldozer sodomizes and destroys Christine.

"I HATE ROCK 'N' ROLL": Christine is scrap metal

Leigh Cabot – the human female lead – has the final say in this masterwork of gender studies, mechanic monstrousness and Faustian wish-fulfilment turned malevolent. She denounces all that Christine – the machine female lead – stands for by declaring that she hates rock 'n' roll. This is a great condensation of everything that we have beared witness to throughout the duration of John Carpenter's savvy and intelligent film: that this classic and time-less majesty of a musical form that revolutionised the culture and ultimately served as a war cry for teenagers (stepping into their own market and form come the fifties (the time of Christine's birth)) is poo-pooed by a teen herself who has been under threat (emotion-ally and physically) by such a liberating instrument of expression. Leigh Cabot hates rock 'n' roll because she senses the destructive-ness of it brought upon by the maniacal machine that is Christine. It is an acute commentary on the recklessness of youth now stunted and pushed into a safe box (the image of Christine now turned into a scrap metal heap) and dropped to the dusty plains, there to collect dust and be rendered unimportant. In essence, Leigh has completely rejected youth and what comes with it, and has opted for a more traditional and "grown up" coda to what might well be an uneventful life anyway. With Dennis Guilder (still hobbling on crutches) by her side, and the stoic and hardened realism represent-ed by Detective Rudolph Junkins along with the young couple-to-be, Leigh has come to represent everything that was not Christine: mannered, a girl of order and principle and almost conservative in a strange way.

When the two junkyard attendants walk past with their ghetto-blaster spewing out Ritchie Valens, it prompts Leigh to make this bold statement and as we bear witness to the trash heap that Chris-tine has now become, we understand that order is in the universe and a new "conservatism" has settled amongst the dust. There is no future for alienated boys who are "good with their hands", they are left to die on the sidelines, while injured football heroes can watch monstrous cars be crushed to pathetic compact metal mounds and hardboiled detectives can soon forget about the deaths of insignificant dead-end suburban kids whose parents may not mourn for too long after. *Christine* presents this cold, dead world so elegantly and sings it out so wistfully sincere; parents don't understand, bullies are true menaces, cars are everything and young teen girls can quickly turn into middle-aged prudes already hating on rock 'n' roll. The sexual energy of Christine herself is also denied and twisted up in this sequence – her once beautiful body now an unrecognizable trash heap, slammed onto the dead grounds. However, in a magically inspired moment of great writing and direction of focus, as the camera closes in we see the metal bands that once served Christine bend and fold, and the sense is: she is still "alive". Christine is not only eager to bring herself back from the "dead", but her spirit and what she represents is well and truly alive: the recklessness of youth, the zeal of teenage rebellion, the soul of rock 'n' roll, the sexual charge of adolescence and the relentless desire to destroy within the realm of creation.

RICHARD KOBRITZ: I really believe that evil never dies. I think it goes away, but always comes back. That's why at the end of *Salem's Lot*, Ben Mears and Mark Petrie are running away from New England and going to South America because the evil has travelled there. Susan Norton is there, now as a vampire. I also wrote the closing shot in myself, where a skull emerges in the moon. That whole section at the end I wrote because Paul Monash was busy working on something else. I also remember on *Salem's Lot*, where the Glick kid pops out of the coffin and that was the end of the first part in the miniseries, I structured it so we could get to that ending. I didn't want to go beyond it, or go before it. Now this was not in the book, but it's something I developed to make sure the audience knew that evil never dies in one spot. I thought the same thing with *Christine*, I mean she is trashed in the end and she is now a bundle of metal, but then you see the last shot where one of the pieces of metal starts to vibrate and pulse and move. All of that is what I wanted – I didn't want the good guys to clearly win, I wanted the audience to know that evil is always omnipresent. I didn't decide on this last moment in *Christine* for any kind of sequel launch, anymore reason that I was doing that ending on *Salem's Lot*, I was just running with the idea that in the history of horror movies is that evil never dies.

JOHN CARPENTER: There was a scene cut out where Bill Phillips, the screenwriter and George Thorogood, who of course sang "Bad to the Bone", in the junkyard doing this dialogue but it was just not right to keep it in there. Marion Rothman the editor was just brilliant. I loved her. What an editor! She worked with me again on movies like *Starman*, and she was just terrific. There were plenty of deleted scenes in *Christine*, and Marion and I went through them, and for the most part it was all about tempo and certain scenes just not making the cut because of mood, pacing and so forth. You would grab a few things here, move them out of the way, that kind of thing.

RICHARD KOBRITZ: The car was the star and I thought the trailer for the film was terrific. It plays out like you're watching the silhouette of a naked girl, and I thought that sold it properly. We were going against Clint Eastwood who was opening the same day with another *Dirty Harry* movie (*Sudden Impact* (1983)), and that was not good, I mean he was at the top of his game, and we had a movie with a car as the star. I think we suffered for that. But we did make the movie for slightly less than ten million dollars so no one was hurting. We always told the people at Columbia as well as the people who made the documentary featurette about the shoot that you have to feature the car, the car is the star and it has to be shown in a beautiful, mysterious, sexual way. Later we can show that this car will look like a shark and look sinister and evil, but right now we want the poster has to be seductive. That's what the campaign artists came up with and we signed off on it. There is talk now of doing another *Christine*, or a sequel, and my only note was 'Just don't make the car fly'. This is something that SFX guys can now do with great ease, today with CGI, and the car can run over a thousand people, the whole Roman army. But don't fall victim to that. Our objective was to go beyond *The Car* with James Brolin which came out a few years before. Everybody talked about *Duel* and I still to this day think it's one of Steven Spielberg's best movies, it goes way beyond a Movie of the Week style film, it keeps you on the edge of your seat. We never felt that *The Car* was good, we didn't care for it, everybody tried to do some kind of a car movie. Stephen King directed *Maximum Overdrive* and that didn't work, so we figured that we succeeded with *Christine*. We were never daunted by previous competition as far as killer car movies go. I hear Christine mentioned in other movies, she is definitely a part of the pop culture landscape. She never dies! In regards to a remake, it is hard to beat what we did where there were no miniatures and nothing that existed outside of the camera.

DONALD M. MORGAN: I don't know of any film that I have done that there are people standing in line asking for my autograph. This was many years ago when the film was released! I think what I am proudest of, was that I knew we had done a good job; that we did what we were hired to do. I haven't seen much of John since we did *Starman*, but I liked working with him. I thought he was a genius. He's involved with the music, he's involved with the editing. He is the real deal!

ALAN HOWARTH: For John right now, it is very challenging. He doesn't want to make another movie. To make another movie, 'First I'd basically need a vault of money that was unlimited and nobody messed with me', and second, he says 'It's too much work!' He doesn't want to work that hard any more. Especially like a movie like *The Thing*. That was a year production, and that was very difficult and going to British Columbia, and the outdoor filming in August and planting all the explosions and the tricks and coming back after it all snowed, so it was all pristine snow with no footprints, and then running those scenes and only having one shot at it, because otherwise the snow was messed up you'd have to wait for it to snow again. All a production challenge. This is not him saying anything, just my observation. If John were on another movie and it didn't supersede his body of work, it would be considered a flop! It's too risky. Miles Davis had this problem. If you want to be Miles, you have to play with a different production level. But the modern Miles that had the synthesisers had the eccos on his trumpet; I just wonder what Miles did originally? Keep doing that, man. They didn't get it.

JOHN CARPENTER: It's hard to say where *Christine* fits in the tradition of killer car movies or evil car movies. It was an odd novel to begin with, a very strange, tricky story. But you can't argue with Stephen King's success, and I am just happy to have made the movie version of it!

ROY ARBOGAST: I had a big cylinder set up with a lever that would spring out and scare the audience for the ending, but John had an entirely different take on the ending. What we ended up doing was using a piece of string to pull up a bendable piece that showed the audience that she was still alive!

DONALD M. MORGAN: I knew that we were going to do a sequel, but we never did. I think a lot of people that were fans of it would have loved to have seen a sequel. I don't know if it was brilliant that we didn't do it or a mistake if we did do it, but there was always a certain mystery about the car being able to come back like that. I think that's what everyone loves most, and comes back to!

ALAN HOWARTH: I sat recently through a screening. I get why – it still holds up! The other interesting things about Carpenter's filmmaking is that he chooses costume and location that could be anytime, anywhere USA, from *Halloween*. The only thing that gives away the timing are the vehicles or the technology. *The Thing* could be released today, except for the clunky computers and the big boxy walkie-talkies. Other than that he completely chooses all the elements so that they don't have markers in time. It's timeless storytelling. He's created that; it's Americana!

KEITH GORDON: I remember really liking one of the trailers for the film. You're going along what looks like a woman's body. It looks like it could have been a trailer for *Body Heat (1981)*, and only at the end of the trailer do you realise that 'Oh, it's a car, not a person.' I remember thinking that was really cool! I don't remember if John did that or was involved with it. He's pretty hands-on, but I don't know if the studio let him run with that. I don't know if it was their idea, but I do remember thinking that that was cool. I do think personally that it should have been a big picture of my face, but you know, that's just me! No, I didn't really think that! Every actor wants it, but I thought the whole idea of playing up the car female... because that is one of the things that I liked best about it thematically. I thought that whole weird sexuality around the car was one of the coolest things about the movie. I had no idea what the campaign was going to be. Again, they don't call you and say, 'You're going to be in the movie. What do you think about the campaign?' So I only saw that when they started putting that stuff out there. I remember really liking it because I was really afraid that they would just advertise it as 'Killer car horror movie!' Even if that was the movie that John made, we've all seen a billion times a campaign that undercuts the intelligence of the movie. One of the things with horror, smart horror movies all have had dumb horror campaigns.

ALEXANDRA PAUL: Who would have thought that this film would be sort of a cult classic? I think that I never had the foggiest idea that thirty-five years later that people would be so interested in this movie and that it actually really holds its own really well, even now. And so I also feel very warm feelings about the whole experience on the film and the part and the people I met. Overall a really good experience. Proud. Very proud to have been involved with John Carpenter on a Stephen King film. It's just all good.

BILL PHILLIPS: I got an autographed copy of the hardcover book, signed by the cast and crew and by Stephen King himself, who wrote: 'Thanks for letting her live.' This referred to the 'twitch' of Christine's metal after she'd been crushed into a cube.

KEITH GORDON: I think the reviews were sort of all over the place. I don't remember many cruelly negative reviews. I think there were some that were like, 'It's fine. It's a fun little horror movie', and there were some that were much more positive. It wasn't like a review driven film. I don't remember anyone being really nervous about the reviews. Some films, when you make a little art movie, the fate completely rests with the reviews. I think with a John Carpenter genre movie, and John had a 'screw the critics' feeling because I think he was so mad because of *The Thing*. He'd been so beat up and so unfairly. Now the film has been recognised as a classic, but at the time you would have thought he had molested a child. The anger that was directed at him for that movie, and the lack of understanding for that movie, and the lack of understanding again for the absurd humour in that movie. For all the gore in that film, it's incredibly effective. That's completely turned around; it's been amazing to watch that process! Now I have read so many critical honours for that movie! I do know that his general attitude about critics, while we were making *Christine*, is, 'I hate them all. I don't care what they think. I don't even want to read their reviews for the movie. Screw the critics!' He felt so unfairly, and I think rightly felt so unfairly attacked because of *The Thing*. So that was his attitude that I think he carried over into everything. I don't remember like trying to run out and read all of the reviews. I mean, I was aware of them, but I don't think I was super focused on them.

ALEXANDRA PAUL: I really love horror fans. I admire them. I love people who have passion about anything. Horror fans have a passion about horror movies and I really just love how much they know, how committed they are and just how loving they are to the folks in the movies that they love and it is great!

JOHN CARPENTER: I am the worst person in the world to ask about my own films! My final thoughts on *Christine* are pretty much as follows: I thought it was pretty good, but I really don't think it was that scary. I thought it was well-made and I am very happy that I did it, and honestly, the best thing about making a movie is when it is finished, it is done! It is out of my hair and I can forget about it. It got done and it got released.

John Stockwell, Alexandra Paul and Harry Dean Stanton watch
Christine drop to the ground, now a solid brick of scrap metal.

A candid on location, with John Stockwell chatting with
screenwriter Bill Phillips and George Thorogood who had
cameos that were minimised in the final cut.

Bill Phillips and George Thorogood on location ready to shoot their cameos.

From the teaser trailer, promising a terrifying Seasonal release.

The invite from Columbia Pictures to the premiere.

The pass for the premiere screening.

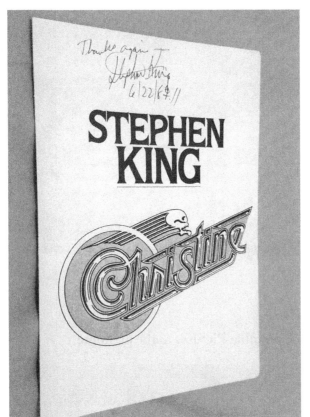

The press kit.

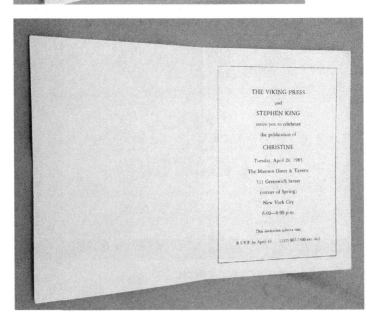

Richard Kobritz and John Carpenter cut the wrap party cake,
celebrating the end of the shoot.

John Carpenter delivers another superb horror classic.

INDEX

199, 200, 212-213, 216-218, 219,
220-221, 246-247, 249, 250-251,
257, 258, 260, 263-264, 265-268,
269-271, 272, 273, 274, 283-284,
298-300
Gottlieb-Walker, Kim 12, 81, 96, 126,
156, 232, 246

Hagen, Earle 191
Halloween 1, 4, 20, 22, 50, 60, 65, 96,
156, 167, 178, 198, 261, 271, 298
Halloween III: Season of the Witch
147, 198
Hanselhoff, Michael 10
Happy Days 6-7
Harris, Thurston 202, 207
Heaven Help Us 64
Heckerling, Amy 45
Henriksen, Lance 192, 225
His Girl Friday 45
Hitchcock, Alfred 7, 8, 154, 167, 177,
229, 268
Hoax 178
Holly, Buddy 7, 20, 26, 103
Howard, Ron 107
Howarth, Alan 11, 127, 132, 136,
141-142, 173, 177-179, 191, 198-
199, 202, 207, 215, 218, 224, 237,
297-298
Hutton, Lauren 9
Hutton, Timothy 185

I Was a Teenage Werewolf 53

Jagger, Mick 236, 239
Jaws 179, 196, 225, 226, 228, 285

Katz, Virginia 80, 125, 245
Kelly, Gene 33

King, Stephen 1, 2, 7, 9, 10, 13, 20,
23, 24, 29, 30, 31, 32-33, 34, 36,
37, 40, 42, 43, 49, 50, 54, 57, 59,
60, 65, 77, 79, 95, 97, 104, 105,
117, 120, 125, 127, 128, 129, 131,
138, 148, 149, 150, 151, 156, 158,
170, 179-180, 181, 193, 201, 203,
214, 215, 217, 230, 234, 236, 237,
253, 256, 263, 275, 276, 277, 297,
298, 299
Knight Rider 12
Kobritz, Richard 1, 8-9, 10, 11, 13,
31-33, 34, 35, 40, 42, 59, 61, 63-64,
68, 79, 93, 95-96, 114, 119-120,
129, 132, 150, 150, 156, 167, 171,
175, 176, 186, 190, 196, 203-204,
215, 216, 229, 232, 234, 236, 246,
250, 256-257, 260, 269, 271-272,
282, 295-297, 305

Lancaster, Bill 61
LaVey, Anton 127, 225
Lee, Bill 232
Lehman, Ernest 7
Lemmon, Jack 250
Leonard, Terry 205, 208, 230, 233
Lewis, Jerry 25, 95
Little Richard 130, 131, 133, 134,
174, 244
Lomino, Daniel 82, 250
Lynch, David 271

MacMurray, Fred 261
"Mangler, The" 131
Mason, James 21, 32
McNichols, Kristy 166
Memoirs of an Invisible Man 125
Midler, Bette 20
Milland, Ray 68

Made in United States
North Haven, CT
12 March 2025

66734096R00176